CISTERCIAN FATHERS SERIES: NUMBER SEVEN

BERNARD OF CLAIRVAUX

Volume Three

ON THE
SONG OF SONGS II

CISTERCIAN FATHERS SERIES: NUMBER SEVEN

THE WORKS OF BERNARD OF CLAIRVAUX

Volume Three

On the Song of Songs II

translated by

Kilian Walsh OCSO

introduction by

Jean Leclercq OSB

CISTERCIAN PUBLICATIONS
Kalamazoo, Michigan
A. R. MOWBRAY & CO. LTD.
LONDON AND OXFORD
1976

The translation here presented is based on the critical Latin edition prepared by Jean Leclercq, C. H. Talbot, and H. M. Rochais under the sponsorship of the S. Order of Cistercians and published by Editiones Cistercienses, Piazza Tempio di Diana 14, I-00143 Rome.

Cistercian Studies Series   ISBN 0-87907-000-5
The Works of Bernard of Clairvaux   ISBN 0-87907-100-1
This volume   ISBN 0-87907-107-9 (*case bound*)
ISBN 0-87907-707-7 (*paper*)
Mowbray edition   ISBN 0-264-66400-0

First published 1976
by
Cistercian Publications, Inc.
1749 West Michigan Avenue, WMU
Kalamazoo, Michigan 49008
and
A. R. Mowbray & Co. Ltd.
The Alden Press, Osney Mead
Oxford, OX2 OEG

Printed in the United States of America

CONTENTS

INTRODUCTION

WERE THE SERMONS ON THE SONG OF SONGS DELIVERED IN CHAPTER

P AST RESEARCH HAS CONCLUDED that St Bernard's *Sermons on the Song of Songs* appeared in book form and were also delivered as talks.[1] But there is a problem here. Anyone reading these *Sermons* today will inevitably see it if he studies the text to any great extent and considers the various difficulties, the same difficulties encountered by copyists, readers and editors in the past, for they perdure. Could such a polished text, one of such consummate literary form and such closely reasoned doctrine ever have been delivered as it stands, and then later have been written down without change either by the speaker or his hearers? Up till recently this has generally been considered to have been the case.[2] However, in the course of the preparation of the critical edition of the *Sermons* a new uncertainty on this point arose. Entire certitude in this matter will be difficult to achieve. At best, one can but suggest reasons which might be adduced in favor of negative and positive opinions, and then propose a solution.

1. "Alloquitur Bernardus fratres Claraeuallense, quibus istum librum scripsit. . . ."—found at the beginning of the *capitulatio* of Durham. "De libro expositionis Cantici canticorum quem idem s. Bernardus exposuit predictis fratribus cisterciensibus, sermocinando scillecet in sui capitulo Claraeuallensi. . . ."—note written by a copyist of La Ferté. See *Recueil d'études sur Saint Bernard,* vol 1 (Rome: Storia et Letteratura, 1962) pp 183, 192.
2. Vacandard, for example, wrote, "This commentary was delivered without formal preparation, as were all the other sermons of St Bernard, after he had long meditated on the text."—*Vie de s. Bernard* (Paris, 1895) 1:472. Vacandard was

This problem does deserve careful study and is worthy of detailed examination. For in one important area a long-held view we have had concerning St Bernard could well be modified by the solution reached. Also, in the course of such research it is possible to glimpse, in its setting, the way in which St Bernard worked. The Abbot of Clairvaux was aware of the fact that he was a great writer.

First of all, it might be well to list the reasons which suggest that the *Sermons* formed a written text and not a series of delivered sermons.

We have, first of all, the explicit statement of Bernard himself. In replying to Bernard de Portes, who had asked for the text of his first *Sermons on the Song of Songs*, Bernard wrote:

> *Sermones paucos in principio Canticorum Solomonis, recens dictatos, en facio transcribi: et tibi, cum necdum ediderim, quam citius mitto. In quo opere cum accepero tempus, Christo imperante curis, tentabo procedere: si tamen me inde confortes.*[3]

None of the words used here by Bernard—*dictare, transcribere, edere, opus*—are words one associates with delivered talks. Rather they suggest a work of literary composition

---

here simply repeating the idea of and even certain terms used by Mabillon, *Preface* to Vol. 4, *S. Bernardi Opera*, A similar view is held by J. Schuck, *Das Hohelied des H1. Bernhard von Clairvaux, Dokumente zur mittelalterlichen Christus-und Brautmystik* (Paderborn, 1926) p 11. This same opinion was held very emphatically by I. Valléry-Radot in *Bernard de Clairvaux* (Paris, 1953) p 462; also in "Le trésor de Citeaux", C Cist. 12 (1950) p 97. Fr C. Haflants speaks rather more simply, *ibid.* 15 (1953) p 250 of SC being "informal family talks" which Bernard gave to his monks. In *S. Bernard mystique* (Paris, 1948) I myself took this traditional opinion for granted.

3. Ep 153:2, PL 182:313: "I am having copied a few sermons I wrote recently on the first verses of the Song of Solomon, and as soon as they are ready I will send them to you. When I have the time, when Christ sees fit to calm the storm of cares that beset me, I shall continue with them, but you must encourage me."— BSJ, Ep 159:2, p. 229. This letter was not written to the Carthusian named Bernard who was then prior of Portes, but to another religious of the same Carthusian monastery, as Mabillon has pointed out, n. 419, PL 182:311. M. Perraud has even more definitely confirmed this in "Notes sur les évêques de Belley: Bernard de Portes," in *Le Buget*, 1930 (offprint of 8 pages).

which has been carefully polished. *Dictare*, moreover, is the same word that Bernard used in referring to some sermons on St Victor, which were never delivered. He had composed them at the request of the Abbot of Montiéramey so that they could be solemnly read during divine office at that monastery.[4] Moreover, in his reply to Bernard de Portes, Bernard never says that he is planning to continue to give talks to his monks on the Song of Songs, but that he will try to continue this "work" when he has the time and the leisure.

In a further letter, Bernard clarifies his plan for this project still more:

> *Sermones super principia Canticorum, quos tu petisti, et ego promiseram, transmitto tibi: quibus lectis peto, ut quam citius opportune poteris, tuo rescripto moneamur vel ad procedendum vel ad supersedendum.*[5]

Clearly, we see here that Bernard says that he is ready to drop his project if, in his friend's opinion, this would be for the best. Evidently he is referring to something quite other than a series of talks begun for the chapter at Clairvaux, talks that the opinion of a stranger would certainly not cause him to discontinue.

Mabillon even wondered—not without reason—whether St Bernard had not actually begun this collection of *Sermons* at the urging of Bernard de Portes.[6] Indeed, Bernard in his first letter to his friend, even before he made the statement quoted above, wrote:

---

4. "Petis, carissime mi Guido abbas, . . . *dictare* me aliqua uobis *legenda* solemniter. . . . De uita Sancti duos sermones *dictaui,* qualicumque sermone meo: illud quantum potui cauens ut nec breuitas obscuros, nec prolixitas redderet onerosos."—Ep 398:1, 3, PL 182:609, 611: "You, my dear Abbot Guy, and your brethren are asking me to compose for you something which can be solemnly recited. . . . I have written two sermons on the life of the saints in my own words but based upon the ancient accounts you sent me. I have tried to avoid obscure brevity on one hand and wearisome prolixity on the other."—BSJ, Ep 430:1, 3, pp. 501-502.

5. Ep 154, PL 182:313: "I am sending you the sermons on the beginning of the Song of Solomon, as you have asked me to do and as I have promised. When you have read them, I beg you to write as soon as you conveniently can and tell me whether you think I should continue with them or not."—BSJ, Ep 160, p. 230.

6. *Preface* to Vol. 4, PL 183:781.

Introduction

Cedo importunitati tuae ut uel exhibitio tollat suspicio-nem. Res est cum amico. Non parco iam uerecundiae: pror-sus dum fiat quod tu uis, insipientiae meae non recorda-bor.[7]

In the statement above, Bernard makes it clear that, in sending him the *Sermons*, he is making good his promise and fulfilling the request of Bernard de Portes: *Quos tu petisti et ego promiseram.* Moreover, at the very beginning of *Sermon One,* Bernard uses a phrase which seems to refer to the request of Bernard de Portes and to the reply which is embodied in the *Sermons* themselves:

Puto autem quod habebit unde aduersum nos murmuret is, qui nobis de uia uenit amicus, cum et tertium istum insump-serit panem.[8]

7. Ep 153:1, PL 182:312: "And so I will accede to your importunity, so that you may have no doubts about my insufficiency. It is a matter between friends. I will not try any more to spare my modesty, I will forget my own foolishness in trying to satisfy your demands."—BSJ, Ep 159, p. 229. Judging from Bernard's reply, it would seem that his friend at Portes had convinced him that the time had come when he should put his powers to the test and create his masterpiece. Indeed the entire letter that Bernard wrote gives the impression that he is referring to a literary work which had been long maturing (*Petis instanter . . .* You earnestly entreat me. . . .), carefully "worked on" (*Utinam tuo studio ingenioque dignum aliquid elaborare possem!* I wish I could compose something worthy of your zeal and intelligence), whose continuation will demand both time and effort (*Ceterum ubi ingenium, aut quando otium mihi suficiens ad id quod petis?* But how can I find the ability, let alone the leisure, to do as you ask?), that it concerned a work which was both lofty and difficult (*Neque enim leue quid aut uile, et quod nos possumus, postulare uideris.* It is not as though you were asking me to do some little thing that would be quite easy and ordinary), destined—and this is always a formidable undertaking—to be offered to the general public and open to the criticism of all (*Quod autem habeo, uereor si in medium uenerit, ne te quoque optasse illud pudeat, paeniteat postulasse.* Were I to give you what I have, I am afraid that you would feel ashamed to have asked for it, and would regret having received it.). Bernard compares himself to a beggar, *Ego potuis illa abs te mendicare debuerim* (It is I who should beg from you.). Now in the first *Sermon on the Song of Songs,* he takes up this comparison again: *Nam et ego unus sum de expectantibus, mendicans et ipse uobiscum. . . .*—SC 1:4, OB 1:4: "For I myself am one of the seekers, one who begs along with you. . . ."—CF 4:3.

8. SC 1:3, OB 1:4: "I am sure that the friend who comes to us on his travels will have no reason to murmur against us after he had shared in this third loaf."—CF 4:3. Moreover, Mabillon, in his *Preface* to Vol. 4 (PL 183:786) wondered if the original instigator of SC might not have been Hugh of St Victor or some other

We have, too, the witness of Bernard's contemporaries. First, we have, for example, that of Aimon de Bazoches who also asked Bernard for the text of the *Sermons* and refers to them as a book: *Liber iste vester uoluitur per ora sinusque omnium.*[9] Now Bernard's other sermons, and we have contemporary testimony for this statement, are never referred to as books.[10]

When Evervin of Steinfeld, around the year 1144, asked Bernard to refute the teachings of the Neo-Manichean heretics who were widely disseminating their theories, especially around Cologne, he suggested that he build his refutation around a verse from the Song of Songs on which Bernard had told him he was writing a commentary:

> It is now time that you draw forth from the five waterpots and publicly make provision against these new heretics, who now almost everywhere through all the churches are bubbling over from the well of the abyss, as if their leader was now beginning to be unleashed and the day of the Lord is at hand. You have told me, Father, that you are now at that place in the bridal song which celebrates the love of Christ and his Church, where you must treat of the verse: "Catch us the little foxes, who destroy the vines."[11] That applies to this mystery and leads you to the five waterpots.

---

commentator on Ecclesiastes or Proverbs. But the allusion that Bernard makes to these two books (SC 1:2) is one which, since the time of Origen, has been a theme traditionally developed in the introduction to the Song of Songs. (*Commentar. in Cant. cant.*, Prol. ed Baehrens, pp 63, 75-79). Bernard is definitely following Origen here: compare particularly the beginning of SC 1:3 with Origen, *loc. cit.* p. 78, 1, 15-19. J. Schuck, *op. cit.* p 7, suggests that the monks of Clairvaux had meditated on Proverbs and Ecclesiastes during 1136 but that when the time came for them to commence using the Song of Songs as the basis for study and growth in their spiritual life Bernard realized that he would have to prepare them for this by explaining it to them. W. Kahles [*Radbert und Bernhard, Zwei Ausprägungen christlicher Frömmigheit* (Emsdetten, 1938) p 60] has already pointed out the fact that this is a realm of useless conjecture and that the traditional theme, inherited from Origen, offers quite sufficient reason for what Bernard said.

9. Among the Ep of St Bernard, Ep 483, PL 182:692: "That book of yours has flown everywhere across land and sea."

10. All this contemporary evidence is brought together in "S. Bernard et ses secrétaires," *Recueil* 11-23. I have indicated other points in *Études sur s. Bernard et le texte de ses écrits* (Rome, ASOC 9, 1953) pp 47-50.

11. Song 2:15.

> Therefore we ask you, Father, to point out all the different aspects of their heresies which have come to your knowledge and to destroy them by bringing against them all the arguments and authorities of our faith. [12]

Evervin then lists the errors of these heretics and concludes by again begging Bernard to take up the "weapon of his pen" against them:

> We ask you, holy Father, in the face of such multifarious evils, to stir up your concern and direct your pen against the savage beasts in the reeds. [13]

In point of fact, Bernard did just what Evervin asked. He composed _Sermons Sixty-five_ and _Sixty-six_ in which he refuted each error in turn, just as they had been enumerated for him. If he had replied to Evervin by writing some sort of a doctrinal letter, this would have been preserved, for it was texts of this sort which were, we find, most frequently preferred and kept in the early collections of his letters.[14] Needless to say, it was in the form of these two long sermons that his reply was couched. R. Manselli has pointed out how precise and complete this reply is. Bernard takes up all the points listed by Evervin, and only these points. He never mentions other heretics of the period, such as Henry whom he had indeed met at Pisa, or the Petrobusians against whom Peter the Venerable, known to Bernard, was in open conflict.[15] The two sermons are a formal reply to a specific request—a request made, not by the monks of Clairvaux, but by a prelate of the Rhineland. Thus, clearly, they were not written with the monks of Clairvaux in mind. They were the medium determined upon by Bernard in the exercise of a role

12. Among the Ep of St Bernard, Ep 472:1, PL 182:677.
13. Ibid. 6, 679.
14. See _Études_, p 95.
15. R. Manselli, _Studi sulle eresie del secolo XII_ (Rome, 1953) pp 103-107. According to the Author, _ibid._ p 99, Bernard's reply to Evervin begins with SC 63-64, in which the danger of bad monks is pointed out. In this case, we see that the carefully developed refutation of the theories of the heretics of Cologne, as Manselli admits himself, p 101, only begins with SC 65. Bernard suggests this himself at the beginning of this _Sermon_, using a play on words: after having spoken of the _vinea domestica_, that is, his monks, he speaks of the _vinea dominica_, that is, the Church.

conceded to him by all, even during his lifetime, his role as doctor and teacher, which no one would permit him to shirk. Evervin makes this point quite clear.[16]

When, sometime before 1156, Geoffroy of Auxerre wrote the third book of the *Life of Saint Bernard,*[17] which had been left unfinished by William of Saint Thierry and Arnaud of Bonneval, he followed the classic plan of biographies which are supposed to glorify the servant of God in question and edify their readers. He speaks of Bernard's deeds, his virtues, his miracles and, finally, of his writings, that is, his "books" and his "letters": *Ceterum longe eminentius in usis ille libris apparet et ex litteris propriis innotescit.*[18] Among the writings, he lists treatises, homilies on *Missus est*, the *Sermo ad milites Templi* (Sermon to the Knights of the Temple), the *Sermons on the Song of Songs*[19] and, last of all, the letters. But it is earlier on, toward the beginning of this same book when Geoffroy of Auxerre is speaking of the virtues and qualities of Bernard and praising his fervent and persuasive eloquence that he dwelt at length on his sermons (*opus praedicationis*).[20] Geoffroy considers therefore that the *Sermons on the Song of Songs* are to be dealt with under the heading of Bernard's literary activity, not under that of his preaching.

Even in the text itself of the *Sermons*, Bernard refers to his

16. All of the first par. of this letter from Evervin, which is too long to quote here in its entirety, shows both Bernard's status and acceptance as a teacher: *Confortare ecclesiam Christi*, it says in the beginning; and it speaks of the agreement of all concerning the high caliber of SC: *Laetabor ego super eloquia tua. . . .*"

17. Concerning the date, see Vacandard. "L'histoire de s. Bernard, Critique des sources," *Rev. des quest. hist.* 43 (1888) p 347.

18. *Vita prima*, 3:8:29, PL 185:320. One can see that the outline plan adopted by Geoffroy of Auxerre is the same as that used by biographers of other holy personages. It corresponds with the three points which are covered by the preliminary inquiries undertaken in view of canonization: life, miracles and writings.

19. *Nam in Sermonibus super Cantica, et inuestigator mysteriorum, et morum aedificator magnificus innotescit.—ibid.* In like manner, Isaac of Stella (fl. 1165) will speak of SC as the best of the *scripturae* of Bernard: *In ejus scripturis. . . ., et maxime in his quae in Canticis canticorum scripsit—*Serm. 52, PL 194:1869 D. About this same period, another writer, and in this case he is an anonymous writer, will say, *in sermonibus super Cantica canticorum conscriptis—*see *Études,* p 123.

20. *Vita prima*, 3:3:6-7, 306-307.

public in the second person singular, not in the second person plural, as he would do if he were speaking to an audience. Here are some examples:

> *Puto, si bene intellexisti . . ., non incongrue me hanc un-*
> *guentariam . . . appellasse testaberis. . . .* SC 23:7; *Vis tibi*
> *denique demonstrem. . . .* SC 25:5; *Et ut scias. . . . Aduerte*
> *adhuc. . . .* SC 28:7; *Quod si probas et tu hanc nostram inter-*
> *pretationem, uide etiam. . . .* SC 30: 6; *Denique aduertisti.*
> *. . .* SC 31:7; *Et primo aduerte . . ., sed nec illud praetereat*
> *te. . . .* SC 33:2; *Vide, autem ne carnaliter cogites. . . . Porro*
> *uerecundiam intellige. . . .* SC 40:1;[21] *Vis tibi per simile*
> *ostendam quod diciture? Attolle oculos. . . .* SC 71:6; *Deni-*
> *que innuitur tibi. . . .* SC 71:7; *Videsne diuersitatem? . . . .*
> *Quamquam, si aduertisti, satis tibi . . . innuitur differentia*
> *unitatum. . . .* SC 71:8.

Now in each of these instances—and in others that are similar—there is no question of an imaginary dialogue between Bernard and his soul or between him and the Bride, but rather Bernard is directly addressing the person for whom he is explaining the text upon which he is commenting or the ideas he is expounding.

Elsewhere, one even wonders if Bernard has not in mind the Carthusian of Portes who had originally asked him to write:

> But that is enough concerning that, for you yourself, if you care to make the effort to look into it, can probably find some others like it in the lofty realms of the Scriptures. (SC 53:2).[22]

---

21. In the entire course of *Sermon 40* we see that Bernard never once uses the second person plural but often speaks in the second person singular as if he were speaking to a specific person. One has the impression from the text that it is a treatise, a meditation or even a letter, as much as it is a sermon.

22. One may well ask oneself, when Bernard substituted a passage of recension M which, in *Sermon 71*, begins with the words *Denique innuitur tibi. . . .* and which has just been mentioned above, if the clearer development of recension A, beginning with *Consensio* and containing the words *Videsne diuersitatem . . . si aduertisti . . . ,* was not made at the suggestion of Bernard de Portes. Several corrections and additions, which distinguish the revised text A from the original text M, could well have been the result of suggestions made to Bernard by others to whom he had submitted his work for evaluation, just as he said he did in the

When Bernard writes, at the beginning of *Sermon Seventy-one: Tu ergo qui haec audis vel legis,* he is thinking in terms of the "listener" at a public reading at least as much as of the scribe writing at his dictation.

In all these instances, it is clear that Bernard has in mind a "reader" for whom he has particularly written this book, although he had previously written other books dealing with this same topic. He states this quite clearly at one point:

> I know that I have explained this text more fully in my book, *On the Love of God,* and gave it a different interpretation. Whether it is better or worse, let the reader decide, unless both are pleasing to him. (SC 51:4)

Seen as a whole, the text of the *Sermons* does not indicate oral delivery. The sermons are long. They take up at least four or five columns of closely printed text in Migne's Patrology. Some run even to ten columns. One simply cannot imagine what period in the Cistercian horarium would have been available during which the monks could hear preached sermons, each of whose texts, if one either read it or delivered it in spoken word, would take up a full hour or more. Moreover, the text is not just long; it is hard to follow. The style is characterized by a great subtlety of phrase and thought in certain places.[23] What audience could fully grasp the nuances?[24] Even though he had prepared his theme by

---

case of Bernard de Portes. There is at Grenoble an old copy (ms. 424, Catal. 243) of *Sermons 40-83.* This copy has marginal or interlinear notations, beginning with *Sermon 63,* which are evidently from recension A. This manuscript belonged to the Correrie of the Grande Chartreuse. One would like to think that it came originally from the Charterhouse of Portes, as did two other manuscripts with some of Saint Bernard's writings, now at Grenoble, 347 (275) and 735 (179).

23. Thus, for example, the ending of SC 17:3; the ending of SC 20:4; SC 50:7; the explanation of the union of the Divine Persons in SC 71; his treatment of the divine image in SC 80-82. Some very long exordiums, such as that of SC 16, have no resemblance whatever to oral preaching addressed to an intimately known audience. Some sermon endings, as that of SC 34, seem planned only to lead up to the final doxology which would be a superfluous device if the reason for their use were not simply to "compose" a sermon, carrying out all the stylistic laws regulating this literary genre.

24. It is true that William of Saint Thierry wrote of the counsels concerning fervor and austerity which Bernard gave to his religious at the beginning of his

deep meditation, could Bernard himself have delivered, extemporaneously, talks whose expression and doctrine are so perfect in content, so closely reasoned and so precise? [25] It is certainly true that the rhetorical formation of men in the Middle Ages prepared them to speak extemporaneously in rhythmic prose and with a literary polish which would astound us today.[26] This is not said by way of putting limits to the genius of Bernard. It is simply to wonder out loud why, some two hundred times during his life time and only those two hundred times, Bernard would have delivered, during chapter at Clairvaux, long and elaborate sermons, these *Sermons* and some hundred and twenty on the liturgical year whose edited text we still have, while usually he gave to his monks warm and intimate little talks, none of whose texts have been preserved save in résumé in the form of a few sentences or "sermons in brief." *Sermon Eighty-six* was never finished, not because Bernard died while he was delivering it,

---

years as abbot: *Sed uiri uere religiosi, et pie prudentes, et praedicatione sermonum eius uenerabantur etiam quae non capiebant.—Vita prima,* 1:6:29, PL 185:243. But, in the context of his remarks, we see that William's intention is simply to show that Bernard later "condescended" to the limitations of the generality of his monks. This is seen even more clearly in the redaction of Alain of Auxerre, *Vita secunda,* 7:21, PL 185:481. For further information concerning Bernard's hearers at Clairvaux and the form in which he addressed them, see *Études,* pp 78-80.

25. As Gilbert of Hoyland has suggested, certain texts and certain problems were sometimes discussed by Bernard most abstrusely! *Et quae uir (utrum eruditior an eloquentior nescio) suis disputauit in homiliis.* . . . SC 22:1, PL 184-114. Gilbert himself sometimes goes in for similar *disputationes* in his *Sermons:* SC 33:9, 114; 44:7, 236. Moreover, John of Salisbury summed up his view of St Bernard's SC by the word *subtilissima; Hist. Pontif.* II, ed R.L. Poole (Oxford, 1927) pp 26-27 (see *Études,* p 123). When speaking of SC, Bernard himself habitually employed the terms *disputare* and *disputatio,* for example, SC 2:9; 4:1; 8:1; 23:3, 17; 27:1; 35:7; 38:5; 40:4; 71:14, etc. One might remark that the terms employed by Evervin toward the end of the text cited above, p 197, n 1. (*distinguere, contra ponere, rationes, auctoritates*) would refer more logically to a *disputatio* than to a "simple talk."

26. This point has been brought out quite clearly by C. Mohrmann, "Le style de s. Bernard," *S. Bernardo* (Milan, 1954) pp 174-175. I should, at this time, like to thank the author of this outstanding study for the light which her talks have given me on the language used by St Bernard.

but because he did not have time to write it down in finished form.[27]

POINTS WHICH WOULD SUGGEST ORAL DELIVERY

There are only two points which would suggest that the *Sermons on the Song of Songs* were actually delivered.

The first indication is to be found in the extremely personal emphasis of these *Sermons*. The speaker refers to the fact that he is tired and ill, that he is busy; he mentions the arrival of guests,[28] and refers to other events taking place during the times when he is speaking,[29] and to the reactions of his hearers, that they grumble, yawn and even go to sleep.[30] He speaks to the monks of Clairvaux who knew his brother Gerard, he mentions their cellarer[31] and those whom he sees sleeping during night office.

These questions call for certain clarifications. The greater part of these allusions to the speaker personally or to his audience are found at the beginning or end of the sermons, in the exordiums or conclusions which precede the doxologies which are themselves introduced with polished skill and form. One should recognize the fact that they simply constitute a "framework" which follows the accepted traditions of oratory, one within which a theme is to be developed. They indicate a framework of procedure which one may consider to be part and parcel of the clearly determined literary style

27. Evervin of Steinfeld has made the continuation of the composition of SC depend not on the preaching of Bernard at Clairvaux, but on the free time left him from his other occupations. Guerric of Igny and Gerhoh of Reichersberg, cited in *Études*, p 123, say the same thing. Bernard actually spoke of the matter no differently himself in the text referred to above, n 3.

28. Mabillon has collected all these suggestive references, *Praeface* of Vol. 4, PL 183:782-783; see also his note 249, PL 183:1155.

29. For example, to his return from Rome, at the beginning of SC 24, to the course of days during which the series of *Sermons* continued, *Heri. . . , hesterno sermone. . . , triduum . . . expensum est* (SC 83:1).

30. *Bene fecistis grunniendo. . . . Quosdam siquidem oscitantes, quosdam et dormitantes intueor.* (SC 35:7).

31. *Sermon 26.* Sermon 26 is particularly artificial in its plan. The beginning (nn 1-2) is as quietly worded as are his other sermons. A single transitional phrase suddenly introduces an outburst of sorrow which tears interrupt in the last phrase (n 14), when all has been said: *Finem uerborum inducunt lacrimae; tu illis, Domine, finem modumque indixeris.*

accepted for a sermon. We know how meticulously Bernard conformed to literary niceties. He plans the *Apologia* in letter form and never infringes on accepted epistolary laws.[32] And when he wrote his *De praecepto*, in a "manner more developed than would be permitted in epistolary form," he makes a lengthy excuse in a dedicatory letter which has no other reason for being than the excuse itself. Here he mentions that he plans to call his work a "book" rather than a "letter."[33] Moreover, when he sets himself to work within the framework of a certain literary style, he is always faithful to its form. The famous "letter to Robert" is as much a propaganda lampoon against Cluny in favor of Cîteaux as it is a composition called for by a given circumstance.[34] However, since it is a letter, the message, which is directed actually to the general reader, must be written as if to an individual. Thus Bernard is saying to his cousin what he wants everyone to know and, in doing so, creates a masterpiece in epistolary style.[35] When Bernard wants to teach mystical theology, refute heretics in Cologne, denounce the errors of Gilbert de la Porée, or explain in sermon form a doctrine of general import, why does he make pretence of speaking to his community? He knows he is composing his *Sermons on the Song of Songs* with the thought of publication in mind but since, in this instance, he plans to have them reach the gen-

32. "If this is going to be a letter, it is time it came to an end."—Apo 15, OB 3:94, CF 1:51.

33. OB 3:253-254, CF 1:103-104.

34. Ep 1, PL 182:67-79; BSJ, pp. 1-10.

35. All this letter, or nearly all of it, seems to have been written with the general public in mind. This can be seen by the examples I gathered together when I published "Les lettres familières d'un moine du Bec", *Analecta monastica* 2 (Rome, 1953) pp 145-150. Here, as elsewhere, the letter writers of the Middle Ages were simply conforming to a tradition inherited from the Patristic Age. To cite but one example, when St Jerome writes his *Letter 125* to the monk Rusticus he writes in a style which is both so polished and, at the same time, so doctrinal that it is in actuality an entire outline for monastic life. He knows that he is writing an open letter. But, as it so often happened, he forgets that he is writing just to an individual and begins to anticipate objections that he thinks the general public may bring up. At such times, he speaks not in the second person singular, as to one person, but uses the plural form: *Scio me offensurum esse quam plurimos . . .*, Ep 125:5. CSEL 56:122.

eral public in sermon form, he conforms to the exigencies of this specific mode of expression. The allusions which make the exordiums and conclusions of his sermons so personal were not of a kind that would mislead his contemporaries who expected to see the laws of the various literary styles observed. To conform to them was a proof of one's deep sincerity and one's careful fidelity to the form one had elected.[36] Moreover, it was customary, when one wrote, to indicate at the beginning the literary form one had chosen.[37] Thus, for example, we see Gilbert of Hoyland in his exordiums and conclusions using the same procedure as Bernard, pretending that he is speaking to monks who have urged him to explain the Song of Songs to them, whereas actually he was leisurely writing a continuation of the work Bernard had begun.[38] Just as Bernard, when he was dictating a treatise in

36. Is it necessary to underline the artificial character of certain allusions, which no one could mistake? Whether or not *Sermon 3* was delivered at an early hour when work was beginning (as would seem to be the case for *Sermon 1:12*) or in the evening (as other endings might suggest), there is very little likelihood that anyone would have come while Bernard was speaking to announce at chapter the arrival of guests, who are, moreover, brought into his talk by an allusion to *diei malitia* (n 6). In any event, the time to announce their arrival would have been said in the formal manner required by the exordium, the development and the conclusion. But our forebears understood better, perhaps, than we can today, that the "composition" of a work of art, as such, includes certain stylistic fictions: *Fingere namque componere dicimus; unde et compositiores luti figulos uocamus,* wrote St Grégory the Great, *Hom. in Eu.* 13:1, PL 76:1282. See *Thes. ling. lat.* "fingo," col 771-774.

37. Thus, Gilbert of Hoyland, when he gathered together some notes at the request of a certain correspondent, reminds his correspondent that he has asked him for *non epistolas sed clausulas uerborum.* PL 184:251D. Since this style is related to oratorical forms (see *Thes. ling. lat.* "clausula," col 1324) he also concludes his "notes" not as letters but as sermons would end. PL 184:258B, 261C, etc. Elsewhere (PL 184:276, 288), Gilbert gives to an abbot, in sermon form, counsels of the same type as those which Bernard wrote in letter form in *De moribus et officio episcoporum,* for in this early collection of the writings of St Bernard, this particular work is included among the letters, not among the series of treatises. Similarly, Geoffrey of Auxerre indicates the style his commentaries on the Song of Songs are based on when he writes, *notulas potius . . . quam dictamen, notulas glossularum.* Seen from this angle, the real preface to SC is actually *Letters 153* and *154,* from St Bernard to Bernard de Portes, which have been mentioned above.

38. For example, Sermon 5:1; 7:1; 26:9; etc. In Sermon 41:4-7, Gilbert inserts a long panegyric on Aelred of Rievaulx, just as St Bernard inserted in *Sermon 26,*

epistolary form, would, from time to time, address himself directly to the person to whom he was supposed to be writing, in like manner, when he was planning a doctrinal exposition in sermon form, he would allude to his hearers, who according to the rules, are considered to be present, seeing him and hearing his talk. His commentary on the Song of Songs, unlike other scholarly commentaries, is not a continuous text, in which there are no divisions. It is a collection of sermons, each standing alone as a finished composition. A series of masterpieces such as this, where one finds such closely knit thought and yet such unity in variety, proves the literary genius of Bernard.[39]

We find, among the texts which have led scholars to believe that the *Sermons on the Song of Songs* were delivered, this explicit statement of Bernard at the beginning of *Sermon Fifty-four*:

> *Super eodem capitulo, quod hesterno sermone uersatum est, dicturus sum et alium intellectum quem hodierno seruaui uos probate, et eligite potiora. Non est opus superiora repetere, quae excidisse non arbitror in tam breui. Si quominus tamen, scripta sunt ut dicta sunt, et excepta stylo, sicut et sermones ceteri, ut facile recuperetur quod forte exciderit.*[40]

This sermon opening, as are so many other exordiums and conclusions, is certainly a literary and fictional form. Indeed, whatever may be the meaning given to the word *ut*, in the last sentence, it still in no way corresponds to fact, as we know it through a great number of other indications. If *ut* is

---

SC, the eulogy on his brother Gerard. Some of Gilbert's sermons are supposedly addressed to consecrated virgins (17:1; 19:1), others to monks (22:7, etc.) Of course, it is not impossible that Gilbert used notes which he had made for sermons he actually preached when he began to set them down in writing.

39. See "Le genre littéraire des Sermones in Cantica," *Études*, p 122.

40. OB 2:102: "In regard to that same chapter which I treated of in yesterday's sermon, I am about to give you a different interpretation from the one I gave you. You examine them and choose which is better. There is no need to repeat what I have already said for I am sure you have not forgotten it so quickly. If however you have forgotten some, it has been written down just as it was preached, except for the style, just as the rest of the sermons, so you can easily recover what you have perhaps forgotten."

a modal conjunction and means "in the same way as," and if it should be translated, "these words are written *just as* they were spoken," this formula can only hold true for the first recension (M), which already contained this statement. Now, in the two authentic recensions we have, there is one passage repeated three times. It does not seem probable that Bernard would have repeated it three times, in the same terms, when speaking to his monks.[41] Moreover, there are in the second recension (A), words, phrases and entire passages, which are not contained in M and which were never delivered. This situation prevails in regard to the style of delivered sermons no less than it does with their content. This is not the place to discuss *ex professo* the moot question of the actual language used by Bernard in speaking to his monks. Suffice it to say that, if his written style manifests already a marked relationship with the *lingua franca*[42] so marked a one that he has been called "the first great writer of French prose,"[43] for yet greater reasons, his oral style, even in Latin, would have manifested even more marked similarities to a romance language and would have differed from that polished Latin which alone was able to furnish Bernard, when he was writing, with the precise and nuanced vocabulary he needed for his thought.[44]

41. This passage, which begins with *siquidem cum dixissent ei: Exultabimus* and ends with a *malis pascuntur,* is found in the first part of both of these two sermons—(24 and 25). In M, they are a commentary on the verse *Recti diligunt te.* (These sermons were written, one before and the other after Bernard's trip to Italy in 1137-1138). They are found in *Sermon 24:2* of recension A where the two sermons are re-worked to form a single sermon together. These two versions of *Sermon 24* are given separately in the critical edition of SC.

42. Cf. C. Mohrmann, "Le style des oeuvres mariales de s. Bernard," *Marie* 7:6 (March-April, 1954) p 26 and "Le style de s. Bernard," *S. Bernardo* (Milan, 1954) p 171.

43. C. Mohrmann, "Le style de s. Bernard," *loc. cit.* p 170.

44. Mabillon (*Praeface of Vol. 3*, PL 183:13-15) has collected evidence and indications which would suggest that Bernard preached in Latin. The question still stands, however, as to what sort of Latin Bernard habitually "spoke." This point will not be cleared up save by philological studies, in depth, on Bernard's "style" and "language," (to borrow a distinction made by the School of Nijmegen) and will not be clarified by studies of his vocabulary alone. Studies such as these V. Lossky. "Etudes sur la terminologie de s. Bernard," *Bulletin Du Cange,* 12 (1942) pp 79-96, has been carrying on with real insight. On the other hand, the characteristic rhythm of Bernard's sermons, one which at times almost sings, a

On the other hand, *ut* cannot mean "when," as if it would be translated: "These words were written down *at the very moment* at which they were spoken." I have shown, elsewhere, that, in the 12th century, no form of stenography, no system of abbreviations, existed, which would permit the exact transcription of a talk as it was being delivered.[45] Thus the *Sermons* were either written out before being delivered, in which case Bernard would simply have come to read to his monks this literary work—all that we know of his psychological make-up, and of the audience of his time, excludes such an hypothesis—or else the *Sermons* were written down after having been delivered as real sermons. Here stands in full light the problem of the relationship between the preached sermon and the written text.[46] This is the problem we must now take up.

SOLUTION

The *Sermons on the Song of Songs* were most certainly not written down while they were being delivered.[47] Were they

---

characteristic which has been very justifiably stressed by C. Mohrmann, can be explained equally well if Bernard is "speaking" them to a secretary—dictation being a quite usual medieval procedure—rather than before an audience which, if we are to believe him, was sometimes drowsy. Bernard's enthusiasm depends less on those to whom he speaks than on the topic matter itself. Concerning the relation that exists between the Latin sermons of St Bernard and their various early translations into romance languages, I have pointed out pertinent ideas in an appendix to an article written in collaboration with H. M. Rochais, "La tradition des sermons de s. Bernard," *Scriptorium,* 15 (1961).

45. See *Études,* p 36.

46. The same problem occurs on the score of some sermons on the psalm *Qui habitat,* of which there are three redactions. These I have described in *Bernard de Clairvaux,* (Paris, 1953) pp 435-446.

47. At the most, the phrase used at the start of *Sermon 54,* cited above, would perhaps mean: "These words are written as if they supposedly had been spoken, as they would actually have been said if the preceding sermon had really been delivered." We would be even more wise if we considered this other phrase from *Sermon 77:2* (OB 2:262) simply as an artificial literary device, when Bernard wrote concerning wicked prelates: "Sine causa tamen uel his uel illis immoraremur, quia non audiunt nos. Set et si litteris forsitan mandentur ista quae dicimus, dedignabuntur legere; aut si forte legerint, mihi indignabuntur, quamvis rectius sibi hoc facerent. Propterea relinquamus istos. . . ." Actually, Bernard did not

written down, "word for word," after actual delivery? A
priori, nothing would indicate this to be the case. We know
that Bernard spoke simply and familiarly with his monks.
The spontaneity with which he then developed his thought in
no way limited his freedom when he was composing, in
sermon form, a doctrinal work destined for the public at
large. Does there then exist no relation between the text of
Sermons on the Song of Songs and Bernard's preaching? One
need not adopt such an extreme position. St Bernard most
certainly spoke to his monks about the Song of Songs and
explained it to them. However we must not attach too much
importance to a single remark of a contemporary of his, who
says that Bernard "spoke" on the Song of Songs.

When Guerric of Igny wrote of St Bernard: "He has planned to *speak* on the whole nuptial canticle and from what he
has already published has given us hope, . . ."[48] he knew
quite well that he was referring to a work which had been
"edited" in view of its presentation to a general public quite
different from the community of Clairvaux. Actually, allusions to monastic life are rare in the *Sermons on the Song* as
they are, too, in Bernard's great sermons on the liturgical
year. They are much more frequent in his short sermons and
the jotted notes from his talks. Still we know that Bernard
loved the Song of Songs. His close friend Geoffrey of
Auxerre tells us that, even in his novitiate days, Bernard liked
to compare himself to the bride.[49] His friend William of
Saint Thierry relates that Bernard, shortly after he was
elected abbot, explained to him the mysteries of this marriage song.[50] We have, among the *De diversis*, seven short
sermons on various verses of the Song.[51] And, finally, the

---

write this before he had previously denounced the morals of bad ecclesiastics and
avaricious prelates in various other places in SC and in his other works. He knows
that he is writing against them yet for them. He is writing in a fashion which, as
literature, is both excellent and expedient.

48. *Third Sermon for the Feast of Saints Peter and Paul,* 1, PL 185:183, tr
Liturgical Sermons of Guerric of Igny, CF 32:160f.

49. Text in *Études,* p 160, 27-32.

50. *Vita prima* 1:12:59, PL 185-259.

51. They have been pointed out and described in *Études,* p 119.

Breuis commentatio in Cantica, which Mabillon published,[52] surely transmits to us a true echo of Bernard's teaching.[53] This text indeed places us in a position to find a solution to our problem.

There are certainly included in the *Sermons on the Song of Songs* fragments of sermons, perhaps even whole sermons, where Bernard has given written and literary form to exegesis which he had already developed in talks to his monks or to other audiences. A close study of the style of the *Sermons* shows an evident difference between certain passages which are subtley nuanced theological dissertations and could not have been delivered in spoken form and others which still have the sound of the spoken word. The latter only needed to be re-worked before being inserted into the general body of his "composed" works, where they fitted well. In any event St Bernard took up again, in these *Sermons,* themes which we know he had developed elsewhere on various occasions. I have already pointed out several of these.[54] Here is still a further instance. We find it in *Sermon Thirty-nine* as well as in parallel passages, where Bernard is giving a symbolic interpretation of the chariots and horses of Pharaoh.

The symbolism of the chariots themselves—and he considers them apart from the horses that draw them—is presented in two typically Bernardine *Sentences,* which show us the outlines or résumés he had made for his sermons. In one (85)[55] he describes four sorts of chariots, those belonging to Pharaoh, each of which represents two vices, and those of the eunuch, of Joseph and of Elijah, each representing two virtues. In the other *Sentence* (142)[56] we find only three chariots mentioned, those of Pharaoh, the eunuch and Elijah,

---

52. PL 184:407-436.

53. See the study devoted to this text in *Études,* p 105-121. A careful comparison of this text with the writings of William of Saint Thierry helps one to determine even more precisely the extent of the latter's role in the redaction he made; see J. Hourlier, in *ASOC* 12 (1956) p 105-114.

54. Concerning the theme of the four temptations of the Church, see *Études,* pp 133-134; concerning the theme of the five kinds of knowledge, *ibid.* pp 73-74.

55.,PL 184:1146.

56. Ibid. 1151.

but here we have each described with its driver, horse and two wheels, all symbolizing some reality in the moral order—a virtue or a vice, a good or evil tendency. If one sets these two *Sentences* in parallel, synoptic tables, it is easily seen that the second *Sentence* develops the initial points of the first, without, however, reproducing exactly its plan and its ideas. In other words, the same topic in the latter has undergone certain variations.

The symbolism of the horses, moreover, furnishes matter for four other *Sentences*. In one (66),[57] three kinds of horses are simply enumerated. In another *Sentence* (150)[58] the three horses still appear, but here the entire equipage is described in detail, the riders, the saddle, the bridle, the bit, the two spurs, the hole into which they run the hazard of falling, all of which suggest, successively, various vices and virtues. Here again we find the second *Sentence* freely developing certain aspects of the first. In two further texts, the symbolic theme of horses has been used again. In *Parable One*, the Son of the King appears, mounted on the steed of Desire, whose trappings are described in detail.[59] Soon the virtues get into a dispute about it, some slowing its course, others speeding it on its way.[60] The steed of Faith will soon intervene.[61] Finally, in the *Sentence* beginning with the words *Quatuor sunt tentationes*, the four horses mentioned in the Apocalypse (6:2-8) are introduced, upon each of whom is a rider carrying arms or bearing banners.[62]

The symbolism of the chariots and the horses forms the theme of a long *Sentence* which some manuscripts have handed down to us as an isolated fragment,[63] and which is also found in the *Breuis commentatio*. The reason for this

57. Ibid. 1145.
58. Ibid. 1152.
59. PL 183:759, n 3.
60. Ibid. n 4.
61. Ibid. 760, n 6.
62. Ed in *Etudes*, p 134, 30-39.
63. For example, in the Vendome ms. 148 (12th century), ff 128-129, following SC 1-24, among a collection of Bernardine *Sentences,* under the title, *De trino curru Dei et de trino diaboli.*

may be either that it was simply lifted from the latter, or, more likely, because the *Breuis commentatio* may well have been composed of a series of *Sentences* joined together by transitional phrases in an ongoing redaction. The *Sentence* is divisible into two parts, which correspond exactly, though in shorter form, to two parts of *Sermon Thirty-nine.* The first is a commentary on the words *Equitatui meo in curribus Pharaonis assimilavi te, amica mea (Song 1:8)*, keeping the same interpretation, and using the same scriptural citations as those given in *Sermon Thirty-nine*, nn. 1-5. The second section describes in detail the three chariots of the devil and the three chariots of God. For each there is given an interpretation of the symbolism of the horse, the rider, the saddle, the bridle, the bit and the spur. Between the two panels of the diptych, as we see them, exists a perfect parallel. Corresponding to each of the things typified by the chariots of the devil, corresponds its opposite as typified by the chariots of God. Moreover, there is a real and carefully built-up balance in the description of all six chariots. No angle is overlooked. All are in the same order and are introduced by parallel formulas. Here the plan is completely worked out, the symbolism of the chariots and the horses being explained in full detail.

In corresponding parts of *Sermon Thirty-nine* we find several of the points contained in the *Breuis commentatio*, but they are worked out within a far less rigorous framework. Here the emphasis is on the princes of Pharaoh. Some are designated by name (*designati*). Others are simply left to be pursued further at the personal inclination of the hearers or reader. [64] The first are Malice, Luxury, Avarice. Each rides in a four-wheeled chariot, drawn by two horses carrying two riders, or one rider, actually, in the case of the third chariot. Other parts of the description vary. Sometimes only the two

---

64. *Ut in his exerceamini, inquirenda relinquo.* —SC 39:9, OB 2:23; below, p 000. A little further on in n 10, Bernard speaks in the second person: *Recordare nunc mihi Moysi et Aethiopissae, et agnoscce... et discerne, si potes....* The theme of the Ethiopian, here simply alluded to, is one which is developed at length in "Une parabole restituée à s. Bernard," *Études*, pp 135-136.

spurs of the rider are singled out for mention, sometimes the tent and the fan, sometimes only the whips are enlarged upon. In the case of Pharaoh's princes, where we are left to our own conjectures, Pride is "one of the greatest." Impiety is Pharaoh's lieutenant, and when it comes to the "inferior satraps," the reader can take a try himself at interpreting the symbolism of their names, their functions, their weapons and their chariots.

The eight texts which we have just anlyzed certainly present us with a theme dear to St Bernard, one peculiarly his own. This theme is developed with such precision and fullness in no other contemporary or earlier text, even though we do find it commented on by the Fathers of the Church. St Bernard is not completely original in his treatment. Origen—and he may well be following Philo[65] in this instance—seems to have been the source from which later commentators on this theme have drawn their own inspiration. In his commentary on Joshua, Origen simply suggests the theme. The chariots and the horses of Pharaoh symbolize demons.[66] In the commentary on Exodus, he enlarges on it more. The four horses of Pharaoh are Luxury, Cruelty, Avarice and Impiety.[67] Again, in *Homily Two* on the Song of Songs, we find a more precise delineation of the temptations to which the soul is subject, the rein of discipline it needs, the yoke that it must bear, the horses and riders of Pharaoh compared with those of God.[68] It is in Bernard's commentary on this same verse that we find these symbols recalled and used in greatest degree, though in very much amplified form.[69] Other

65. *De agricultura,* 15-19, ed L. Cohn (Berlin, 1896) 1:102-107.

66. Hom 15:3, ed Baehrens, p 384.

67. Hom. 6:3, ed Baehrens, p 194. Gregory of Nyssa, *De uita Moysi,* PG 44:364, also enumerates, in speaking of the passage of the Red Sea, the vices which are buried in the waters of baptism.

68. Ed Baehrens, p 151.

69. In his commentary on this same verse of the Song, Aponius (who relies on Origen in his exegesis; critics have not yet determined whether he lived in the 4th century or, later, in the 7th) speaks of the chariots of Elisha, the one seen by Zechariah and the chariot of which Habakkuk speaks. According to his thinking, the horses and riders of the chariot of Christ are the Angels and the Apostle who

patristic commentators are more cautious, particularly the Latin Fathers.[70] Ambrose applies the symbolism of the chariot of Isaiah to the soul[71] Elsewhere he compares the soul to the chariot of Aminadab where the horses, both good and bad, signify the passions which war among themselves.[72] Jerome says that the chariot is voluptuousness, that its wheels signify instability and its horses pride.[73] Gregory the Great, commenting on the Song, sets up four virtues over against four opposing vices, which are the horses drawing Pharaoh's chariot,[74] but he says nothing of the bit, the saddle and the other comparisons of which Origen and Bernard speak.[75] In later times the theme is scarcely ever found. Bede, we see, still retains the fundamental idea that Pharaoh represents the devil and the sea the waters of Baptism.[76] So does Rabanus Maurus.[77] Between the years 1114 and 1117, Rupert of Deutz again takes up the basic idea which all these interpretations presuppose, but deals with it most cursorily and, actually, in a rather unimaginative fashion.[78] Bernard's treatment, therefore, is quite original. Here he approaches the

---

were victors over Pharoah's riders, that is, over the abettors of heresy. *In Cant.* ed H. Bottino-J. Martini (Rome, 1845) p 42-43. Bernard does not follow Aponius here, though he seems to in other places.

70. Gregory of Nyssa, when he discusses this same verse, brings up the chariot of Elijah, the chariot Zechariah speaks of, and the victory of Israel over the chariots of Pharoah. For him they all signify the victory of the Word within the soul to which he unites himself; *In Cant.,* Hom. 3, PG 44:809-813.

71. *De Uirginitate* 3, PL 16-295.

72. *De Isaac* 8:65, PL 14:527; *In Ps. CXVIII,* 2:33-35, PL 15:1287.

73. *In Ps XIX,* PL 26-876. Moreover, Jerome speaks of a tandem of four virtues which the *auriga Christi* drives, EP 52:13, CSEL 54:437. The virtues here enumerated—prudence, justice, temperance, fortitude—are those whose distinction Jerome, elsewhere, attributes to the Stoic School, after having let it be understood that he borrowed the comparison of the chariots and the horses from Ezechiel and Habakkuk. Ep 66:2, ibid. 54:649. —The symbolism of the horses is developed, without allusion to the virtues in *Comment. in Abacuc,* 2:111, PL 25:1318, 1319.

74. *In Cant.* 1:29, PL 79:491.

75. Moreover, the symbolism of the chariot and the riders is developed differently when dealing with the virtues (*In I Reg.* 4:7, PL 79:239-249) than when dealing with bad thoughts. (ibid. 5:7, 340-341).

76. *In Exod.* 14 PL 91:310.

77. *Allegoriae in S. Scripturam,* PL 112:905; *De uniuerso,* 22:30, PL 111:551.

78. *De Trinitate et eius operibus, In Ex.* 3:31, PL 167:640.

seminal thought of Origen more closely than the thought of any other writer, and, nevertheless, he has created a new imagery which would, henceforth, influence both future literary works [79] and religious art. [80]

Among the eight texts, in which mention is made of chariots, the text of *Breuis commentatio* holds, more than any other, the various basic elements which have passed into the *Sermons on the Song of Songs*. But in the earlier text there is a strict parallelism developed between the symbolic themes within like groups of chariots and between different groups. The plan was artificial, but it permitted a full development in which nothing was omitted. Actually in a spoken exposition, it was logical—and easy—having once spoken of each of Pharaoh's chariots to compare each, in turn, with the chariots of God. In the *Sermons on the Song* Bernard has only retained the points which refer to the chariots of Pharaoh, that is to say, only the first part of the exposition. Moreover he has only developed the symbolism of three chariots. He had evidently been quite content simply to suggest what might be the corresponding possibilities of the fourth, as well as of various other details. When speaking of the three chariots, he uses parts which are also in the *Breuis commentatio*, but quite freely adds, eliminates and modifies the thought with a liberty which is indeed the mark of genius. He avoids over-emphasizing his point or enlarging on details which could well be in poor taste. The chariot theme, like that of the four temptations of the Church, is a theme on which he could give free rein to his imagination—

79. The direct influence of SC 39 on the *Divine Comedy,* where the chariot theme is intermingled with that of the temptations of the Church, has been established by A. Masseron, *Dante et saint Bernard* (Paris, 1953) pp 177-180: c 5: "Les assauts de char mystique et un sermon de saint Bernard."

80. The representation of the chariot of Pharaoh, in the group of frescoes at Saint-Savin de Gartempe (frequently reproduced, for example, in H. Focillon, *Peintures romanes des églises de France* [Paris, 1938] plates 32-33) is still quite simply handled, but it dates from the beginning of the 12th century (see P. H. Michel, "La Psychomachie, thème littéraire et plastique," *Gazette des Beaux-Arts,* 99 (1952) p 326), and thus executed some forty years earlier than SC 39. On the other hand, in his *Trionfi,* Petrarch, who is known to have greatly admired the writings of St Bernard (see *Études* pp 183-184), inspired a whole symbolic iconography of chariots and steeds, much exploited at the time of the Renaissance.

and one on which the editors of his *Sentences* could, too. His was the theme. He changed it about and others, after him and like him, did the same. But when Bernard wrote down the *Sermons on the Song of Songs*, he wisely kept his vivid imagination in check as only a true artist can do.

This example throws a great deal of light on things. The conclusions reached concerning the chariot symbolism are valid, as well, for the entire series of *Sermons on the Song of Songs*. First of all, one must weigh again the importance of the *Breuis commentatio*, which shows itself ever more clearly to be the frame on which Bernard wove his work on the *Sermons*. We do not have the actual spoken sermons which Bernard delivered on the Song of Songs. But we can well believe that they were more developed than the text of the *Breuis commentatio*, and on the other hand less polished than the text of the published *Sermons*.

To sum up, one can now really appreciate the excellence of these *Sermons on the Song of Songs*. Certain passages, as has been said, approximate, to a greater or lesser degree, the oral style of Bernard's delivery. The Abbot of Clairvaux, as we know, was fully engrossed in the composition of the Sermons. People were constantly asking him about their progress and he was well aware of the importance of his undertaking. During the years when he was composing this work, he must surely have spoken on the Song of Songs to his monks more frequently than before. But even though he spoke on the same text and on the same themes which inspired his written work, the latter differs from his talks. In the published *Sermons*, he shows himself in the fullest stature of his genius. He never disappoints his admirers, and this is why he ever pressed on with his task, which was interrupted by his death. [81] In this work we see the writer, his perfect taste, his genius, giving to a long composition which could well have become dull, an inexhaustible color and variety.

---

81. We must also realize that Bernard may well have been considered a Doctor of the Church even during his life and immediately after his death. In substantiation of this point, I have gathered together supporting testimony in "S. Bernard, docteur," C Cist 16 (1954) pp 284-286.

ON THE SONG OF SONGS

SERMONS 21-46

SERMON 21

THE LOVE OF THE BRIDE, THE CHURCH, FOR CHRIST

"DRAW ME AFTER YOU; we shall run in the odor of your ointments."[1] What does this mean? Is the bride an unwilling lover, even of her Bridegroom? Does she have to be drawn to him because she lacks freedom to follow him? But not everyone drawn is reluctant to be drawn. Invalids and people in frail health who find walking difficult do not object to being carried to the bath or to a meal, but a criminal will not enjoy being taken to court or to the scaffold. She who asks to be drawn wills to be drawn; she would not have asked if she possessed the power to follow her loved one of her own free will. But why should she be unable? Must we understand that the bride is weak? If one of the maidens complained of weakness and asked to be drawn, it would not have surprised us. But the bride herself who was so strong and healthy that she seemed able to draw others—is it not hard to believe that she herself needs to be drawn like a person sick or indisposed? Is it possible to regard any person as strong and healthy if we apply the term weak to one who is named bride of the Lord because of her unique perfection and peerless virtue? Is it perhaps the Church who spoke these words as her eyes followed the ascent of her Bridegroom into heaven, filled with desire to

1. Song 1:3 Scripture references are given according to the Latin Vulgate, the text known to Bernard, which sometimes varies slightly in its enumeration from other versions, especially in regard to the Psalms.

3

follow him and be assumed with him into glory?[2] For no matter how great the perfection to which one attains, as long as one is burdened with this mortal body,[3] as long as one is confined in the prison of this evil world, cramped by necessities and tormented by sinful urges, the contemplation of sublime truths can be achieved only little by little and in weariness of spirit; one is certainly not free to follow the Bridegroom wherever he goes.[4] And so we have that tearful cry of the distressed heart: "What a wretched man I am! Who will rescue me from this body doomed to death?"[5] Hence too that supplication: "Free me from this imprisonment."[6] Even the bride herself may repeat out of her distress: "Draw me after you;[7] for a perishable body presses down the soul, and this tent of clay weighs down the active mind."[8] Does she say this because she wants "to be gone and to be with Christ,"[9] especially since she sees that those for whom she might have felt it necessary to continue her earthly life, are making definite progress in the love of the Bridegroom, and safely grounded in charity? She had already referred to this when she said: "Therefore the maidens love you beyond measure."[10] Now she would seem to say: "See, the maiden love you, and this love binds them to you firmly; they no longer have any need of me, there is no longer any reason for me to continue living in this life;" and so she says: "Draw me after you."

2. This is what I should have thought if she had said: "Draw me *to* you."

II. But because she says "after you, " she seems rather to appeal for the grace to follow the example of his way of life, to emulate his virtue, to hold fast to a rule of life similar to his and achieve some degree of his self-control. This is a work for which she needs all possible aid in order to deny herself, take up her cross, and follow Christ.[11] Here surely the bride

2. Col 3:4
3. Rom 7:24
4. Rev 14:4
5. Rom 7:24
6. Ps 141:8

7. Song 1:3
8. Wis 9:15
9. Phil 1:23
10. Song 1:2
11. Mt 16:24

needs to be drawn, and drawn by no other than he who said: "Without me you can do nothing."[12] "I know," she says, "that I have no hope of joining you except by walking after you; and even in this I am helpless unless helped by you. Therefore I entreat you to draw me after you. Happy the man whose help is from you. He prepared in his heart in this valley of tears his going up,[13] to attain to union with you one day in the mountains where joys abound. How few there are, Lord, who wish to follow you, and yet there is not one who does not wish to reach you, because all know that at your right hand are everlasting pleasures.[14] All men therefore wish to enjoy you, but not to the extent of following your example; they will reign with you but not suffer with you.[15] One of these said: 'May I die the death of the just! May my end be one with theirs!'[16] He wanted his last days to resemble those of the just, but not the years of early manhood. Even worldly men who know that a saint's death is an event dear to God[17] want to die with the dispositions of spiritual men whose holy lives repel them; for 'when sleep comes to the loved ones, the Lord's heritage is at hand.'[18] 'Happy are those who die in the Lord,'[19] but on the contrary, in the Prophet's words: 'The death of the wicked is an evil one.'[20] They are not concerned to search for the Lord though they should like to find him; they want to get to him without following him. Not so those to whom Christ said: 'You are the men who have stood by me faithfully in my trials.'[21] Happy those, dear Jesus, who are privileged to have you as their witness. They followed after you in very truth, with their feet and with their hearts. You have revealed to them the paths of life,[22] calling them after you because you are the way and the life.[23] 'Follow me,' you said, 'and I will make you fishers of men;'[24] and again: 'If a man serves me

---

12. Jn 15:5
13. Ps 83:6
14. Ps 15:11
15. Rom 8:17
16. Num 23:10
17. Ps 115:15
18. Ps 126:2-3

19. Rev 14:13
20. Ps 33:22
21. Lk 22:28
22. Ps 15:11
23. Jn 14:6
24. Mt 4:19

he must follow me; wherever I am, my servant will be there too.'[25] And hence that ring of triumph in their words: 'See, we have left everything and followed you.'[26]

3. "So too with the one you love. For your sake she has left all things, eager always to journey after you, ever to walk in your footsteps, to follow you wherever you go.[27] She knows that your ways are delightful ways, that your paths all lead to contentment,[28] that anyone who follows you will not walk in darkness.[29] She requests, however, to be drawn, because 'your righteousness is like the mountains of God,'[30] and she cannot attain to it of her own strength. She requests to be drawn because she knows that no one comes to you unless your Father draws him.[31] But those whom the Father draws are drawn also by you, for whatever works the Father does the Son does too.[32] There is a more intimate note however about her request to be drawn by the Son, for he is her Bridegroom, sent before her by the Father as leader and teacher.[33] He would be the exemplar of her moral life, preparing the way of virtue;[34] he would teach her to become like himself, and share with her his prudence;[35] and having thus given her the law of life and discipline,[36] he would inevitably be attracted by her beauty.[37]

4. " 'Draw me after you; we shall run in the odor of your ointment.'[38] It is indeed necessary that we be drawn, because the fire of your love has quickly cooled within us. We cannot run now, because of this cold,[39] as we did in former days. But we shall run again when you restore to us the joy of knowing you are our Savior,[40] when the benign warmth of grace will have returned with the renewed shining of the Sun of Justice. The troubles that hide him from us like clouds will then pass, the soft breath of the caressing breeze

25. Jn 12:26
26. Mt 19:27
27. Rev 14:4
28. Prov 3:17
29. Jn 8:12
30. Ps 35:7
31. Jn 6:44
32. Jn 5:19
33. Is 55:4
34. Ps 104:22
35. Is 40:14
36. Sir 45:6
37. Ps 44:12
38. Song 1:3
39. Ps 147:17
40. Ps 50:14

will melt the ointments and the perfumes will rise to fill the air with their sweet odor. Then we shall run, run with eagerness where the wafted perfumes draw us. The lethargy that now numbs us will vanish with the return of fervor, and we shall no longer need to be drawn; stimulated by the perfumes we shall run of our own accord. But now again, draw me after you."

III. Thus you see that he who is guided by the Spirit[41] does not always remain in the same state.[42] He does not always advance with the same facility. "The course of man is not in his control."[43] It rather depends on the guidance of the Spirit who sets the pace as he pleases, sometimes torpidly, sometimes blithely, teaching him to forget the past and to strain ahead for what is still to come.[44] If you have been attentive I think you will have seen that your inward experience re--echoes what I have outwardly described.

5. Therefore when you feel weighed down by apathy, lukewarmness and fatigue, do not yield to cowardice or cease to study spiritual truths, but look for the hand of the one who can help you, begging like the bride, to be drawn, until finally, under the influence of grace, you feel again the vigorous pulse of life. Then you will run and shout out: "I run the way of your commandments since you have enlarged my heart."[45] But while this state of happiness remains, you must not use it as if you possessed God's gift by right of inheritance, secure in the conviction that you could never lose it; for if he should suddenly withdraw his hand and withhold his gift, you would be plunged into dejection and excessive unhappiness. When you feel happy beware of boasting: "Nothing can ever shake me!"[46] For you may be compelled to repeat for yourself the Psalmist's sad comment: "But then you hid your face and I was terrified."[47] If you are wise you will try to follow the advice of the Wise Man: in the time of

41. Gal 16:25
42. Job 14:2
43. Jn 10:23
44. Phil 3:13

45. Ps 118:32
46. Ps 29:7
47. Ps 29:8

adversity not to be unmindful of prosperity, and in the time of prosperity not to be forgetful of adversity.[48]

6. Do not, then, pin your hopes on ephemeral well-being, but cry to God like the Prophet and say: "Do not desert me when my strength is failing."[49] Be consoled in the time of trial and say with the bride: "Draw me after you; we shall run in the odor of your ointments." This will keep your hopes buoyant in times of hardship, and give you foresight when fortune favors you. You will ride above the vicissitudes of good and evil times with the poise of one sustained by values that are eternal, with that enduring, unshakeable equanimity of the man of faith who thanks God in every circumstance.[50] Even amid the fluctuating events and inevitable shortcomings of this giddy world you will ensure for yourself a life of durable stability, provided you are renewed and reformed according to the glorious and original plan of the eternal God, the likeness of him in whom there is no such thing as alteration, no shadow of a change.[51] Even in this world you will become as he is:[52] neither dismayed by adversity nor dissolute in prosperity. Living thus, this noble creature, made to the image and likeness of his Creator,[53] indicates that even now he is re-acquiring the dignity of that primal honor, since he deems it unworthy to be conformed to a world that is waning. Instead, following Paul's teaching, he strives to be reformed by the renewal of his mind,[54] aiming to achieve that likeness in which he knows he was created. And as is proper, this purpose of his compels the world itself, which was made for him, to become conformed to him by an admirable change of relationship, according as all things in their true and natural form begin to co-operate for his good.[55] They become aware of the Lord for whose service they were created, and shed every trace of degeneracy.

48. Sir 11:27
49. Ps 70:9
50. Ps 33:2
51. Jas 1:17

52. 1 Jn 4:17
53. Gen 1:26
54. Rom 12:2
55. Rom 8:28

IV. 7. For this reason the words uttered by God's Only-Begotten Son about himself: "And when I am lifted up from the earth, I shall draw all things to myself,"[56] can also be true of all his brothers, all those whom the Father "foreknew and predestined to be conformed to the image of his Son, in order that he might be the first-born among many brothers."[57] And therefore if even I be lifted up from the earth, I say unflinchingly that I shall draw all things to myself. For it is not rash for me to make my Brother's words my own if I have put on his likeness.[58] If this be true, the rich of this world[59] must not imagine that because Christ said: "Blessed are the poor in spirit, for theirs is the kingdom of heaven,"[60] that the brothers of Christ possess heavenly gifts only. If the promise mentions only heavenly things, it does not follow that these alone are meant. They do possess earthly things, but with the spirit of men who possess nothing;[61] in reality they possess all things, not like unhappy beggars who get what they beg for, but as masters, masters in the best sense because devoid of avarice. To the man of faith the whole world is a treasure-house of riches: the whole world, because all things, whether adverse or favorable, are of service to him; they all contribute to his good.[62]

8. The miser hungers like a beggar for earthly possessions, the man of faith has a lordly independence of them. The first is a beggar no matter what he owns, the latter by his very independence is a true owner. Ask any man whose heart is insatiably bent on earthly riches[63] what he thinks of those who, by selling their possessions and giving the proceeds to the poor, bartered their earthly goods for the kingdom of heaven.[64] Did they do wisely or not? Almost certainly he will say: "Wisely." Then ask him why he in turn does not practice what he approves of. He will answer: "I cannot." And why? Simply because avarice is his mistress and will not

56. Jn 12:32
57. Rom 8:29
58. Gen 27:1-40
59. 1 Tim 6:17
60. Mt 5:3

61. 2 Cor 6:10
62. Rom 8:28-29
63. Ps 100:5
64. Mt 19:21

allow it; he is not free because the things he seems to possess are not his own, he is not his own master. "If they are really yours, spend them profitably and exchange earthly goods for those of heaven. If you cannot, then admit that you are not the master of your money but its slave; a caretaker, not an owner. In short you adapt yourself to your purse like a slave to his mistress; he must be happy when she is happy, sad when she is sad. And you: when your purse swells your mood expands, when it grows slack you are deflated. When it is empty you are crushed with misery; when it is full you melt with joy, or rather become puffed up with pride." Such is the miser.

V. We, however, must be more concerned to imitate the liberty and constancy of the bride who, well taught on every topic, her heart schooled in wisdom,[65] knows how to handle riches and how to suffer want.[66] When she asks to be drawn she shows that she stands in need not of money but of strength. But since she is consoled by the hope that grace will return to her, she proves that despite her need she is not disheartened.

9. Let her say then: "Draw me after you; we shall run in the odor of your ointments." Where is the wonder that she needs drawing who chases after a giant, striving to catch him as he goes "leaping on the mountains, bounding over the hills"?[67] "His word runs swiftly."[68] She is not able to match his running, cannot compete in swiftness with him "who exults like a giant to run his race;"[69] it is beyond her own strength, so she asks to be drawn. "I am tired," she says, "I grow weak; do not desert me, draw me after you or I shall begin to stray after strange lovers,[70] I shall be running aimlessly.[71] Draw me after you, for it is better that I be drawn by you, that you use any force you please against me, terrifying me with threats or harassing me with scourges, rather

---

65. Ps 89:12
66. Phil 4:12
67. Song 2:8
68. Ps 147:15

69. Ps 18:6
70. Song 1:6
71. 1 Cor 9:26

than spare my lukewarmness and abandon me to false security. Draw me even against my will, and make me docile; draw me despite my indolence and make me run. A day will come when I shall not need to be drawn, when we shall run with a will and with all speed. For I shall not be running alone even though I ask that I alone be drawn: the maidens will be running with me. We shall run at equal pace, we shall run together, I in the odor of your ointments, they under the stimulus of my example and encouragement, and hence all of us running in the odor of your ointments." The bride has her followers just as she is the follower of Christ,[72] so she does not speak in the singular: "I run," but: "we shall run."

10. But the question comes up: why did she not include the maidens along with herself when she asked to be drawn? Why did she say "draw me" and not "draw us"? Does she have need to be drawn and the maidens do not? O beautiful, O happy, O blessed one, explain to us the meaning of this distinction. "Draw me", she says. "Why 'me,' and not 'us'? Do you envy us this favor? Surely not. You would not have mentioned so soon that the maidens would run with you if you had wished to travel alone after the Bridegroom. If therefore you intended to add 'we shall run' in the plural, why did you formulate in the singular the request to be drawn?" She answers: "Charity demanded this. Learn from me by means of these words to expect a twofold help from above in the course of your spiritual life: correction and consolation. One controls the exterior, the other works within; the first curbs arrogance, the latter inspires trust; the first begets humility, the latter strengthens the faint-hearted; the first makes a man discreet, the latter devout. The first imbues us with fear of God,[73] the latter tempers that fear with the joy of salvation, as the words of Scripture indicate: 'Let my heart rejoice that it may fear your name;'[74] and 'Serve the Lord with fear, and rejoice before him with reverence.'[75]

72. 1 Cor 4:16
73. Ps 33:12

74. Ps 85:11
75. Ps 2:11

11. "We are drawn when we are tested by temptations and trials; we run when inwardly suffused by consolations, breathing-in the ointment-scented air. Therefore when I encounter what is hard and austere I confine it to myself, being strong and healthy and perfect, and I speak in the singular: 'Draw me.' What is pleasant and sweet I share with you, the weak one, and I say: 'We shall run.' I know quite well that girls are delicate and tender, ill- equipped to endure temptations; so I want them to run in my company, but not to be drawn in my company. I will have them as companions in hours of consolation, but not in times of trial.[76] Why so? Because they are frail, and I fear they may tire and lag behind. It is me that you must correct, my Bridegroom" she says, "me that you must test, put on trial and draw after you, because I am ready for the lash and strong enough to persevere.[77] Apart from that we shall run together; I alone shall be drawn, together we shall run. So let us run and run, but in the odor of your ointments, not by trusting in our own worth. We pin our hopes for the race, not in the durability of our powers but in the abundance of your mercies.[78] For although when we ran we did so willingly, it depended not upon man's will or exertion but upon God's mercy.[79] Let mercy but return and we shall run again. You with your giant's power can run with your own strength;[80] we can run only when your ointments breathe their scent. You whom the Father has anointed 'with the oil of gladness above your fellows,'[81] run by virtue of that anointing; we run in the odor it diffuses. You enjoy the fullness, we the fragrance." This should be the time to fulfill a promise about the ointments of the Bridegroom that I recall having made to you so long ago, but the length of this sermon forbids it. It must be postponed, for the exalted nature of the theme will not brook the distortion of an abbreviated treatment. Pray therefore to the Lord who confers this anointing, that he may

76. 2 Cor 1:7
77. Ps 37:18
78. Ps 68:17

79. Rom 9:16
80. Ps 18:6
81. Ps 44:8

bless the instructions that I so willingly impart,[82] that I may fill your desires with the memory of the generous kindness of him[83] who is the Church's Bridegroom, our Lord Jesus Christ.

82. Ps 118:108
83. Ps 144:7

SERMON 22

ON THE FOUR OINTMENTS OF THE BRIDEGROOM AND THE
FOUR CARDINAL VIRTUES

IF THE OINTMENTS OF THE BRIDE are as precious and exquisite as you have heard them portrayed, how matchless must those of the Bridegroom be! And though any exposition of mine will fail to do justice to them, we must accept that their power is great and their grace efficacious, since their odor alone is enough to make not only the maidens but even the bride run. As you notice, she has not dared to make any such promise about her own ointments. She does indeed rejoice that they are flawless; but she does not say that they have inspired her to run, or that they will do so. This she attributes solely to the Bridegroom's ointments. But if the merest fragrance of these so excites her that she must run, what would the consequences be if she should experience the ointment itself being poured out in her? What wonder if she should even fly! But some of you must want to say: "Desist now from praising these gifts. When you begin to explain them we shall see clearly enough what they are." But no. I make no such promise. For believe me, I have not as yet decided whether I ought to express all the thoughts that suggest themselves. My opinion is that the Bridegroom has a varied and plentiful stock of perfumes and ointments. Some are solely for the pleasure of the bride who enjoys more intimate and familiar relations with him: others are wafted out to the maidens; and others again reach out to strangers afar off, so that "nothing can escape his heat."[1] For although "the Lord is good to all,"[2] he is especially kind to

1. Ps 18:7   2. Ps 144:9

14

those who live in his house, and the more one is assimilated to him by a virtuous life and an upright will, the more sensitive I think he will be to the fragrance of the newer perfumes and the sweeter ointments.

2. In matters of this kind, understanding can follow only where experience leads, and I shall be the last to intrude rashly where the bride alone may enter. The Bridegroom knows the delights with which the Holy Spirit charms the one he loves, the inspirations with which he reanimates her affections, the perfumes that enhance her loveliness. Let her be as a fountain entirely his own, unshared by any stranger, untouched by unworthy lips: for she is "a garden enclosed, a sealed fountain,"[3] though rivulets flow from it into the streets.[4] These I may use, though I want no trouble or ingratitude from anyone[5] if I offer what I draw from a public source. I shall even pay myself a mild compliment in this matter, for no small effort and fatigue are involved in going out day by day to draw waters from the open streams of the Scriptures and provide for the needs of each of you, so that without exerting yourselves you may have at hand spiritual waters for every occasion, for washing, for drinking, for cooking of foods. God's word is a water of the wisdom that saves;[6] when you drink it you are made clean, as the Lord himself points out: "You are already made clean by the word which I have spoken to you."[7] The word of God, winged with the Holy Spirit's fire, can cook the raw reflections of the sensual man, giving them a spiritual meaning that feeds the mind, and inspiring him to say: "My heart became hot within me, and as I meditated a fire burst forth."[8]

3. Far from disapproving of those whose purer mind enables them to grasp sublimer truths than I can present, I warmly congratulate them, but expect them to allow me to provide a simpler doctrine for simpler minds. How I wish that all had the gift of teaching: I should be rid of the need to preach these sermons! It is a burden I should like to transfer

3. Song 4:12
4. Prov 5:16
5. Gal 6:17

6. Sir 15:3
7. Jn 15:3
8. Ps 38:4

to another, or rather I should prefer that none of you would need to exercise it, that all would be taught by God,[9] and I should have leisure to contemplate God's beauty.[10] Now however I must confess, not without tears, that I have no time to seek after God, much less to contemplate him; no time to see the king in his beauty[11] seated upon the Cherubim, on a throne raised aloft;[12] to see him in that form in which, as the Father's equal, he was born before the dawning amid the sacred splendors.[13] This is the form in which the angels long to contemplate him forever,[14] God with God;[15] and I, a man, describe him to men according to the human form that he adopted in order to reveal himself with the maximum of esteem and love; "made lower than the angels,"[16] he came out of his chambers like a Bridegroom and pitched a tent in the sun.[17] I present him as attractive rather than sublime, as God's appointed servant and not a remote deity, as the one whom the Spirit of the Lord anointed and sent "to bring good news to the poor, to bind up hearts that are broken, to proclaim liberty to captives, freedom to those in prison; to proclaim a year favorable to the Lord."[18]

II. 4. Every person, therefore, is free to pursue the thoughts and experiences, however sublime and exquisite, that are his by special insight, on the meaning of the Bridegroom's ointments. For my part, I offer for the common good what I have received from a common source. He is the fountain of life,[19] a sealed fountain, brimming over from within the enclosed garden[20] through the pipe of St Paul's mouth. This is that true wisdom which Job says, "is drawn out of secret places,"[21] divides into four streams and flows into the streets,[22] where it indicates to us him who has been made by

9. Jn 6:45
10. Ps 45:11
11. Is 33:17
12. Is 6:1
13. Ps 109:3
14. 1 Pet 1:12
15. Jn 1:1

16. Heb 2:9
17. Ps 18:6
18. Is 61:1-2; Lk 4:18
19. Ps 35:10
20. Song 4:12
21. Job 28:18
22. Prov 5:16

God "wisdom and righteousness, and holiness, and redemption."[23] From these four streams as from priceless perfumes —there is nothing to prevent us seeing them either as water or as perfume, water because they cleanse, perfume because of their scent— from these four as from priceless perfumes blended from heavenly ingredients "upon the spicy mountains,"[24] so sweet an odor fills the nostrils of the Church, that she is roused even to the four corners of the earth by its sheer delightfulness. She hurries to meet her heavenly Bridegroom, like the Queen of the South who hastened from the ends of the earth to hear the wisdom of Solomon, drawn by his fame as by a sweet scent.[25]

5. The Church was devoid of the power to run in the odor of her Solomon until he who from all eternity was the Wisdom begotten of the Father, became Wisdom from the Father for her in time,[26] and so enabled her to perceive his odor. Thus he has become for her righteousness and holiness and redemption, that she might run in the odor of these gifts too, since these also were equally in him before all things began. "In the beginning was the Word,"[27] but the shepherds hurried to see him only when his human birth was announced.[28] Then it was that they said to each other: "Let us go to Bethlehem and see this word that was made, which the Lord has made known to us."[29] Scripture adds that "they came in haste."[30] Before that, while the Word remained solely with God,[31] they did not stir. But when the Word, which was, was made, when the Lord accomplished this and revealed it, then they came with haste, they ran. And therefore, just as the Word was in the beginning, but with God, so, when he began to live among men he was made. Even in the beginning he was wisdom and righteousness and holiness and redemption, but only for the angels; in order that he might become so to men as well, the Father made him all these

23. 1 Cor 1:30
24. Song 8:14
25. 1 Kings 10:1
26. 1 Cor 1:30
27. Jn 1:1

28. Lk 2:16
29. Lk 2:15
30. Lk 2:16
31. Jn 1:1

things because he is the Father. Therefore it says he became our Wisdom from God. It does not say merely that he became Wisdom, but that he became Wisdom for us, because all that he was to the angels he became in turn to us. [32]

6. But you will say: "I cannot see how he could have brought redemption to the angels. The Scriptures give no grounds for thinking that they were ever the captives of sin or doomed to death, [33] and therefore in need of liberation, excepting only those who incurred the incurable sin of pride, and afterwards could not merit to be redeemed. If therefore the angels were never set at liberty, some not needing it because they never fell, others not meriting it because fallen irrevocably, on what grounds do you say that Christ the Lord is their redemption? " Listen for a moment. He who raised up fallen man and freed him from slavery, enabled the angels not to fall by guarding them from slavery. Thus he was equally the liberator of both, providing release for one, protection for the other. [34] It is clear then that just as the Lord Christ was righteousness and wisdom and holiness for the angels, so too he was their redemption; it is also clear that he was made flesh with these four gifts for the sake of men, who can contemplate the invisible things of God only by studying the things he has made. [35] All that he was for the angels, he became for us. What? Wisdom and righteousness, and holiness and redemption: wisdom in preaching, righteousness in forgiving of sins, holiness in social contacts with sinners and redemption in the passion he endured for sinners. When therefore he was made these by God, then the Church perceived the odor, then it ran.

III. 7. Take note therefore of the fourfold anointing, recognize the superabundant and indescribable sweetness of him whom the Father has anointed with the oil of gladness

32. 1 Cor 1:30
33. 2 Sam 19:28
34. St Bernard upholds here preventive redemption in the case of the angels.
35. Rom 1:20

above his fellows.[36] You lived, O man, in darkness and the shadow of death[37] through ignorance of the truth; you were a prisoner and your sins were your shackles. He came down to you in your prison, not to torture you but to liberate you from the power of darkness.[38] And first of all, as the Teacher of Truth, he banished the murk of your ignorance by the light of his wisdom. By "the righteousness that comes of faith,"[39] he loosed the bonds of sin,[40] justifying the sinners by his free gift.[41] By this twofold favor he fulfilled those words of David: "The Lord sets the prisoners free; the Lord opens the eyes of the blind."[42] Furthermore, by living holily in the midst of sinners he laid down a pattern of life that is a pathway back to the fatherland. As a supreme gesture of love he surrendered himself to death[43] and from his own side produced the price of satisfaction that would placate his Father, thus clearly making his own the verse: "It is with the Lord that mercy is to be found, and a generous redemption."[44] Utterly generous, for not a mere drop but a wave of blood flowed unchecked from the five wounds of his body.

8. What should he have done for you and has not done?[45] He gave sight to the blind, set captives free,[46] led the wanderers back, reconciled sinners. Who would not run spontaneously and eagerly after him who sets men free from error, overlooks their blundering,[47] bestows merits by his mode of life and acquires rewards for them by his death? What excuse can anyone have for not running in the fragrance of your perfumes, except that the fragrance has not reached him? But the fragrance of your life[48] has gone into every land,[49] because "the earth is full of the steadfast love of the Lord,[50] and his compassion is over all that he has made."[51] Therefore the man who fails to perceive this life-

36. Ps 44:8
37. Lk 1:79
38. Col 1:13
39. Rom 9:30
40. Ps 118:61
41. Rom 3:24
42. Ps 145:7-8
43. Is 53:12
44. Ps 129:7
45. Is 5:4
46. Ps 145:8
47. Wis 11:24
48. 2 Cor 2:16
49. Ps 18:5
50. Ps 32:5
51. Ps 144:9

giving fragrance that permeates all places, and does not run
on that account, must be dead or even corrupt. Fragrance
signifies fame. When the fragrance of his fame arrives it
excites men to run, it leads to the experience of inward grace,
to the reward of vision. The joyous throng who attain to it
shout all together: "As we have heard so have we seen in the
city of the Lord of hosts."[52] If we run after you, Lord Jesus,
it is entirely because of the meekness associated with your
name,[53] because you do not spurn the poor nor recoil from
the sinner. You did not reject the repentant thief,[54] the
weeping sinner,[55] the importunate Chanaanite woman,[56] the
woman caught in adultery,[57] the man who sat at the customs
house,[58] the humble tax collector,[59] the disciple who denied
you,[60] the man who persecuted your followers,[61] even those
who crucified you.[62] We run in the fragrance that these dif-
fuse. The fragrance of your wisdom comes to us in what we
hear, for if anyone needs wisdom let him but ask of you and
you will give it to him.[63] It is well known that you give to all
freely and ungrudgingly. As for your justice, so great is the
fragrance it diffuses that you are called not only just but even
justice itself, the justice that makes men just. Your power to
make men just is measured by your generosity in forgiving.[64]
Therefore the man who through sorrow for sin hungers and
thirsts for justice,[65] let him trust in the One who changes the
sinner into a just man,[66] and, judged righteous in terms of
faith alone, he will have peace with God.[67] Your holiness, for
its part, is sweetly and richly radiated not only by your mode
of life, but even by your conception. You have neither committed sin nor been contaminated by it. Repentant sinners
therefore who wish to attain to that holiness essential for the

52. Ps 47:9
53. Ps 44:5
54. Lk 23:40-43
55. Lk 7:37-50
56. Mt 15:21-28
57. Jn 8:2-11
58. Mt 9:9-13
59. Lk 18:9-14
60. Mt 26:69-75
61. Acts 8:3, 9-11
62. Lk 23:34
63. Jas 1:5
64. Is 55:7
65. Mt 5:6
66. Rom 4:5
67. Rom 5:1

vision of God,[68] should listen to your warning: "Be holy, for I am holy."[69] Let them pay attention to your ways for you are just in all your ways and holy in all your doings.[70] Finally, how many are inspired to run by the sweet odor of your redemption! When you are lifted up from the earth you draw all things to yourself.[71] Your Passion is the ultimate refuge, a remedy that is unique. When our wisdom lets us down, when our righteousness falls short, when the merits of our holiness founder, your Passion becomes our support. Who would presume that his own wisdom, or righteousness or holiness suffices for salvation? "Not that we are sufficient of ourselves to claim anything as coming from us; our sufficiency is from God."[72] Therefore when my strength is spent I shall not be troubled,[73] I shall not lose heart. I know what I shall do:[74] "I will lift up the cup of salvation and call on the name of the Lord."[75] Enlighten my eyes, O Lord,[76] that I may learn what is pleasing to you at all times,[77] and then I am wise. "Remember not the sins of my youth, or my transgressions,"[78] and then I am righteous. "Teach me your way,"[79] and then I am holy. And yet, unless your blood cries out on my behalf, I am not saved. To obtain all these gifts we run after you: forgive us, because we cry after you.[80]

IV. 9. All of us do not run with equal ardor in the fragrance of all the perfumes; some are more eager for the study of wisdom, others concentrate on doing penance in the hope of pardon, others again are inspired to practise the virtues by the example of Christ's life and behavior, while yet others are roused to fervor more by the memory of his Passion. Is it possible for us to find examples of each kind? Those ran in the fragrance of wisdom who had been sent by the Pharisees and returned to them saying: "No man ever spoke like this man!"[81] They admired his doctrine and praised his wisdom.

68. Heb 12:14
69. Lev 19:2
70. Ps 144:17
71. Jn 12:32
72. 2 Cor 3:5
73. Ps 70:9
74. Lk 16:4
75. Ps 115:13
76. Ps 12:4
77. Wis 9:10
78. Ps 24:7
79. Ps 85:11
80. Mt 15:23
81. Jn 7:46

Nicodemus also was lured into running by this fragrance
when he came to Jesus by night, in the clear light of his
wisdom, and went back reformed, instructed in many
things.[82] Mary Magdalene ran in the fragrance of justice:
many sins were forgiven her because she loved much.[83] She
had ceased to be the sinner taunted by the Pharisee,[84] and
become a virtuous and holy woman. He did not realize that
righteousness or holiness is a gift of God, not the fruit of
man's effort, and that the man "to whom the Lord imputes
no iniquity"[85] is not only just but blessed. Had he forgotten
how the Lord had cured his or some other man's bodily
leprosy with a touch without contracting it? [86] So, when the
Just One is touched by the sinner, he imparts rather than
loses righteousness, nor is he tarnished with the stain of the
sin from which he cleanses her. The tax collector ran in
similar fashion; and Justice himself bears witness that after he
had humbly implored forgiveness for his sins, he ¨went home
again at rights with God.[87] Peter ran when, after his fall, he
wept bitterly to wash away his sin and be restored to righteousness.[88] David ran when he acknowledged and confessed
his crime and was privileged to be told: "The Lord has put
away your sin."[89] Paul testifies that he ran in the fragrance of
holiness, when he glories in being an imitator of Christ. He
said to his followers: "Take me for a model as I take
Christ."[90] And all those were running, too, who said: "We
have left everything and followed you."[91] It was because of
the desire to follow Christ that they had left all things. A
general exhortation to everyone to follow in this fragrance is
contained in the words: "He who says he abides in Christ
ought to walk in the same way in which he walked."[92] Finally, if you wish to hear of those who ran in the fragrance of
the Passion, behold all the martyrs. Such, then, is my ex-

82. Jn 3:1-2
83. Lk 7:47
84. Lk 7:39
85. Ps 31:2
86. Mt 26:6
87. Lk 18:14

88. Lk 22:62
89. 2 Sam 12:13
90. 1 Cor 11:1
91. Mt 19:27
92. 1 Jn 2:6

planation of the four ointments: the first, wisdom; the second, righteousness; the third, holiness; and the fourth, redemption.

V. Remember their names and enjoy their fragrance, but forbear to question the manner in which they are made or the number of ingredients they contain. For the knowledge of the nature of the ointments of the Bridegroom cannot be as easily ascertained by us as was that of the ointments of the bride, that we have previously discussed. For in Christ these are in their fullness, unnumbered and unmeasured. His wisdom is infinite,[93] his righteousness is like the mountains of God,[94] mountains that are eternal,[95] his holiness is unique, his redeeming work inexplicable.

10. It must be remarked too that the wise of this world have multiplied arguments about these four virtues to no purpose;[96] they had no chance of grasping their true meaning, because they knew nothing of him whom God made our wisdom in order to teach us prudence, our righteousness to forgive our sins, our holiness through his example of chaste and temperate living, and our redemption through patience in his resolute acceptance of death.[97] Perhaps one of you will say: "They are all suitably applied except holiness, which seems to bear no proper relation to temperance." To this I answer, first, that temperance and continence imply the same thing. Secondly, scriptural usage identifies continence or cleanliness with holiness. And finally, what else were those frequent rites of sanctification decreed by Moses but purifications consisting of abstinence from food, from drink, from sexual intercourse and similar things?[98] But take special note of the freedom with which the Apostle attributed this meaning to the word holiness: "What God wants is for you all to be holy so that each one of you might know how to possess his body in holiness, not giving way to selfish passion;"[99] and again: "God did not call us into uncleanness, but into holi-

---

93. Ps 146:5
94. Ps 35:7
95. Ps 75:4
96. 1 Cor 1:20

97. 1 Cor 1:30
98. See Lev 22ff
99. 1 Thess 4:3

ness."[100] It is clear that he identifies holiness with temperance.

11. Now that I have thrown light on what seemed obscure, I return to the point from which I digressed. What have you to do with righteousness if you are ignorant of Christ, who is the righteousness of God? Where, I ask, is true prudence, except in the teaching of Christ? Or true justice, if not from Christ's mercy? Or true temperance, if not in Christ's life? Or true fortitude, if not in Christ's Passion? Only those can be called prudent who are imbued with his teaching; only those are just who have had their sins pardoned through his mercy; only those are temperate who take pains to follow his way of life; only those are courageous who hold fast to the example of his patience when buffeted by sufferings. Vainly therefore will anyone strive to acquire the virtues, if he thinks they may be obtained from any source other than the Lord of the virtues, whose teaching is the seed-bed of prudence, whose mercy is the well-spring of justice,[101] whose life is a mirror of temperance, whose death is the badge of fortitude. To him be honor and glory for evermore. Amen.[102]

---

100. 1 Thess 4:7
101. Is 32:17
102. Rom 16:27

SERMON 23

IN THE ROOMS OF THE KING

"THE KING HAS BROUGHT ME into his rooms."[1] This is where the fragrance comes from, this is the goal of our running. She had said that we must run, drawn by that fragrance, but did not specify our destination. So it is to these rooms that we run, drawn by the fragrance that issues from them. The bride's keen senses have been quick to detect it, so eager is she to experience it in all its fullness. But first of all we ought to give thought to the meaning of these rooms. To begin with, let us imagine them to be perfume-laden places within the Bridegroom's quarters, where varied spices breathe their scents,[2] where delights are manifold. The more valuable products of garden and field are consigned for preservation to store-rooms like these. To these therefore people run, at least those who are aglow with the Spirit.[3] The bride runs, so do the maidens; but the one to arrive first is the one whose love is most ardent, because she runs more quickly.[4] On arrival she brooks no refusal, not even delay. The door is promptly opened to her as to one of the family, one highly esteemed, loved with a special love, uniquely favored. But what of the maidens? They follow at a distance;[5] they are still undeveloped, they can neither run with an energy to match that of the bride, nor achieve the ardor of her desire. Conse-

1. Song 1:3
2. Rev 5:8
3. Rom 12:11
4. Jn 20:4
5. Mt 26:58

25

quently they arrive late and remain outside.[6] But the charity of the bride will not allow her to be indifferent, nor does pride in her accomplishments blind her, as it does so many, and cause her to forget them. On the contrary, she consoles them and exhorts them to be patient, to tolerate calmly both the rebuff and her absence. She tells them how great is her happiness, for the sole reason that they may share in her joy, and be inspired with the confidence that they will not at all be excluded from the favors bestowed on their mother. She is never so bent on her own progress as to overlook their interest, nor desirous of promoting her own welfare at their expense. Though the excellence of her merits puts a barrier between them, it is certain that she is always with them through her love and holy solicitude. She has to be thus conformed to her Bridegroom, who ascended into heaven and yet promised to be with his followers on earth until the end of the world.[7] So too with the bride; however great her progress or the graces with which she is endowed, never, whether in her concern for them, in her forethought or in her love, is she separated from those whom she has begotten through the Gospel,[8] never does her heart forget them.

2. She speaks to them therefore as follows: "Be happy, be confident: 'the King has brought me into his bedroom.'[9] You may regard yourselves as introduced too. Even though I alone seem to have been introduced, it is not for my sole advantage. Every preferment I enjoy is a joy for you all; the progress that I make is for you, and with you I shall divide all that I shall merit above your measure." Do you wish for unquestionable proof that these words express her intention and her love? Then listen to their answer: "You will be our joy and gladness."[10] "You," they say, "will be our joy and gladness, for we are not yet fit to rejoice in ourselves." And they go on to say: "remembering your breasts," that is: "We

---

6. Mt 25:10-11
7. Mt 28:20
8. 1 Cor 4:15
9. Song 1:3 Here he uses *cubiculum* instead of *cellaria*.
10. Song 1:3

persevere quietly until you come, knowing that you will return to us with overflowing breasts. We are confident that then we shall rejoice and be glad,[11] but meanwhile we keep remembering your breasts." By adding: "more than wine," they reveal that because of their imperfection they are still disturbed by the remembrance of carnal desires, designated by the wine, but that these desires are overcome by recalling the abundant sweetness[12] which, experience assures them, flows from those breasts. Now would be a time to speak about these if I had not done so previously.[13] But now see how the maidens anticipate their own reward in that of their mother, how they regard her recompense and enjoyment as their own, how her admission consoles them for the bitterness of their rebuff. They would never have this confidence if they did not accept her as their mother. Here is a point for the ear of those superiors who wish always to inspire fear in their communities and rarely promote their welfare. Learn, you who rule the earth.[14] Learn that you must be mothers to those in your care, not masters; make an effort to arouse the response of love, not that of fear:[15] and should there be occasional need for severity, let it be paternal rather than tyrannical. Show affection as a mother would, correct like a father. Be gentle, avoid harshness, do not resort to blows, expose your breasts: let your bosoms expand with milk, not swell with passion. Why impose in addition your yoke[16] on those whose burdens you ought rather to carry? [17] Why will the young man, bitten by the serpent, shy away from the judgment of the priest, to whom he ought rather to run as to the bosom of a mother? If you are spiritual, instruct him in a spirit of gentleness, not forgetting that you may be tempted yourselves.[18] Otherwise he shall die in his sin, but, says the Lord, "I will hold you responsible for his death."[19] We shall speak of this again.

11. Ps 117:14
12. Ps 144:7
13. Sermon Nine.
14. Ps 2:10
15. RB, Chap 64

16. Is 47:6
17. Gal 6:2
18. Gal 6:1
19. Ezek 3:18

II. 3. Since the implications of the text are clear from what
I have said, let us now try to discover the spiritual meaning of
the storerooms. Further on there is mention of a garden[20]
and a bedroom,[21] both of which I join to these rooms for the
purpose of this present discussion. When examined together
the meaning of each becomes clearer. By your leave then, we
shall search the Sacred Scriptures for these three things, the
garden, the storeroom, the bedroom. The man who thirsts
for God eagerly studies and meditates on the inspired word,
knowing that there he is certain to find the one for whom he
thirsts. Let the garden, then, represent the plain, unadorned,
historical sense of Scripture, the storeroom its moral sense,
and the bedroom the mystery of divine contemplation.

4. For a start I feel that my comparison of scriptural
history to a garden is not unwarranted, for in it we find men
of many virtues, like fruitful trees in the garden of the Bridegroom, in the Paradise of God.[22] You may gather samples of
their good deeds and good habits as you would apples from
trees. Who can doubt that a good man is a tree of God's
planting? Listen to what St David says of such a man: "He is
like a tree that is planted by a stream of water, yielding its
fruit in season, and its leaves never fade."[23] Listen to Jeremiah, speaking to the same effect and almost in similar
words: "He is like a tree that is planted by a stream of water
that thrusts its roots to the stream: when the heat comes it
fears not."[24] Likewise the Prophet: "The virtuous flourish
like palm trees and grow as tall as the cedars of Lebanon."[25]
Of himself he says: "I, for my part, am like an olive tree
growing in the house of God."[26] History therefore is a garden
in which we may recognize three divisions. Within its ambit
we find the creation, the reconciliation, and the renewal of
heaven and earth. Creation is symbolized in the sowing or
planting of the garden; reconciliation by the germination of

20. Song 5:1
21. Song 3:4
22. Ezek 31:9
23. Ps 1:3

24. Jer 17:8
25. Ps 91:13
26. Ps 51:10

what is sown or planted. For in due course, while the heavens
showered from above and the skies rained down the Just
one,[27] the earth opened for a Savior to spring up, and heaven
and earth were reconciled.[28] "For he is the peace between us,
and has made the two into one,"[29] making peace by his
blood between all things in heaven and on earth. Renewal
however is to take place at the end of the world. Then there
will be "a new heaven and a new earth,"[30] and the good will
be gathered from the midst of the wicked like fruit from a
garden, to be set at rest in the storehouse of God. As Scripture says: "In that day the branch of the Lord shall be beautiful and glorious, and the fruit of the land raised on high."[31]
Here you have the three aspects of time represented by the
garden in the historical sense.

III. 5. In its moral teaching too, three things are to be taken
into account, three apartments as it were in the one storeroom. It was for this reason perhaps that she used the plural,
rooms, instead of room, since she must have been thinking
about these apartments. Later on she glories in being admitted to the wine-room.[32] We therefore, in accord with the
advice: "Give occasion to a wise man and he will be still
wiser,"[33] take occasion from the name given by the Holy
Spirit to this room, and give names to the other two: the
room of spices and the room of the ointments. Afterwards
we shall see the reason for these names. For the moment take
note that all these possessions of the Bridegroom are wholesome and sweet: wine, ointments and spices. "Wine," says
Scripture, "gladdens the heart of man."[34] We read too that
oil gives him a merry countenance,[35] and it is with oil that
the various powders are mixed to produce ointments. Spices
are useful, not only for the attractive sweetness of their

27. Is 45:8
28. Eph 2:14
29. Col 1:20
30. Rev 21:1
31. Is 4:2

32. Song 2:4
33. Prov 9:9
34. Ps 103:15
35. Ps 103:15

scent, but also for their powers of healing. Rightly then the bride's happiness abounds on being admitted to a place filled to overflowing with such rich graces!

6. But I can give them other names, whose application seems more obvious. Taking them in due order, I name the first room discipline, the second nature, and the third grace. In the first, guided by moral principles, you discover how you are inferior to others, in the second you find the basis for equality, in the third what makes you greater; that is: the grounds for submission, for co-operation, for authority; or if you will: to be subject, to co-exist, to preside. In the first you bear the status of learner, in the second that of companion, in the third that of master. For nature has made all men equal. But since this natural moral gift was corrupted by pride, men became impatient of equal status. Driven by the urge to surpass their fellows, they spared no efforts to achieve this superiority; with an itch for vainglory and prompted by envy, they lived in mutual rivalry. [36] Our primary task is to tame this wilfulness of character by submission to discipline in the first room, where the stubborn will, worn down by the hard and prolonged schooling of experienced mentors, is humbled and healed. The natural goodness lost by pride is recovered by obedience, and they learn, as far as in them lies, to live peacefully and sociably with all who share their nature, with all men, no longer through fear of discipline but by the impulse of love. When they pass from here into the room of nature, they discover what is written: "How good, how delightful it is to live together as one like brothers: fine as oil on the head." [37] For when morals are disciplined there comes, as to spices pounded together, the oil of gladness, [38] the good of nature; the resulting ointment is good and sweet. The man who is anointed with it becomes pleasant and temperate, a man without a grudge, who neither swindles nor attacks nor offends another; who never exalts himself nor promotes himself at their

36. Gal 5:26   38. Ps 44:8
37. Ps 132:1-2

expense,[39] but offers his services as generously as he willingly accepts theirs.[40]

7. If you have adequately grasped the characteristics of these two rooms, I think you will admit that I have appropriately named them the spice room and the ointment room. In the former, just as the vigorous pounding with a pestle presses and extracts the strong fragrance of the spices, so the power of authority and strictness of discipline elicit and reveal the natural strength of good morals. In the latter, a sweet refinement arising from innate and ready affection inspires one to serve with courteous promptitude, like the oil which anoints the head and runs down and flows over the whole body[41] when exposed to a little heat. Accordingly, in the storeroom of discipline, the various dried ingredients of the spicy mixtures are stored up, and hence I thought it ought to be called the room of spices. But because the ointments are stored and preserved ready for use in the storeroom of Nature, it is called the room of ointments. With regard to the wine room, I do not think there is any other reason for its name than that the wine of an earnest zeal for the works of love is found there. One who has not been admitted to this room should never take charge of others. This wine should be the inspiring influence in the lives of those who bear authority, such as we find in the Teacher of the Nations, when he said: "Who is weak and I am not weak? Who is made to fall and I am not indignant?"[42] Your desire is venal if you hanker to rule over others without the will to serve them; your ambition is unprincipled if you would hold men in subjection without concern for their salvation. I have also named this the room of grace; not because a man may enter the other two without the aid of grace, but because grace is especially found here in its fullness. For "love is the fullness of the law"[43] and if you love your brother you have fulfilled the law."[44]

39. 2 Cor 7:2; Lk 3:14
40. Phil 4:15
41. Ps 132:2

42. 2 Cor 11:29
43. Rom 13:10
44. Rom 13:8

8. Now that I have given you an explanation of the names, let us see how the rooms differ from each other. To check the petulant, dreamy senses with the fear a superior can inspire, to curb with firm discipline the flesh's immoderate appetites, is by no means as easy or manageable as to live in the harmony of spontaneous affection with our companions; to live agreeably with them at the prompting of the will is different from a life where the rod is the check on manners. No one will maintain that the ability to live sociably and to govern beneficially are of equal importance or demand the same sort of virtue. Hence there are so many living peacefully under a superior who, when freed from their inferior status, are unable to control themselves or refrain from abusing their equals. Lots of men, too, can spend their days uprightly and peacefully among their brothers, but if given authority over them they become not only useless but foolish and unworthy. People of this kind are meant to be content with a moderate measure of goodness, this is their allotted grace from God; they have little need of guidance from a superior but are not themselves capable of leadership. These latter are endowed with a finer character than those previously referred to as devoid of self-control, but leaders blest with competence surpass them both. They qualify to receive what the Lord has promised to those who govern well; that he will place them over all his possessions.[45] Those who exercise authority for the welfare of others are comparatively few, and fewer still those whose power rests in humility. These both are achieved easily by the man of perfect discretion, the mother of the virtues, the man who is drunk with the wine of charity even to contempt for his own good name, to forgetfulness of self and indifference to self-interest.[46] This is the unique and exquisite lesson of the Holy Spirit infused in the wine room. Without the fervor of charity the virtue of discretion is lifeless, and intense fervor goes headlong without the curb of discretion. Praiseworthy the man then who possesses both, the fervor that enlivens discretion, the discretion that regulates fervor. A man in a position of authority ought to

45. Mt 24:47   46. 1 Cor 13:5

be so constituted. But the man whose character I most admire, who has attained supreme success in the way of life I have portrayed, is the man to whom it is given to sprint through or ramble round all these rooms without stumbling, who never contends with his superiors nor envies his equals, who does not fail in concern for his subjects nor use his authority arrogantly. To be obedient to superiors, obliging to one's companions, to attend with kindness to the needs of one's subjects—these sure marks of perfection I unhesitatingly attribute to the bride. We infer this from the words she speaks: "The king has brought me into his rooms,"[47] which show that she was introduced, not to any room in particular but to the whole complex of rooms.

IV. 9. Let us at last enter the bedroom. What can be said of it? May I presume that I know all about it? Far from me the pretension that I have experienced so sublime a grace, nor shall I boast of a privilege reserved solely to the fortunate bride. I am more concerned to know myself, as the Greek motto advises,[48] that with the Prophet, "I may know what is wanting to me."[49] However, if I knew nothing at all there is nothing I could say. What I do know I do not begrudge you or withhold from you; what I do not know may "he who teaches men knowledge"[50] supply to you. You remember that I said the bedroom of the King is to be sought in the mystery of divine contemplation.[51] In speaking of the ointments I mentioned that many varieties of them are to be found in the Bridegroom's presence, that all of them are not for everybody's use, but that each one's share differs according to his merits; so too, I feel that the King has not one

47. Song 1:3
48. "Know thyself"—Socrates claims to have received this precept from the Delphic oracle: Xenophon, *Memorabilia* 4, 2, 24-25. It was inscribed on one of the columns of the peristyle in the front of the temple: Plato, *Charmides* 164d. It is frequently used by the Cistercian Fathers.
49. Ps 38:5
50. Ps 93:10
51. See above, Sermon 23:3. The word translated "divine" in both these places is *theoricae,* indoubtedly harking back to the Greek θεωρια.

bedroom only, but several. For he has more than one queen;
his concubines are many, his maids beyond counting.[52] And
each has her own secret rendezvous with the Bridegroom and
says: "My secret to myself, my secret to myself."[53] All do
not experience the delight of the Bridegroom's private visit in
the same room, the Father has different arrangements for
each.[54] For we did not choose him but he chose us and
appointed places for us;[55] and in the place of each one's
appointment there he is too. Thus one repentant woman was
allotted a place at the feet of the Lord Jesus,[56] another —if
she really is another —found fulfillment for her devotion at
his head.[57] Thomas attained to this mystery of grace in the
Savior's side,[58] John on his breast,[59] Peter in the Father's
bosom,[60] Paul in the third heaven.[61]

10. Who among us can see the difference between these
various merits, or rather rewards? But in order to draw attention to what is known to us all, I suggest that the first woman
took her rest on the secure ground of humility, the second on
the seat of hope, Thomas in firm faith, John in the breadth
of charity, Paul in the insights of wisdom, Peter in the light
of truth. There are many rooms therefore in the Bridegroom's house;[62] and each, be she queen, or concubine or one
of the bevy of maidens,[63] finds there the place and destination suited to her merits until the grace of contemplation
allows her to advance further and share in the happiness of
her Lord,[64] to explore her Bridegroom's secret charms. Rely-
ing on the light it may please him to give me, I shall try to

52. Song 6:7
53. Is 24:16
54. Mt 20:23
55. Jn 15:16
56. Lk 10:39
57. Mt 26:7. See note 42, Sermon Twelve, CF 4:82.
58. Jn 20:27
59. Jn 13:25
60. Mt 16:17
61. 2 Cor 12:2
62. Jn 14:2
63. Song 6:7
64. Mt 25:21

demonstrate this more clearly in its proper place.[65] For the moment it suffices to know that no maiden, or concubine, or even queen, may gain access to the mystery of that bedroom which the Bridegroom reserves solely for her who is his dove, beautiful, perfect and unique.[66] Hence it is not for me to take umbrage if I am not admitted there, especially since I can see that even the bride herself is at times unable to find fulfillment of her desire to know certain secrets. At such times she craves to be shown where he pastures his flock, where he rests it at noon.[67]

11. But I shall tell you how far I have advanced, or imagine I have advanced; and you should not accuse me of boasting, because I reveal it solely in the hope of helping you. The Bridegroom who exercises control over the whole universe, has a special place from which he decrees his laws and formulates plans as guidelines in weight, measure and number for all things created.[68] This is a remote and secret place, but not a place of repose. For although as far as in him lies he arranges all things sweetly[69] —the emphasis is on arranging— and the contemplative who perchance reaches that place is not allowed to rest and be quiet. In a way that is wondrous yet delightful he teases the awe-struck seeker till he reduces him to restlessness. Further on the bride beautifully describes both the delight and the restlessness of this stage of contemplation when she says that though she sleeps her heart is awake.[70] She means that in her sleep she experiences a repose full of sweetest surprise and wondrous peace, but her wakeful heart endures the lassitude of avid desire and laborious effort. Job referred to this when he said: "Lying in bed I wonder, 'When will it be day?' Having risen I think, 'How slowly evening comes!' "[71] Do you gather from these words that a person in pursuit of holiness sometimes finds sweetness bitter and wants to be rid of it, and at other times finds that same bitterness attractive? For he would not have said:

65. See Sermon 68:7
66. Song 6:8
67. Song 1:6
68. Wis 11:20

69. Wis 8:1
70. Song 5:2
71. Job 7:4

"When will it be day? " if that contemplative repose entirely satisfied him; but if it had been entirely displeasing he would not have longed for the quiet of evening. This place then, where complete repose is not attainable, is not the bedroom.

V 12. There is another place from which God, the just Judge,[72] "so much to be feared for his deeds among mankind,"[73] watches ceaselessly with an attention that is rigorous yet hidden, over the world of fallen man. The awe-struck contemplative sees how, in this place, God's just but hidden judgment neither washes away the evil deeds of the wicked nor is placated by their good deeds. He even hardens their hearts lest they should repent, take stock of themselves, and be converted and he would heal them.[74] And he does this in virtue of a certain and eternal decree, all the more frightening from its being unchangeably and eternally determined. The contemplative's fears are intensified if he recalls God's words to the angels as recorded in the Prophet: "Shall we show favor to the wicked? " And when they ask with dismay: "Will he not, then, learn to do justice? " God answers: "No," and gives the reason: "He does evil in the land of the upright, and he will not see the glory of the Lord."[75] Let the clerics, let the ministers of the Church, who are guilty of impious conduct in their benefices, be filled with fear. Discontented with the stipends that ought to suffice them,[76] they sacrilegiously retain the surplus income that is meant for the upkeep of the needy; they are not afraid to squander the sustenance of the poor in pandering to their own pride and luxury. They are guilty of a double wickedness: they pilfer the property of others and prostitute the goods of the Church to serve their lusts and vanities.

13. Who will want to rest in such a place when he sees that he, whose judgments are like the mighty deep,[77] only spares and shows mercy to these sinners in this life that he may not do so in eternity? This kind of vision inspires a terror of

72. Ps 7:12
73. Ps 65:5
74. Jn 12:40

75. Is 26:10
76. Lk 3:14
77. Ps 35:7

judgment, not the secure confidence of the bedroom. That place is awe-inspiring,[78] and totally devoid of quiet. I am horror-stricken when suddenly pitched into it, and over and over I think on the words: 'What man knows whether he deserves love or hate? "[79] What wonder if I should be stumbling there, I who am but a leaf blown in the wind, a sapless stalk,[80] when even the greatest contemplative confessed his feet were on the point of stumbling. He almost slipped, and said: "I envied the wicked, seeing the peace of sinners."[81] Why should he have felt like this? "They do not suffer as other men do, no human afflictions for them! So pride upholds them."[82] Hence they will not stoop to repentance, and are to be damned for their pride with the proud devil and his angels. Those not involved in the toil of men will be involved in the work of the devil. To them the Judge will say: "Go away from me, your cursed, to the eternal fire prepared for the devil and his angels."[83] However, that is a place where we find God working, it is nothing less than the house of God and the gate of heaven.[84] In it we learn the fear of God, that his name is holy and terrible;[85] it is the anteroom to glory, for "the fear of the Lord is the beginning of wisdom."[86]

14. Do not be surprised that I have assigned the beginning of wisdom to this place and not to the first. For there we listen to Wisdom as a teacher in a lecture-hall, delivering an all-embracing discourse,[87] here we receive it within us; there our minds are enlightened, here our wills are moved to decision. Instruction makes us learned, experience makes us wise. The sun does not warm all those for whom it shines; and so, though Wisdom gives light to many to see what they should do, it does not immediately spur them on to action. To know where great wealth is to be found is not the same as possessing it; it is possession, not knowledge, that makes a man rich. And so with God: to know him is one thing, to fear him is

78. Gen 28:17
79. Eccles 9:1
80. Job 13:25
81. Ps 72:2-3
82. Ps 72:5-6

83. Mt 25:41
84. Gen 28:17
85. Ps 110:9
86. Ps 110:10
87. 1 Jn 2:27

another; nor does knowledge make a man wise, but the fear that motivates him. Would you then call him wise who is puffed up by his own knowledge? [88] Who but the most witless would consider those wise who, "although they knew God, did not honor him as God or give thanks to him"? [89] I share the opinion of the Apostle, who did not hesitate to declare their heart foolish. How truly is the fear of the Lord the beginning of wisdom,[90] because the soul begins to experience God for the first time when fear of him takes hold of it, not when knowledge enlightens it. You fear God's justice, you fear his power; and so you experience God as just and powerful because fear of him is itself an experience. Experience makes a wise man, as knowledge makes a learned man and wealth a rich man. What then of the place first mentioned? It makes one ready for wisdom. There you are prepared, here you are initiated. The preparation lies in knowing things. But a proud conceit easily follows on this knowledge unless repressed by fear, which is rightly called the beginning of wisdom, because from the beginning it is a barrier to foolishness. In the first place we are set on the way to wisdom, here we enter its doors. But neither here nor there does the contemplative find rest, because there he discovers a busied God, here an angry God. Hence you must not look for the bedroom in these places, one of which resembles a teacher's auditorium, the other a bar of justice.

VI. 15. But there is a place where God is seen in tranquil rest, where he is neither Judge nor Teacher but Bridegroom. To me —for I do not speak for others —this is truly the bedroom to which I have sometimes gained happy entrance. Alas! how rare the time, and how short the stay! There one clearly realizes that "the Lord's love for those who fear him lasts forever and forever."[91] It is there that one may happily say: "I am a friend to all who fear you and observe your precepts."[92] God's purpose stands fast, the peace he has

88. 1 Cor 8:1   91. Ps 102:17
89. Rom 1:21   92. Ps 118:63
90. Ps 110:10

planned for those who fear him is without recall. Overlooking their faults and rewarding their good deeds, with a divine deftness he turns to their benefit not only the good they do but even the evil.[93] He alone is happy "whom the Lord accuses of no guilt."[94] There is no one without sin, not even one. "For all have sinned and forfeited God's glory."[95] But "could anyone accuse those that God has chosen? "[96] I ask no further pledge of righteousness if he is on my side whom alone I have offended.[97] If he decrees that a sin is not to be imputed to me, it is as if it never existed. Inability to sin constitutes God's righteousness; God's forgiveness constitutes man's. When I grasped this I understood the truth of the words: "We know that anyone who has been begotten by God does not sin, because a heavenly birth protects him."[98] Heavenly birth is eternal predestination, by which God loved his chosen ones and endowed them with spiritual blessings in his beloved Son before the world was made.[99] Thus appearing before him in his holy place,[100] they would see his power and his glory, and become sharers in the inheritance of the Son to whose image they were to be conformed.[101] I think of such as these as if they had never sinned, because the sins they committed in time do not appear in eternity, for the love of the Father covers a multitude of sins.[102] "Happy is the man whose fault is forgiven, whose sin is blotted out."[103] When I say these words I am suddenly inspired with so great a confidence, filled with such joy, that it surpasses the fear I experienced in the place of horror,[104] that place of the second vision, and I even look upon myself as one of that blessed band. Would that this moment lasted! Again and again visit me, Lord, in your saving mission; let me see the goodness of your chosen, let me rejoice in the joy of your nation.[105]

93. Rom 8:28
94. Ps 31:2
95. Rom 3:23
96. Rom 8:33
97. Ps 50:6
98. 1 Jn 5:18
99. Eph 1:16; 1:4

100. Ps 62:3
101. Rom 8:29
102. 1 Pet 4:8
103. Ps 31:1
104. Deut 32:10
105. Ps 105:4-5

16. O place so truly quiet, so aptly called a bedroom where God is not encountered in angry guise nor distracted as it were by cares, but where his will is proved good and desirable and perfect.[106] This is a vision that charms rather than terrifies; that does not arouse an inquisitive restlessness, but restrains it; that calms rather than wearies the senses. Here one may indeed be at rest. The God of peace pacifies all things, and to gaze on this stillness is to find repose. It is to catch sight of the King who, when the crowds have gone after the day-long hearing of cases in his law-courts, lays aside the burden of responsibility, goes at night to his place, and enters his bedroom with a few companions whom he welcomes to the intimacy of his private suite. He is all the more secure the more secluded his place of rest, all the more at ease when his placid gaze sees about him none but well-loved friends. If it should ever happen to one of you to be enraptured and hidden away in this secret place, this sanctuary of God, safe from the call and concern of the greedy senses, from the pangs of care, the guilt of sin and the obsessive fancies of the imagination so much more difficult to hold at bay —such a man, when he returns to us again, may well boast and tell us: "The King has brought me into his bedroom."[107] Whether this be the same room that makes the bride so jubilant I do not dare to affirm. But it is a bedroom, the bedroom of the King, and of the three that I have described in the three visions, it is the only place where peace reigns.[108] As was clearly shown, in the first there is but a modicum of quiet, in the second none; for in the first God's glorious appearance fires our curiosity to explore deeper truths, and in the second the terror he inspires shatters our weakness. In the third place however, he is neither fearsome nor awe-inspiring, he wills to be found there in the guise of love, calm and peaceful, gracious and meek,[109] filled with mercy for all who gaze on him.

17. This sermon has been so protracted that for your memory's sake I must summarize briefly what I have said about

106. Rom 12:2   108. Ps 75:3
107. Song 1:3   109. Ps 85:5

the storeroom, the garden, the bedroom. Remember the three divisions of time, three kinds of merit and three rewards. The times are connected with the garden, the merits with the storeroom, the reward with the threefold contemplation of one who seeks the bedroom. I am satisfied that I have said enough about the storeroom. With regard to the garden and bedroom, if I discover new ideas or feel the need to modify what I have already said, I shall inform you in due course. If not, what has been said must suffice, not to be repeated lest I make wearisome what has been spoken for the praise and glory of the Church's Bridegroom, our Lord Jesus Christ, who is God over all, blessed for ever. Amen.[110]

110. Rom 9:5

SERMON 24

DETRACTION AND MAN'S RIGHTEOUSNESS[1]

ON THIS THIRD RETURN from Rome,[2] my brothers, a more merciful eye has looked down from heaven and a more serene countenance has smiled on us. The Lion's rage has cooled,[3] wickedness has ceased, the Church has found peace. The reprobate, the man who for almost eight years has bitterly embroiled her in schism, has been brought to nothing in her sight.[4] But have I returned from so great dangers to be useless to you? I have been granted to your desires; I am ready to serve your advancement. Through your merits I am still alive, so I wish to live for your welfare, for your salvation. And because you wish me to continue the sermons I began a while back on the *Song of Songs*, I gladly acquiesce, thinking it better to resume where I broke off than to commence with something new. But I fear that my mind, alienated all that time from a doctrine so sublime and preoccupied with manifold affairs of much less consequence, may prove inept for the task. But if I give you what I have,[5] then God can take account of my

---

1. In some manuscripts *Sermon Twenty-Four* is divided into two short sermons, one interrupted by his journey to Rome in 1137, the other a resumption of the same theme on his return in 1138. In other manuscripts the *Sermon* begins as here, has the same content as the two short sermons, and is considered to be the definitive construction from Bernard's own hand. See J. Leclercq, "Introduction" in *Sancti Bernardi Opera*, vol. 1 (Rome, 1957), pp. XV ff.

2. That of 1138.

3. Anacletus II was known as Peter the Lion. He died on January 25, 1138.

4. Ps 14:4

5. Acts 3:6

well-meant effort and enable me to give even what I have not. If events should prove otherwise, the fault will lie in the skill, not the will.

2. We ought to begin, if I be not mistaken, with the words: "The righteous love you."[6] Before we begin to explain what this means, let us take a look at its origin, see who spoke it. For we are expected to understand what the author omits to say. Perhaps it is better to assign it to the maidens, as a continuation of their previous conversation. For when they said: "We will exult and rejoice in you as we remember your breasts, more delightful than wine,"[7] it is certain they were speaking to their mother; and they continued with the words: "The righteous love you." I think they may have said this because of members of their party who were not of the same mind[8] although they travelled in their company, who insisted on their own way,[9] their lives being neither simple nor sincere.[10] These were filled with envy of their mother's unique glory and took occasion to murmur against her on the grounds that she alone had entered the storehouses. This is the situation described in the Apostle's words: "Danger from false brothers."[11] It is against their reproaches that she is later compelled to justify herself with the answer: "I am black but lovely, daughters of Jerusalem."[12] It is because of these murmurers, these blasphemers, that the good and the simple, the humble and the meek, try to console the bride by telling her; "The righteous love you." "Do not be disturbed," they say, "by the wicked words of these blasphemers, because the righteous do love you." When we are reviled for doing good by evil-minded men, it is a sweet consolation if the righteous love us. The esteem of the good and the testimony of our conscience[13] make full amends for lying mouths.[14] "My soul glories in the Lord, let the humble hear and rejoice."[15] Let the humble rejoice, he said; let me but

6. Song 1:3
7. Song 1:3
8. Rom 12:16
9. 1 Cor 13:5
10. Prov 11:20

11. 2 Cor 11:26
12. Song 1:4
13. 2 Cor 1:12
14. Ps 62:12
15. Ps 33:3

please the humble and I shall bear with equanimity whatever the envy of wicked men may fling in my face.

3. I think this to be the meaning of the appendage: "The righteous love you." Nor is it mere fantasy, for in almost any group of young maidens I find some who curiously watch the bride's actions, not to imitate but to disparage them. They are embittered by their elders' good deeds, they feed on what is evil. You may see them walking apart, banding together, sitting in a huddle and immediately unleashing their wanton tongues in odious gossip. They are linked, one to the other, without an air space between them, so great is the desire to smear or listen to the smear. They combine in intimate groups whose end is slander, their unions promote disunion. Among themselves they develop most mischievous friendships, and equally impelled by unanimous malevolence, fête each other in a camaraderie of spite. Herod and Pilate once behaved just like this, for the Gospel says of them that "they became friends with each other that very day,"[16] that is, on the day of the Lord's passion. When they meet thus together it is not to eat the Lord's supper,[17] but rather to offer to others "the cup of demons"[18] and to drink of it themselves. They bear on their tongues the virus of death for their fellows, and gladly welcome the death that enters by their own ears. When with prattling mouths and itching ears[19] we busy ourselves in administering the poisoned cup of slander to each other, we fulfil the Prophet's words: "Death has climbed in at our windows."[20] I have no wish to be trapped in the plots of detractors, for the Apostle tells us they are hated by God: "Detractors, hateful to God."[21] God himself through the Psalm confirms this judgement: "Him who slanders his neighbour secretly I will destroy."[22]

4. No wonder if he should, since this vice is known to assail and victimize more bitterly than the others the love which is

16. Lk 23:12
17. 1 Cor 11:20
18. 1 Cor 10:20
19. 2 Tim 4:3

20. Jer 9:21
21. Rom 1:30
22. Ps 100:5

God,[23] as you can see for yourselves. For every slanderer first of all betrays that he himself is devoid of love. And secondly, his purpose in slandering can only be to inspire hatred and contempt in his audience for the victim of his slander. The venomous tongue strikes a blow at charity in the hearts of all within hearing, and if possible kills and quenches it utterly; worse still, even the absent are contaminated by the flying word that passes from those present to all within reach. See how easily and in how short a time this swift-moving word[24] can infect a great multitude of men with its sickly malice. Hence the inspired Prophet said of such: "Their mouth is full of cursing and bitterness; their feet are swift to shed blood."[25] Swift with the speed of news that brooks no delay. One man speaks, one word is spoken; but that one word, in one moment, penetrates the ears of the multitude and destroys their souls. For a heart embittered by the poison of envy can use the tongue to broadcast only bitter words, just as the Lord said: "A man's words flow out of what fills his heart."[26] This malady has varying forms. Some will spew out, with barefaced disrespect, any wicked slander that enters their heads; others try to hide an irrepressible evil purpose under the guise of simulated modesty. See the prelude of deep sighs, the mingled gravity and reluctance blazoned on his unhappy face, the downcast eyes and sombre tones, as the slanderer tells his tale, all the more persuasive the more the audience believes that he speaks with regret and with sympathy rather than malice. "I am really sorry for him," he says, "because I like him so much, but I could never induce him to set himself right in this matter." "I knew well," says another "that he was guilty of that fault, though I should never have been the one to reveal it. But now that it has been divulged by another I cannot deny that it is true; it pains me to say it, but facts are facts." And he goes on: "It's a great pity, he has so many good qualities; but if we are to be candid, he cannot be excused in this particular thing."

23. 1 Jn 4:8
24. Ps 147:15
25. Ps 13:3
26. Lk 6:45

II. 5. I have said my few words about this most deadly vice, so let me return to the theme I set out to explain, and show who are to be understood here as the "righteous." I am sure that nobody here with a right understanding would hold that those who love the bride are being spoken of in regard to physical perfection. It is spiritual righteousness, that of the soul, that must be explained. It is the Spirit who teaches, interpreting spiritual truths to those who possess the Spirit.[27] Therefore God made man righteous in his soul,[28] not in the body made of earthly slime. He created him according to his own image and likeness.[29] He is the one of whom you sing: "The Lord our God is righteous, and there is no iniquity in him."[30] God in his righteousness made man righteous like himself, without iniquity, since there is no iniquity in him. Iniquity is a fault in the heart, not in the flesh, and so you should realize that the likeness of God is to be preserved or restored in your spirit, not in the body of gross clay. For "God is a spirit,"[31] and those who wish to persevere in or attain to his likeness must enter into their hearts, and apply themselves spiritually to that work, until "with unveiled face, beholding the glory of the Lord," they "become transfigured into the same likeness, borrowing glory from that glory, as the Spirit of the Lord enables them."[32]

6. God indeed gave man an upright stance of body, perhaps in order that this corporeal uprightness, exterior and of little account, might prompt the inward man, made to the image of God, to cherish his spiritual uprightness; that the beauty of the body of clay might rebuke the deformity of the mind. What is more unbecoming than to bear a warped mind in an upright body? It is wrong and shameful that this body shaped from the dust of the earth should have its eyes raised on high, scanning the heavens at its pleasure and thrilled by the sight of sun and moon and stars, while, on the contrary, the heavenly and spiritual creature lives with its eyes, its

27. 1 Cor 2:13
28. Eccles 7:29
29. Gen 1:26

30. Ps 91:16
31. Jn 4:24
32. 2 Cor 3:18

inward vision and affections centred on the earth beneath; the mind that should be feasting on dainties is wallowing in the mire, rolling in the dung like a pig.[33] The body says: "Look on me, my soul, and blush for shame. Blush, my soul, that you have exchanged the divine for a bestial likeness; blush that despite your heavenly origin you now wallow in filth. Created upright and in your Creator's likeness, you received me as a helper like to yourself,[34] at least in bodily uprightness. Whatever way you turn,[35] to God above or to me below—'for no man ever hates his own flesh'[36]—everywhere you encounter reminders of your own beauty,[37] everywhere you find the friendly admonitions that wisdom imparts, intimating the dignity of your state. If I have retained and preserved the prerogative that I received for your sake, why are you not dismayed at losing yours? Why should the Creator continue to behold the loss of his likeness in you, at the same time that he ceaselessly preserves yours in me? All the help due to you from me you have turned to your own disgrace, you abuse my service to you; a brutish and bestial spirit, you dwell unworthily in this human body."

7. Those whose souls are warped in this fashion cannot love the Bridegroom, because they are not friends of the Bridegroom, they belong to this world. Scripture says: "Whoever wishes to be a friend of the world makes himself an enemy of God."[38] Therefore to pursue and enjoy the worldly warps the soul,[39] while, on the contrary, to meditate on or desire the things that are above constitutes its uprightness.

III. But if this is to be perfect, it must be not only a conviction of the mind, but a habit of life. I shall judge you to be righteous if your opinions are correct and your deeds do not contradict them. For the state of the invisible soul is made known by one's belief and practice. You may consider a man righteous if you prove him just by his work and Catholic by

33. Lam 4:5
34. Gen 2:18
35. 1 Kings 2:3
36. Eph 5:29

37. Ps 49:2
38. Jas 4:4
39. Col 3:2

faith. If otherwise, do not hesitate to appraise him as warped.
For Scripture says: "If you offer rightly, but do not divide rightly, you have sinned."[40] You offer rightly either of these,
faith or good work, however you do not rightly separate one
from the other. Be not one who is righteous in offering but
unrighteous in dividing. Why should there be a division between your faith and your conduct? It is a wrong division, it
destroys your faith, for "faith without good works is
dead."[41] The gift you offer to God is dead. For if devotion is
the soul of faith, what is faith that does not work through
love but a dead corpse?[42] Can you pay due honor to God
with a gift that stinks? Can you who murder your faith hope
to please him? What becomes of the sacrifice of peace where
this cruel discord reigns? What wonder if Cain attacked his
brother when he had already slain his own faith?[43] Why be
surprised, O Cain, if your gift is refused by him who holds
you in contempt?[44] Divided as you are against yourself, it is
no surprise that he pays you no heed. If you set your hand to
the sacrifice, why yield your mind to envy? You cannot be
reconciled with God while at odds with yourself; you do not
please him, rather you sin, not yet because of the impious
blow but because of the unrighteous division in your life.
Though not yet your brother's murderer, you have murdered
your own faith. How can you be right when, while raising up
your hand to God, your heart is drawn to earth by envy and
fraternal hate? How can you be right when your faith is
dead, your purpose to kill, your heart empty of devotion and
laden with bitterness? There was faith indeed in your act of
worship, but faith devoid of love: the offering was right but
the division cruel.

8. The death of faith is the departure of love. Do you
believe in Christ? Do the works of Christ so that your faith
will live; love will animate your faith, deeds will reveal it. Let
no earthly preoccupation bend down the mind that is raised
on high by faith. If you say you abide in Christ you ought to

40. Gen 4:7 (Septuagint)   43. Gen 4:8
41. Jas 2:20   44. Gen 4:5
42. Gal 5:6

walk as he walked.[45] But if you seek your own glory,[46] envy the successful, slander the absent, take revenge on those who injure you, this Christ did not do. You profess to know God, yet reject him by your deeds.[47] There is certainly nothing righteous, but plainly impious, in giving Christ your tongue while surrendering your soul to the devil. Listen then to what he says: "That man honors me with his lips, but his heart is far from me."[48] You are obviously not righteous in maintaining this unrighteous division. You cannot lift a head upwards that is weighed down by the devil's yoke. You have no means at all of raising yourself, for you are held by an evil power. Your iniquities have gone over your head; they weigh like a burden too heavy for you.[49] Iniquity sits upon a talent of lead.[50] You see then that right faith will not make a man righteous unless it is enlivened by love.[51] The man who has no love has no means of loving the bride. But on the other hand, deeds, however righteous, cannot make the heart righteous without faith. Who would call that man righteous who does not please God? But "without faith it is impossible to please God."[52] And God cannot please the man who is not pleasing to him; for if God is pleasing to a man, that man cannot displease God. Furthermore, if God is not pleasing to a man, neither is his bride. How then can he be righteous who loves neither God nor God's Church, to whom is said: "The righteous love you"? If therefore neither faith without good works nor good works without faith suffice for a man's righteousness,[53] we, my brothers, who believe in Christ, should strive to ensure that our behavior and desires are righteous.[54] Let us raise up both our hearts and hands to God,[55] that our whole being may be righteous, our righteous faith being revealed in our righteous actions. So we shall be lovers of the bride and loved by the Bridegroom Jesus Christ our Lord, who is God, blessed for ever. Amen.[56]

45. 1 Jn 2:6
46. Jn 7:18
47. Tit 1:16
48. Mt 15:8
49. Ps 37:5
50. Zech 5:7-8
51. Gal 5:6
52. Heb 11:6
53. Jas 2:20
54. Jer 7:3
55. Lam 3:41
56. Rom 1:25

SERMON 25

WHY THE BRIDE IS BLACK BUT BEAUTIFUL

I MENTIONED IN THE PREVIOUS SERMON[1] that the bride was compelled to give an answer to her envious assailants, who seemed to be physically part of the group of maidens,[2] but alienated from them in spirit. She said: "I am black but beautiful, daughters of Jerusalem."[3] It would appear that her dark skin is the object of their slanderous taunting. But we cannot help noting her patience and kindness. She not only refrained from hurling back curse for curse,[4] but gave them a friendly answer, calling them daughters of Jerusalem when for their wickedness she might properly have called them daughters of Babylon,[5] or daughters of Baal, or any other disreputable name. She had learned from the Prophet, and from Christ himself, the teacher of gentleness,[6] that the crushed reed must not be broken nor the wavering flame be quenched.[7] Hence she decided not to provoke to further outbursts people who had already so upset themselves, nor to add fuel to the fires of envy that tormented them. Conscious of her obligation even to the foolish,[8] she took pains to be peaceful with those who hated

1. Sermon 24:2
2. Song 6:7
3. Song 1:4
4. 1 Pet 3:9
5. Ps 136:8
6. 1 Jn 2:27
7. Is 42:3
8. Rom 1:14

peace.[9] She preferred therefore to soothe them with a kind word, because she felt it her duty to labor for the salvation of the weak rather than gratify personal spite.

2. Perfection of this kind is commendable for all, but is the model for prelates who wish to be worthy. Good and faithful superiors know that they have been chosen, not for the vain prestige of holding office, but to take care of ailing souls. And when they detect the presence of inward discontent by the voicing of complaints, even to the point of insult and contumely, they must see themselves then as physicians, not masters, and rather than retaliate, prepare a medicine for the fevered mind. This is why the bride addressed the scornful and malevolent maidens as daughters of Jerusalem; her soothing words would captivate the malcontents, calm their anger and banish their envy. It is written: "A peaceful tongue appeases strife."[10] Nor did she give them a false name, for in a certain sense these are truly daughters of Jerusalem. For whether because of the sacraments of the Church which they carelessly receive with the good, or because of a communal profession of faith, or the bodily unity of all the faithful, or even the hope of future salvation from which they are never wholly excluded as long as they live and of which they must not despair here below however recklessly they live, they are not unfittingly called daughters of Jerusalem.

II. 3. Let us next examine what was meant by saying: "I am black but beautiful." Is this a contradiction in terms? Certainly not. These remarks of mine are for simple persons who have not learned to distinguish between color and form; form refers to the shape of a thing, blackness is a color. Not everything therefore that is black is on that account ugly. For example blackness in the pupil of the eye is not unbecoming; black gems look glamorous in ornamental settings, and black locks above a pale face enhance its beauty and charm. You may easily verify this in any number of things, for instances

9. Ps 119:7
10. Prov 15:18; 25:15

abound in which you will find beautiful shapes with disagreeable colors. And so the bride, despite the gracefulness of her person, bears the stigma of a dark skin, but this is only in the place of her pilgrimage.[11] It will be otherwise when the Bridegroom in his glory will take her to himself "in splendor, without spot or wrinkle or any such thing."[12] But if she were to say now that her color is not black, she would be deceiving herself and the truth would not be in her.[13] So there is no reason to be surprised that she said: "I am black," and yet nonetheless gloried that she is beautiful. How can she be other than beautiful since it is said to her: "Come my beautiful one"?[14] Since she is invited to come, she has not yet arrived. So no one should think that the invitation was addressed to a blessed one who reigns without stain in heaven, it was addressed to the dark lady who was still toiling along the way.

4. But let us try to see why she calls herself black, and why beautiful. Is she black because of the benighted life she formerly led under the power of the prince of this world,[15] still modelled on the image of the earthly man,[16] and lovely because of the heavenly likeness into which she was afterwards changed as she began to live a new life?[17] If that were so would she not have spoken of the past and said: "I was black," and not "I am black"? But if anybody wishes to see it in this light, then in the case of the words that follow: "like the tents of Kedar, like the curtains of Solomon,"[18] the tent of Kedar should be understood of her former life, the tent of Solomon of the new. That curtains may have the same meaning as tent is shown by the Prophet when he says: "My tents are suddenly destroyed, in one moment my curtains have gone."[19] Formerly she was black like the wretched tents of Kedar, but later beautiful like the curtains of the renowned King.

11. Ps 118:54
12. Eph 5:27
13. 1 Jn 1:8
14. Song 2:10
15. Jn 12:31 ff

16. 1 Cor 15:49
17. Rom 6:4
18. Song 1:4
19. Jer 4:20

III. 5. But let us see how both of these refer rather to her present state of life. If we consider the outward appearance of the saints, all that our eyes may discern, how lowly and abject it is, how slovenly through want of care; yet at the same time, inwardly, "with unveiled faces reflecting like mirrors the brightness of the Lord, they grow brighter and brighter as they are turned by the Spirit of the Lord into the image that they reflect."[20] May not such a soul justly answer those who reproach her for being black:[21] "I am black but beautiful"? Shall I point out to you a person at once both black and beautiful? "They say he writes powerful and strongly-worded letters, but when he is with you, you see only half a man and no preacher at all."[22] This was St Paul. Daughters of Jerusalem, do you measure Paul in terms of his bodily presence, and despise him as blemished and ugly because you see only a runt of a man who has suffered hunger and thirst, cold and nakedness, the hardship of constant labor, countless beatings, often to the verge of death? [23] These are the experiences that denigrate Paul; for this the Doctor of the Nations is reputed abject, dishonorable, black, beneath notice, a scrap of this world's refuse.[24] But surely this is the man who is rapt into paradise,[25] who, traversing the first and second heavens, penetrates by his purity to the third? O soul of surpassing beauty, even though dwelling in a sickly little body, heaven's own loveliness had not scorned your company, the angels on high did not cast you out, God's brightness did not repudiate you! Is this soul to be called black? It is black but beautiful, daughters of Jerusalem. Black in your estimation, but beautiful in the eyes of God and the angels. The blackness you observe is merely external. Not that it makes the slightest difference to Paul whether you find him worthy or not,[26] you who judge according to appearances.[27] "Man looks at appearances but God looks at the heart."[28] Hence though black without, he

20. 2 Cor 3:18
21. Ps 118:42
22. 2 Cor 10:10
23. 2 Cor 11:27, 23
24. 1 Cor 4:13
25. 2 Cor 12:4
26. 1 Cor 4:3
27. Jn 7:24
28. 1 Sam 16:7

is beautiful within, intent on pleasing him to whom he must prove himself; for if he still endeavored to be pleasing to you he would not be the servant of Christ.[29] Happy the darkness that begets radiance in the mind, a light of knowledge and cleanness of conscience.

6. And finally, listen to what God promises through his Prophet to those blemished with this kind of blackness, those who seem discolored as by the sun's heat through the lowliness of a penitential life, through zeal for charity. He says: "Though your sins are like scarlet, they shall be as white as snow; though they are red as crimson, they shall be white as wool."[30] The outward blemishes that we may discern in holy people are not to be condemned, because they play a part in the begetting of interior light, and so dispose the soul for wisdom. For wisdom is described by the wise man as "a reflection of eternal life,"[31] and brightness befits the soul in which it decides to dwell. If the soul of the righteous man is the seat of wisdom,[32] I may certainly refer to such a soul as bright. Righteousness itself can be called brightness. Paul was a righteous man for whom was laid up "a crown of righteousness."[33] Therefore the soul of Paul was adorned with brightness, and wisdom dwelt there, to enable him to impart wisdom among the mature,[34] a wisdom hidden in mystery, which none of the rulers of this world understood.[35] This wisdom and righteousness of Paul were either produced or merited through the outward impairment of his little body,[36] worn out by constant labors,[37] by frequent fastings and vigils. Hence this ugliness of Paul is more beautiful than jewelled ornaments, than the raiment of kings. No physical love-

---

29. Gal 1:10
30. Is 1:18
31. Wis 7.26. This is probably a slip on Bernard's part; all the known sources give "light" not "life".
32. Prov 12:23 (Septuagint)
33. 2 Tim 4:8
34. 1 Cor 2:6
35. 1 Cor 2:7-8
36. 2 Cor 10:10
37. 2 Cor 11:23

liness can compare with it, no skin however bright and glowing; not the tinted cheek for which corruption waits, nor the costly dress that time wears out; not the lustre of gold nor sparkle of gems, nor any other creature: all will crumble into corruption.

IV. 7. It is with good reason then that the saints find no time for the glamor of jewellery and the elegance of dress, that lose their appeal with the passing hour;[38] their whole attention is fixed on improving and adorning the inward self that is made to the image of God,[39] and is renewed day by day.[40] For they are certain that nothing can be more pleasing to God than his own image when restored to its original beauty. Hence all their glory is within,[41] not without; not in the beauty of nature[42] nor in the praises of the crowd, but in the Lord. With St Paul they say: "Our boast is this, the testimony of our conscience;"[43] because the sole judge of their conscience is God, whom alone they desire to please, and pleasing him is their sole, true and highest glory. There is nothing mean about that inward glory, for, as David points out, the Lord of glory takes his delight in it: "All his glory is within the daughter of the king."[44] Each one's glory is all the more secure when in his own keeping, and not in another.[45] And the saints glory not only in their inward light but even in the unsightliness of their outward appearance; nothing in them is without its use, "everything works for good."[46] Sufferings are their joy equally with their hope.[47] St Paul says: "I will all the more gladly boast of my weaknesses, that the power of Christ may rest upon me."[48] How desirable that weakness for which the power of Christ compensates. Let me be not merely weak, then, but entirely resourceless, utterly helpless, that I may enjoy the support of the power of the Lord of hosts. "For virtue is perfected in weakness."[49] And

38. 2 Cor 4:16
39. Gen 1:26
40. 2 Cor 4:16
41. Ps 44:14
42. 1 Pet 1:24
43. 2 Cor 1:12

44. Ps 44:14
45. Gal 6:4
46. Rom 8:28
47. Rom 5:2-3
48. 2 Cor 12:9
49. 2 Cor 12:9

Paul adds: "It is when I am weak that I am strong and power-ful."[50]

8. This being so, how aptly the bride accepted as an en-hancement of her glory the insult hurled by those who envied her, rejoicing not only in her loveliness but even in her black-ness. She is not ashamed of this blackness, for her Bride-groom endured it before her, and what greater glory than to be made like to him? Therefore she believes that nothing contributes more to her glory than to bear the ignominy of Christ. And hence that note of gladness and triumph as she says:[51] "Far be it from me to glory except in the cross of our Lord Jesus Christ."[52] The ignominy of the cross is welcome to the man who will not be an ingrate to his crucified Lord. Though it involves the stigma of blackness, it is also in the pattern and the likeness of the Lord. Listen to St Isaiah, and he will describe him for you as he saw him in spirit: "A man of sorrows and afflicted with suffering,[53] without beauty, without majesty."[54] And he adds: "We thought of him as a leper, struck by God and brought low. Yet he was pierced through for our faults, crushed for our sins, and through his wounds we are healed."[55] This is the reason for his blackness. But think at the same time of those words of St David: "You are the fairest of the sons of men,"[56] and you will find in the Bridegroom all the traits that the bride, in the words of our text, ascribes to herself.

9. Does it not seem to you, in accord with what has been said, that he could have replied to the envious Jews: "I am black but beautiful, sons of Jerusalem"? Obviously black, since he had neither beauty nor majesty;[57] black because he was "a worm and no man, scorned by men and despised by the people."[58] If he even made himself into sin,[59] shall I shirk saying he was black? Look steadily at him in his filth-covered cloak, livid from blows, smeared with spittle, pale as

50. 2 Cor 12:10
51. Ps 117:15
52. Gal 6:14
53. Is 53:3
54. Is 53:2

55. Is 53:4-5
56. Ps 44:3
57. Is 53:2
58. Ps 21:7
59. 2 Cor 5:21

death: surely then you must pronounce him black. But enquire also of the apostles in what guise they found this same man on the mount,[60] and ask the angels to describe him on whom they long to gaze,[61] and the beauty you discover will compel your admiration. Beautiful in his own right, his blackness is because of you. Even clad in my form, how beautiful you are, Lord Jesus! And not merely because of the miracles of divine power that render you glorious, but because of your truth and meekness and righteousness.[62] Happy the man who, by attentive study of your life as a man among men,[63] strives according to his strength to live like you. The Church in her loveliness has already received from you this blessed gift, the first fruits of her dowry; she is not slow to pattern herself on what is beautiful in you, nor ashamed to endure your ignominies. All this we must recall when she says: "I am black but beautiful, daughters of Jerusalem;" to which she adds the comparison: "like the tents of Kedar, like the curtains of Solomon." This dictum is obscure however, and beyond the reach of those already wearied. But it is a door on which you are given time to knock. Those who are sincere will there encounter him whose light illumines mysteries; and he will open at once, because he invites you to knock.[64] He it is who opens and no man shuts,[65] the Church's Bridegroom, Jesus Christ our Lord, who is blessed for ever. Amen.[66]

60. Mt 17:2
61. 1 Pet 1:12
62. Ps 44:5
63. Bar 3:38

64. Lk 11:9
65. Rev. 3:7
66. Rom 1:25

SERMON 26

THE BLACKNESS OF THE BRIDE COMPARED TO THE TENTS OF KEDAR
BERNARD'S LAMENT FOR HIS BROTHER

"AS THE TENTS OF KEDAR, as the curtains of Solomon."[1] This is our starting-point, since it is where the last sermon ended. You are waiting to hear what these words mean, and in what way they are connected with the text of our previous discourse in chapter, because they do bear comparison. They can be so connected that both parts of the comparison refer solely to the first clause of that text: "I am black;" or the two parts may correspond to the two parts there, one to each. The former interpretation is the more simple, the latter the more obscure. But let us try both, and for a start the one that seems more difficult. For the difficulty lies, not in the first term of the comparison, but in the last. It is obvious that Kedar,[2] meaning darkness, corresponds to blackness; but not so obvious that the curtains of Solomon signify beauty. All must be able to see that tents can suggest the notion of darkness. For what is meant by tents but our bodies, in which we wander as pilgrims?[3] "For we have not here a lasting city, but we seek one that is to come."[4] We even wage war in them, like soldiers in tents, like violent men taking the kingdom by force.[5] In a word, "the

1. Song 1:4
2. See St Jerome, *Liber interpretationum hebr. nom.*, ed. P. de Lagarde (Paris, 1887), no. 41, p. 30.
3. 2 Cor 5:6
4. Heb 13:14
5. Mt 11:12

life of man upon earth is a warfare,"[6] and as long as we do
battle in this body "we are away from the Lord,"[7] away
from the light. For "God is light,"[8] and to the extent that a
man is not with him, to that extent he is in darkness,[9] that is,
in Kedar. Hence he may recognize as his own that tearful
outcry: "Woe is me that my sojourning is prolonged! I have
dwelt with the inhabitants of Kedar; my soul has been long a
sojourner."[10] Our bodily dwelling-place therefore, is neither a
citizen's residence nor one's native home, but rather a sol-
dier's tent or traveller's hut. This body, I repeat, is a tent, a
tent of Kedar, that now intervenes to deprive the soul for a
while of the vision of the infinite light, permiting that it be
seen "in a mirror dimly," but not face to face.[11]

2. Do you not see whence blackness appears on the
Church's body, why persons of the greatest beauty are
tainted by defects? It is because of the tents of Kedar, the
waging of wearisome war, a life of prolonged misery, the
distresses of bitter exile, in a word, a body that is both frail
and burdensome: "for a perishable body weighs down the
soul, and this earthly tent burdens the thoughtful mind."[12]
Hence some souls long to die, that freed from the body, they
may fly to the embraces of Christ.[13] One of these unhappy
people said out of his misery: "Wretched man that I am, who
will deliver me from this body of death? "[14] A man such as
this is aware that one cannot dwell in a tent of Kedar and
lead a pure life, free of stain, a life without a wrinkle,[15]
without some degree of blackness; so he longs to die and be
divested of it. This is why the bride said she is black like the
tents of Kedar. But how can she be beautiful like the curtains
of Solomon? I feel that something beyond imagining, something sublime and sacred is so caught up in these curtains of
Solomon, that I dare not approach them at all, except at the
bidding of him who hid it there and sealed it. For I have read

6. Job 7:1

7. 2 Cor 5:6

8. 1 Jn 1:5

9. 1 Jn 2:9

10. Ps 119:5-6

11. 1 Cor 13:12

12. Wis 9:15

13. Phil 1:23

14. Rom 7:24

15. Eph 5:27

"he that is a searcher of majesty shall be overwhelmed by glory."[16] So I shall not pursue the matter now, but leave it to another time. Meantime let it be your concern to ask this grace for me by your accustomed prayers, that we may return with greater confidence and greater eagerness to a subject that demands more than normal attention. And one may hope that a respectful knock will discover to us what rash curiosity could not achieve. Besides all that, the sorrow that oppresses me since my bereavement compels me to come to an end.[17]

II. 3. How long shall I keep my pretence while a hidden fire burns my sad heart, consumes me from within? A concealed fire creeps forward with full play, it rages more fiercely. I, whose life is bitterness, what have I to do with this canticle? Overpowering sorrow distracts my mind, the displeasure of the Lord drains my spirit dry.[18] For when he was taken away, he who enabled me to attend to the study of spiritual doctrine so freely and so frequently, my heart departed from me too. But up till now I have done violence to myself and kept up a pretence,[19] lest my affection should seem stronger than my faith. While others wept, I, as you could not but see, followed with dry eyes in the wake of the cruel bier, stood with dry eyes at the graveside till the last solemn funeral rite was performed. Clothed in priestly vestments, with my own mouth I recited the accustomed prayers over him till the end; with my own hands I cast the clay over the body of him I loved, destined soon to be at one with the clay. The eyes that beheld me were filled with tears, and the wonder was that I did not weep, since all took pity, not so

---

16. Prov 25:27
17. Job 6:2 Here begins Bernard's lament for his brother Gerard, cellarer or bursar of the Abbey of Clairvaux. It reveals one more aspect of the extremely passionate nature of St Bernard. It was preached in 1138.
18. Job 6:4
19. Ps 39:13

much on him who had gone as on me who had lost him. Who would not be moved, even with iron for a heart, at seeing me there living on without my Gerard. All had experienced the loss, but regarded it as nothing in comparison with mine. And I? With all the force of faith that I could muster I resisted my feelings, striving, against my will, not to be vainly upset by what is but our natural destiny, a debt that all must pay by the law of our condition, by the command of God and his just judgment; the God we must fear because it is he who strikes, his will we must accept. Since then all the time I have forced myself to refrain from much weeping, though inwardly much troubled and sad. I could control my tears but could not control my sadness; in the Scripture's words: "I was troubled and did not speak."[20] But the sorrow that I suppressed struck deeper roots within, growing all the more bitter, I realized, because it found no outlet. I confess, I am beaten. All that I endure within must needs issue forth. But let it be poured out before the eyes of my sons, who, knowing my misfortune, will look with kindness on my mourning and afford more sweet sympathy.

4. You, my sons, know how deep my sorrow is, how galling the wound it leaves. You are aware that a loyal companion has left me alone on the pathway of life:[21] he who was so alert to my needs, so enterprising at work, so agreeable in his ways. Who was ever so necessary to me? Who ever loved me as he? My brother by blood, but bound to me more intimately by religious profession. Share my mourning with me, you who know these things. I was frail in body and he sustained me, faint of heart and he gave me courage, slothful and negligent and he spurred me on, forgetful and improvident and he gave me timely warning. Why has he been torn from me? Why snatched from my embraces, a man of one mind with me, a man according to my heart?[22] We loved each other in life: how can it be that death separates us? And how bitter the separation that only death could bring

20. Ps 76:5
21. Ps 76:5
22. Acts 13:22, 2 Sam 1:23

about! While you lived when did you ever abandon me? It is totally death's doing, so terrible a parting. Who would dare refuse to spare so sweet a bond of mutual love —who but death, that enemy of all that is sweet! Death indeed, so aptly named, whose rage has destroyed two lives in the spoliation of one. Surely this is death to me as well? Even more so to me, to whom continued life is more wretched than any form of death. I live, and I die in living: and shall I call this life? How much more kind, O cruel death, if you had deprived me of life itself rather than of its fruit! For life without fruit is a more terrible death. The tree that bears no fruit is faced with a twofold doom: the axe and the fire.[23] And because you envied the works that I performed, you removed beyond my reach him who was both friend and neighbor;[24] for if these works were fruitful it was because of his zeal. How much better for me then, O Gerard, if I had lost my life rather than your company, since through your tireless inspiration, your unfailing help and under your provident scrutiny I persevered with my studies of things divine. Why, I ask, have we loved, why have we lost each other? O cruel circumstance! But pity pertains to my lot only, not to his.

III. And the reason, dear brother, is that though you have lost your loved ones, you have found others more lovable still. As for me, already so miserable, what consolation remains to me, and you, my only comfort, gone? Our bodily companionship was equally enjoyable to both, because our dispositions were so alike; but only I am wounded by the parting. All that was pleasant we rejoiced to share; now sadness and mourning are mine alone: anger has swept over me,[25] rage is fastened on me.[26] Both of us were so happy in each other's company, sharing the same experiences, talking together about them; now my share of these delights has ceased and you have passed on, you have traded them for an immense reward.[27]

23. Mt 3:10   26. Ps 87:8
24. Ps 87:19   27. Ps 18:12
25. Ps 87:17

5. What a harvest of joys, what a profusion of blessings is yours. In place of my insignificant person you have the abiding presence of Christ, and mingling with the angelic choirs you feel our absence no loss. You have no cause to complain that we have been cut off from you, favored as you are by the constant presence of the Lord of Majesty and of his heavenly friends. But what do I have in your stead? How I long to know what you now think about me, once so uniquely yours, as I sink beneath the weight of cares and afflictions, deprived of the support you lent to my feebleness! Perhaps you still give thought to our miseries, now that you have plunged into the abyss of light, become engulfed in that sea of endless happiness. It is possible that though you once knew us according to the flesh, you now no longer know us[28] and because you have entered into the power of the Lord you will be mindful of his righteousness alone, forgetful of ours.[29] Furthermore, "he who is united to the Lord becomes one spirit with him,"[30] his whole being somehow changed into a movement of divine love. He no longer has the power to experience or relish anything but God, and what God himself experiences and relishes, because he is filled with God. But God is love,[31] and the deeper one's union with God, the more full one is of love. And though God cannot endure pain, he is not without compassion for those who do; it is his nature to show mercy and pardon. Therefore you too must of necessity be merciful, clasped as you are to him who is Mercy; and though you no longer feel the need of mercy, though you no longer suffer, you can still be compassionate. Your love has not been diminished but only changed; when you were clothed with God you did not divest yourself of concern for us, for God is certainly concerned about us.[32] All that smacks of weakness you have cast away, but not what pertains to love. And since love never comes to an end,[33] you will not forget me for ever.[34]

28. 2 Cor 5:16
29. Ps 70:15-16
30. 1 Cor 6:17
31. 1 Jn 4:8

32. 1 Pet 5:7
33. 1 Cor 13:8
34. Ps 12:1

6. It seems to me that I can almost hear my brother saying: "Can a woman forget the son of her womb? And if she should forget, yet I will not forget you."[35] This is how it must be. You know how I am situated, how dejected in spirit, how your departure has affected me; there is none to give me a helping hand.

IV. In every emergency I look to Gerard for help, as I always did, and he is not there. Alas! then I can only sigh in my misery, like a man deprived of all resources.[36] To whom shall I turn for advice when perplexed? In whom shall I confide when fortune is against me? who will carry my burdens? [37] Who will save me when danger threatens? Were not Gerard's eyes an unfailing guide to my feet? Were not my worries, O Gerard, better known to your heart than to mine, their inroads more penetrating, their pressure more acute? How often did you not free me from worldly conversations by the adroitness of your gifted words, and return me to the silence that I loved? The Lord endowed him with a discernment that enabled him to speak with due propriety,[38] and this prudence in his responses, accompanied by a certain graciousness given to him from above, made him acceptable both to his fellow monks and to people in the world, and anybody who spoke to Gerard had rarely need to see me. He made a point of meeting visitors to forestall and prevent them from inopportune intrusion on my solitude. When he did lack the competence to satisfy the needs of some, he brought them to me; the others he dealt with and dismissed. What a busy man he was! What a trustworthy friend! Though always glad to be in the company of friends, he was never thereby prevented from answering the call of charity. Who ever went away from him empty-handed? The rich found enlightenment, the poor were given alms. Nor did he seek his own advantage,[39] he who shouldered every burden that I might be free. In his great humility he hoped for more fruit

35. Is 49:15
36. Ps 87:5
37. Gal 6:2
38. Is 50:4
39. 1 Cor 13:5

from our quiet than if he himself had leisure. Yet he did sometimes ask to be discharged from his office, that a more efficient administrator might take over. But where could such a man be found? Charity alone, and not, as so often happens, mere wanton desire for position, detained him there. Nobody worked so hard as he, and nobody received less in return; and quite often, after he had supplied everybody's needs, he himself stood in need in many ways, for example in food and clothing. And when he knew that he was close to death, this is what he said: "O God, you know that in as far as it was possible for me I have wanted a tranquil life, the freedom to be with you. But fear of you, the community's will and my own desire to obey, and above all my deep love for one who was both my abbot and my brother, kept me involved in the business of the house." That is how it was. So I may thank you, dear brother, for what fruits may result from my studies of the things of God. What progress I have made, what good I have done, I owe to you. Your involvement in the business of the house gave me the leisure and privacy for more prayerful absorption in divine contemplation, for more thorough preparation of doctrine for my sons. Why should I not rest secure in my cell when I knew that you were my spokesman with the people, my right-hand man, the light of my eyes,[40] my heart and my tongue? A tireless hand, a candid eye,[41] a wise heart, a judicious tongue, just like Scripture says: "The mouth of the righteous utters wisdom and his tongue speaks what is right."[42]

V. 7. But why have I described Gerard as a mere extern worker, as if he were ignorant of the interior life and devoid of spiritual gifts? Spiritual men who knew him knew that his words bore a spiritual aroma. His comrades knew that his dispositions and propensities were anything but worldly,[43] they were alive with a spiritual power.[44] Who was more uncompromising than he in the maintenance of discipline? Who were more austere in bodily mortification, more absorbed

40. Ps 37:11
41. Mt 6:22
42. Ps 36:30

43. Rom 8:5
44. Rom 12:11

in contemplation, more skilled in discussion? How often when talking with him have I increased my knowledge; I who approached to enlighten him came away enlightened instead! And no surprise that I should experience this, since men of learning and consequence testify to similar experiences when meeting with him. He had no knowledge of literature;[45] but he possessed the intelligence that is its source and the Holy Spirit who is the mind's light. And whether the occasion was small or great, he displayed an equal standard of excellence. For example, did anything ever escape the skilled eye of Gerard in the buildings, in the fields, in gardening, in the water systems, in all the arts and crafts of the people of the countryside? With masterly competence he supervised the masons, the smiths, the farm workers, the gardeners, the shoemakers and the weavers. And yet, he whom all esteemed as supremely wise, was devoid of wisdom in his own estimation. One could mightily wish that so many people, all of them less than wise, would cease to expose themselves to that scriptural reproach: "Woe to those who are wise in their own eyes."[46] I speak to men who are aware of these facts,[47] who know that finer things still might be said of him. I shall not say them however, because he is my blood-brother.[48] But I do say without a qualm: I found him helpful above all others and in every situation, helpful on small occasions and great, in private and in public, in the world and in the cloister. It was only right that I should depend entirely on him, he was all in all to me. He left me little more than the name and honor of provider, he did the work. I was saluted as abbot, but he was the one who watched over all with solicitude.[49] I could not but feel secure with a man who enabled me to enjoy the delights of divine love,[50] to preach with greater facility, to pray without anxiety. I must repeat that through you, my dear brother, I enjoyed a peaceful mind and a welcome peace; my preaching was more effective, my prayer more fruitful, my study more regular, my love more fervent.

45. Ps 70:15
46. Is 5:21
47. Rom 7:1
48. Gen 37:27
49. Rom 12:8
50. Ps 36:4

8. Alas! You have been taken away and these good offices too. All my delights, all my pleasures, have disappeared along with you. Already cares rush in upon me, troubles press about me on every side;[51] manifold anxieties have found me companionless, and, since you departed, have stayed with me in my solitude. In my loneliness I groan under the burden. Because your shoulders are no longer there to support it, I must lay it down or be crushed. O, if I could only die at once and follow you! Certainly I would not have died in your stead, I would not deprive you of the glory that is yours. But to survive you can mean only drudgery and pain.[52] My life, if you can call it that, will be one of bitterness and mourning;[53] it will even be my comfort to endure this painful grief. I shall not spare myself, I shall even co-operate with the hand of the Lord: for "the hand of the Lord has touched me."[54] It is I who am touched and stricken, not he, for it has but summoned him to repose; in cutting short his life it has brought me death. One can scarcely speak of him as dead! Was he not rather transplanted into life? At least what was for him the gateway to life is simply death to me; for by that death it is I who died, not he; he has but gone to sleep in the Lord.[55] Flow on, flow on, my tears, so long on the point of brimming over; flow on, for he who dammed up your exit is here no longer. Let the flood-gates of my wretched head be opened,[56] let my tears gush forth like fountains, that they may perchance wash away the stains of those sins that drew God's anger upon me.[57] When the Lord shall have been appeased in my regard, then perhaps I shall find the grace of consolation, but without ceasing to mourn: for those who mourn shall be comforted.[58]

VI. Therefore my request to every good man is that he look on me with kindness, and in a spirit of gentleness which is

51. Dan 13:22
52. Ps 89:10
53. Job 3:20
54. Job 19:21

55. Acts 7:60
56. Gen 7:11
57. Job 6:2
58. Mt 5:5

spiritual support to me in my lament.[59] And I implore you, let not mere conventional respect, but your human affection, draw you to me in my sorrow. Day after day we see the dead bewailing their dead:[60] floods of tears, but all to no pupose. Not that I condemn the affection they show, unless it be out of all proportion, but the reason that inspires it. The former springs from nature, the disturbance it causes is but a consequence of sin; the latter however is sinful vanity. Their weeping, if I mistake not, is solely for the loss of earthly glory, because of the misfortunes of the present life. Those who so weep should themselves be wept for. Can it be possible that I am one of them? My emotional outburst is certainly like theirs, but the cause, the intention, differs. I make no complaint at all about the ways of this world.[61] But I do lament the loss of a loyal helper, one whose advice on the things of God was ever reliable. It is Gerard whom I weep for. Gerard is the reason for my weeping, my brother by blood, but closer by an intimate spiritual bond, the one who shared all my plans.

9. My soul cleaved to his.[62] We were of one mind, and it was this, not blood relationship, that joined us as one. That he was my blood-brother certainly mattered; but our spiritual affinity, our similar outlooks and harmony of temperaments, drew us more close still. We were of one heart and one soul;[63] the sword pierced both my soul and his,[64] and cutting them apart,[65] placed one in heaven but abandoned the other in the mire. I am that unhappy portion prostrate in the mud, mutilated by the loss of its nobler part, and shall people say to me: "Do not weep"? My very heart is torn from me and shall it be said to me: "Try not to feel it"? But I do feel it intensely in spite of myself, because my strength is not the strength of stones nor is my flesh of bronze.[66] I feel it and go on grieving; my pain is ever with me.[67] He who

59. Gal 6:1
60. Mt 8:22
61. 1 Cor 7:32-34
62. 1 Sam 18:1
63. Acts 4:32

64. Lk 2:35
65. Dan 13:55
66. Job 6:12
67. Ps 37:18

chastises me will never be able to accuse me of hardness and insensibility, like those of whom it was said: "You have struck them; they have not felt it."[68] I have made public the depth of my affliction, I make no attempt to deny it.[69] Will you say then that this is carnal? That it is human, yes, since I am a man. If this does not satisfy you then I am carnal. Yes, I am carnal, sold under sin,[70] destined to die, subject to penalties and sufferings. I am certainly not insensible to pain; to think that I shall die, that those who are mine will die, fills me with dread. And Gerard was mine, so utterly mine. Was he not mine who was a brother to me by blood, a son by religious profession, a father by his solicitude, my comrade on the spiritual highway, my bosom friend in love? And it is he who has gome from me. I feel it, the wound is deep.

10. My sons, forgive me; or better still, as sons, grieve for your father's misfortune. "Have pity on me, at least you my friends,"[71] for you can see how heavy the penalty I have received from God's hand for my sins. With the rod of his anger he struck me,[72] justly because I deserve it, harshly because I can bear it. Can any man lightly say that I can get along without Gerard, unless he be ignorant of all that Gerard meant to me? I have no wish to repudiate the decrees of God,[73] nor do I question that judgment by which each of us has received his due; he the crown he had earned, I the punishment I deserved. Shall I find fault with his judgment because I wince from the pain? This latter is but human, the former is impious. It is but human and necessary that we respond to our friends with feeling: that we be happy in their company, disappointed in their absence. Social intercourse, especially between friends, cannot be purposeless; the reluctance to part and the yearning for each other when separated, indicate how meaningful their mutual love must be when they are together.

68. Jer 5:3
69. Jn 1:20
70. Rom 7:14

71. Job 19:21
72. Lam 3:1
73. Job 6:10

VII. I grieve for you, my dearest Gerard,[74] not for the sake of grieving, but because you have been separated from me. Perhaps my grieving should be on my own account, because the cup I drink is bitter. And I grieve by myself because I drink by myself: for you cannot join me. All by myself I experience the sufferings that are shared equally by lovers when compelled to remain apart.

11. Would that I have not lost you, but have sent you on before me! Would that one day, however far off, I may follow you wherever you go! [75] One cannot doubt but that you have gone to those whom you invited to sing God's praise in the middle of your last night on earth, when with face and voice all joyful,[76] to the astonishment of those about you, you burst into that hymn of David: "Let heaven praise the Lord, praise him in the heights."[77] Even then, for you, dear brother, the midnight dark was yielding to the dawn, the night was growing bright like the day.[78] Surely that night was your light in your pleasures! [79] I was summoned to witness this miracle, to see a man exulting in the hour of death, and mocking its onset. "O death, where is your victory? "[80] A sting no longer but a shout of joy. A man dies while he sings, he sings by dying. Begetter of sorrow, you have been made a source of gladness; an enemy to glory, you have been made to contribute to glory; the gate of hell, you have been made the threshold of heaven; the very pit of perdition, you have been made a way of salvation, and that by a man who was a sinner. Justly too, because in your rashness you wickedly grasped at power over man in his state of innocence and justice. You are dead, O death, pierced by the hook you have incautiously swallowed,[81] even as the Prophet said: "O death, I will be your death; O hell, I will be your destruction."[82] Pierced by that hook, you open a broad and happy exit to life for the faithful who pass through your

74. 2 Sam 1:26
75. Rev 14:4
76. Ps 41:5
77. Ps 148:1
78. Ps 138:12

79. Ps 138:11
80. 1 Cor 15:55
81. Job 40:20-21
82. Hos 13:14

midst. Gerard had no fear of you, shadowy phantom that you are. Gerard passes on to his fatherland through your jaws, not only secure but filled with overflowing joy.[83] So when I arrived, and heard him finishing the last verses of the Psalm in a clear voice, I saw him look toward heaven and say: "Father, into your hands I commend my spirit."[84] Sighing frequently, he repeated the same word: "Father, Father;" then turning to me, his face lit up with joy, he said: "How great the goodness of God, that he should become a father to men! How great a glory for men, that they are sons of God, heirs of God! For if sons, then heirs too."[85] This is how he sang, the man we mourn for; and he could well have changed my mourning into song, for with my mind fixed on his glory, the sense of my own misery had begun to fade.

12. But the pang of sorrow quickly recalls me to myself from that serene vision; I am roused, as from a light sleep, by a gnawing anxiety. I continue to lament, but over my own plight, because reason forbids me to mourn for him. I feel that given the occasion, he would now say to us: "Do not weep for me, but weep for yourselves."[86]

VIII. David rightly mourned for his parricidal son,[87] because he knew all exit from the pit of death was denied to him forever by the greatness of his sin. Rightly he mourned over Saul and Jonathan, for whom, once engulfed by death, there seemed no hope of deliverance.[88] They will rise indeed, but not to life: or if to life, only to die more miserably in a living death, though one must reasonably hesitate to apply this judgment to Jonathan. As for me, though my mourning may not be for this reason, it is not without reason. In the first place I bewail my own wounds and the loss this house has suffered; I bewail the needs of the poor, to whom Gerard was a father; I bewail above all the state of our whole Order, of our religious life, that derived no small support from your

83. Is 35:2
84. Lk 23:46
85. Rom 8:17

86. Lk 23:28
87. 2 Sam 19:1-2
88. 2 Sam 1:17-27

zeal, your wisdom and your example, O Gerard; and finally, though my mourning is not for you, it is because of you. My deepest wound is in the ardor of my love for you. And let no one embarrass me by telling me I am wrong in yielding to this feeling, when the kind-hearted Samuel poured out the love of his heart for a reprobate king,[89] and David for his parricidal son, without injury to their faith, without offending the judgment of God. Holy David cried out: "Absalom, my son, my son, Absalom! "[90] And see, a greater than Absalom is here.[91] Our Savior too, looking at Jerusalem and foreseeing its destruction, wept over it.[92] And shall I not feel my own desolation that even now presses upon me? Shall I not grieve for the heavy blow so recently received? David's tears were tears of compassion, and shall I be afraid to weep in my suffering? At the tomb of Lazarus Christ neither rebuked those who wept nor forbade them to weep, rather he wept with those who wept.[93] The Scripture says: "And Jesus wept."[94] These tears were witnesses to his human kindness, not signs that he lacked trust. Moreover, he who had been dead came forth at once at his word,[95] lest the manifestation of sorrow be thought harmful to faith.

13. In the same way, our weeping is not a sign of a lack of faith, it indicates the human condition. Nor do I rebuke the striker if I weep on receiving the blow, rather do I invite his mercy, I try to mitigate his severity. You hear the heavy note of sorrow in my words,[96] but I am far from murmuring. Have I not been completely fair when I said that the one who was punished deserved it, the one who was crowned was worthy of it? And I still aver that the sweet and just Lord acted fairly to us both.[97] "My song, O Lord, shall be of mercy and judgment."[98] Let that mercy poured out by you on your servant Gerard sing to you;[99] and let that judgment that I endure sing to you as well.[100] I praise your goodness to him,

89. 1 Sam 16:1
90. 2 Sam 18:33
91. Mt. 12:42
92. Lk 19:41
93. Rom 12:15
94. Jn 11:35

95. Jn 11:44
96. Job 6:3
97. Ps 24:8
98. Ps 100:1
99. Ps 118:124
100. Gal 5:10

your justice to me. Shall goodness alone merit praise, and not justice? "You are righteous indeed, O Lord, and all your judgments are right."[101] You gave me Gerard, you took him away:[102] and if his removal makes me sad, I do not forget that he was given to me, and offer thanks for my good fortune in having had him. My regret at his departure is but in accord with the need it has exposed.

14. I will meditate, O Lord, on my covenant with you, and on your mercy,[103] that you may be justified in passing sentence on me, and blameless in your judgments.[104] Last year when we were at Viterbo on the Church's business, Gerard became ill, so ill that it seemed God was about to call him to himself. I felt it unthinkable that my companion on my journeys, and so wonderful a companion, should be left behind in a foreign land. I had to restore him to those who had entrusted him to me. All of them loved him because he was so utterly lovable.[105] So I began to pray in the midst of my tears and said: "Wait O Lord, till we return home. Let me give him back to his friends, then take him if you wish, and I shall not complain." You listened to me O God,[106] his health improved, we finished the work you had enjoined on us,[107] and, laden with the fruits of peace, [108] returned in great happiness. Since then I lost sight of my agreement with you, but you did not forget. I am ashamed of these sobs of grief that go to prove my unfaithfulness. What more shall I say? You entrusted Gerard to us, you have claimed him back; you have but taken what was yours. These tears prevent me speaking further; impose a limit on them O Lord, bring them to an end.

101. Ps 118:137
102. Job 1:21
103. Ezek 16:60
104. Ps 50:6

105. 2 Sam 1:26
106. Ps 16:6
107. Jn 4:34
108. Ps 125:6

SERMON 27

THE BEAUTY OF THE BRIDE COMPARED TO THE CURTAINS OF SOLOMON
WHY SHE IS CALLED A HEAVEN

MY BROTHERS, OUR FRIEND HAS GONE back to his homeland, we have paid the full tribute of human affection to his memory, so I take up again the instruction which I then discontinued. As he is now in the state of happiness it is improper to prolong our mourning for him, it is out of place to appear in tears before a man enjoying a banquet. Even though we do shed tears in our troubles, our grief should not be excessive, or it will seem to express our regret for the service we have lost rather than our love for him. To think that the one we love is in a state of bliss must ease the pain of our bereavement; to realize that he is with God must make his absence from us more bearable. And so, trusting in the aid of your prayers, I shall attempt to throw light on the secret hidden by those curtains that portray the beauty of the bride. We touched on this, as you recall, but did not delve into it,[1] though we had discussed and discovered how she is black like the tents of Kedar. But in what way can she be beautiful like the curtains of Solomon, as if Solomon in all his glory could even remotely resemble the beauty of the bride,[2] or possessed anything to match the splendor of her adornment? Even if I were to say that these mysterious curtains refer to the quality of blackness as well as to the tents of Kedar, I should perhaps be

1. Sermon 26: 1-2   2. Mt 6: 29

correct; there are arguments to support this, as I shall show later. But if we suppose that the beauty of any sort of curtains is to be compared to the glory of the bride, then we need the help for which you have been praying, if we are to be worthy to unveil this mystery. For must not outward loveliness, no matter how radiant, seem to an enlightened mind to be cheap and ugly, when compared with the inward beauty of a holy soul? What qualities can we find within the framework of this passing world[3] that can equal the radiance of a soul that has shed its decrepit, earthly body,[4] and been clothed in heaven's loveliness,[5] graced with the jewels of consummate virtue,[6] clearer than mountain air because of its transcendence, more brilliant than the sun? So do not look back to the earthly Solomon when you wish to investigate the ownership of those curtains whose beauty delights the bride because so like her own.

2. What does she mean then by saying: "I am beautiful like the curtains of Solomon"?[7] I feel that here we have a great and wonderful mystery, provided that we apply the words, not to the Solomon of this *Song*, but to him who said of himself: "What is here is greater than Solomon."[8] This Solomon to whom I refer is so great a Solomon that he is called not only Peaceful—which is the meaning of the word Solomon—but Peace itself; for Paul proclaims that "He is our Peace."[9] I am certain that in this Solomon we can discover something that we may unhesitatingly compare with the beauty of the bride. Note especially what the Psalm says of his curtains: "You have spread out the heavens like a curtain."[10] The first Solomon, though sufficiently wise and powerful, did not spread out the heavens like a curtain; it was he, rather who is not merely wise but Wisdom itself, who both created them and spread them out. It was he, and not the former Solomon, who spoke these words of God his Father: "When he set the heavens in their place, I was

3. 1 Cor 7:31
4. 1 Cor 15:42
5. 2 Cor 5:2
6. Is 61:10

7. Song 1:4
8. Mt 12:42
9. Eph 2:14
10. Ps 103:2

there."[11] His power and his wisdom were undoubtedly present at the establishing of the heavens.[12] And do not imagine that he stood by idle, as merely a spectator, because he said "I was there," and not "I was cooperating." Search further on in this text and you will find that he clearly states he was with him arranging all things.[13] Therefore he said: "Whatever the Father does, the Son does too."[14] He it was who spread out the heavens like a curtain, a curtain of superlative beauty that covers the whole face of the earth like a huge tent, and charms our human eyes with the variegated spectacle of sun and moon and stars. Is there anything more lovely than this curtain? Anything more bejewelled than the heavens? Yet even this can in no way be compared to the splendor and comeliness of the bride. It fails because it is a physical thing, the object of our physical senses; its form will pass away.[15] "For the things that are seen are transient, but the things that are unseen are eternal."[16]

II. 3. The bride's form must be understood in a spiritual sense, her beauty as something that is grasped by the intellect; it is eternal because it is an image of eternity. Her gracefulness consists of love, and you have read that "love never ends."[17] It consist of justice, for "her justice endures forever."[18] It consists of patience, and Scripture tells you "the patience of the poor shall not perish forever."[19] What shall I say of voluntary poverty? Of humility? To the former an eternal kingdom is promised,[20] to the latter an eternal exaltation.[21] To these must be added the holy fear of the Lord that endures for ever and ever;[22] prudence too, and temperance and fortitude and all other virtues; what are they but pearls in the jewelled raiment of the bride, shining with unceasing radiance? I say unceasing, because they are the basis, the very foundation of immortality. For there is no place for

11. Prov 8:27
12. 1 Cor 1:24
13. Prov 8:30
14. Jn 5:19
15. 1 Cor 7:31
16. 2 Cor 4:18

17. 1 Cor 13:8
18. Ps 111:3
19. Ps 9:19
20. Mt 5:3
21. Lk 14:11
22. Ps 18:10

immortal and blissful life in the soul except by means and mediation of the virtues. Hence the Prophet, speaking to God who is eternal happiness, says: "Justice and judgment are the foundation of your throne."[23] And the Apostle says that Christ dwells in our hearts, not in any and every way, but particularly by faith.[24] When Christ, too, was about to ride on the ass, the disciples spread their cloaks underneath him,[25] to signify that our Savior, or his salvation, will not rest in the naked soul until it is clothed with the teaching and discipline of the apostles.[26] Therefore the Church, possessing the promise of happiness to come,[27] now prepares for it by adorning herself in cloth of gold, girding herself with a variety of graces and virtues,[28] in order to be found worthy and capable of the fulness of grace.

4. Though this visible, material heaven, with its great variety of stars is unsurpassingly beautiful within the bounds of the material creation, I should not dare to compare its beauty with the spiritual and varied loveliness she received with her first robe when being arrayed in the garments of holiness. But there is a heaven of heavens to which the Prophet refers. "Sing to the Lord who mounts above the heaven of heavens, to the east."[29] This heaven is in the world of the intellect and the spirit; and he who made the heavens by his wisdom,[30] created it to be his eternal dwelling-place.[31] You must not suppose that the bride's affections can find rest outside of this heaven, where she knows her Beloved dwells: for where her treasure is, there her heart is too.[32] She so yearns for him that she is jealous of those who live in his presence; and since she may not yet participate in the vision that is theirs, she strives to resemble them in the way she lives. By deeds rather than words she proclaims: "Lord, I love the beauty of your house, the place where your glory dwells."[33]

23. Ps 88:15
24. Eph 3:17
25. Mt 21:7
26. 2 Cor 5:4
27. 1 Tim 4:8
28. Ps 44:10

29. Ps 67:33-34
30. Ps 135:5
31. Is 40:22
32. Mt 6:21
33. Ps 25:8

III.   5. She has no objection whatever to being compared to this heaven, made glorious by the marvellous and manifold works of the Creator, that reaches out like a curtain,[34] not over mighty spaces but over the hearts of men. Any distinctions that exist there do not consist of colors but of degrees of bliss.[35] Among its inhabitants we find Angels, Archangels, Virtues, Dominations, Principalities, Powers, Thrones, Cherubim and Seraphim.[36] These are that heaven's sparkling stars, these are that curtain's shining glories. We are dealing with only one of the curtains of my Solomon, but the one that surpasses all in the radiance of its multiform glory. This immense curtain contains within itself many other curtains of Solomon, for every blessed and saint who dwells there is indeed a curtain of Solomon. They overflow with kindness, their love reaches out till it comes down even to us. Far from begrudging us the glory they enjoy, they want us to share it, and hence find it no burden to accompany us for that purpose, sedulously watching over us and our concerns. They are all spirits whose work is service, sent to help those who will be the heirs of salvation.[37] Therefore, since the multitude of the blessed, taken as a unit, is called the heaven of heavens, so, when taken individually, they are called the heavens of heavens, because each is a heaven, and we may apply to each the words: "You have spread out heaven like a curtain."[38] You now see, I hope, what these curtains are to which the bride so assuredly compares herself, and to which Solomon they belong.

IV.   6. Contemplate what a glory is hers who compares herself to heaven, even to that heaven who is so much more glorious as he is divine. This is no rashness, taking her comparison from whence her origin comes. For if she compares herself to the tents of Kedar because of her body drawn from the earth, why should she not glory in her likeness to heaven because of the heavenly origin of her soul, especially since

34. Ps 103:2   37. Heb 1:14
35. Ex 36:35   38. Ps 103:2
36. 1 Cor 12:28; Eph 4:11

her life bears witness to her origin and to the dignity of her nature and her homeland? She adores and worships one God, just like the angels; she loves Christ above all things, just like the angels; she is chaste, just like the angels, and that in the flesh of a fallen race, in a frail body that the angels do not have. But she seeks and savors the things that they enjoy, not the things that are on the earth.[39] What can be a clearer sign of her heavenly origin than that she retains a natural likeness to it in the land of unlikeness, than that as an exile on earth she enjoys the glory of the celibate life, than that she lives like an angel in an animal body? These gifts reveal a power that is more of heaven than of earth. They clearly indicate that a soul thus endowed is truly from heaven. But Scripture is clearer still: "I saw the holy city, the new Jerusalem, coming down out of heaven from God, prepared as a bride adorned for her husband. And I heard a great voice from the throne saying: 'Behold the dwelling of God is with men. He will dwell among them.' "[40] But why? In order to win a bride for himself from among men. How wonderful this? He came to seek a bride, but did not come without one. He sought a bride, but she was with him. Had he then two brides? Certainly not. "My dove is only one,"[41] he says. Just as he wished to form one flock of the scattered flocks of sheep, that there might be one flock and one shepherd,[42] so, although from the beginning he had for bride the multitude of angels, it pleased him to summon the Church from among men and unite it with the one from heaven, that there might be but the one bride and one Bridegroom. The one from heaven perfects the earthly one; it does not make two. Hence he says: "My perfect one is only one."[43] Their likeness makes them one, one now in their similar purpose, one hereafter in the same glory.

7. These two then have their origin in heaven—Jesus the Bridegroom and Jerusalem the bride. He, in order to be seen by men, "emptied himself taking the form of a servant, being

39. Col 3:2
40. Rev 21:2-3
41. Song 6:8

42. Jn 10:16
43. Song 6:8

born in the likeness of men."[44] But the bride—in what form
or exterior loveliness, in what guise did St John see her
coming down? [45] Was it perhaps in the company of the angels
whom he saw ascending and descending upon the Son of
Man? [46] It is more accurate to say that he saw the bride when
he looked on the Word made flesh, and acknowledged two
natures in the one flesh.[47] For when that holy Emmanuel
introduced to earth the curriculum of heavenly teaching,
when we came to know the visible image and radiant comeliness of that supernal Jerusalem,[48] our mother, revealed to
us in Christ and by his means, what did we behold if not the
bride in the Bridegroom? What did we admire but that same
person who is the Lord of glory,[49] the Bridegroom decked
with a garland, the bride adorned with her jewels? [50] "He
who descended is he also who ascended,"[51] since "no one has
ascended into heaven but he who descended from heaven,"[52]
the one and same Lord who as head of the Church is the
Bridegroom, as body is the bride. This heaven-formed man
did not appear on earth in vain,[53] since he endowed a multitude of earthly followers with his own heavenly image.[54] As
Scripture says: "the heavenly Man is the pattern of all the
heavenly."[55] From that time the lives of many on earth have
been like the lives of heaven's citizens, as when, after the
example of that exalted and blessed bride, she who came
from the ends of the earth to hear the wisdom of Solomon,[56]
embraced the heavenly Bridegroom with a chaste love.
Though, unlike the blessed bride, not yet united to him by
vision, she is still espoused to him by faith, as God promised
through the Prophet's words: "I will betroth you to me in
steadfast love and mercy, I will betroth you to me in faithful-
ness."[57] Hence she strives more and more to resemble her
who came from heaven, learning from her to be modest and

44. Phil 2:7
45. Rev 21:2
46. Jn 1:51
47. Gen 2:24
48. Gal 4:26; Ps 49:2
49. 1 Cor 2:8
50. Is 61:10

51. Eph 4:10
52. Jn 3:13
53. Bar 3:38
54. 1 Cor 15:47
55. 1 Cor 15:48
56. 1 Kings 10:1-10
57. Hos 2:19-20

prudent, learning to be chaste and holy, to be patient and compassionate, and ultimately to be meek and humble of heart.[58] By these virtues she endeavors, even while absent,[59] to be pleasing to him on whom the angels long to look.[60] With a love angelic in its fervor she shows herself to be a fellow-citizen with the saints and a domestic of God,[61] she shows that she is beloved, that she is a bride.

V. 8. I believe that all persons such as I have described are not only heavenly because of their origin but that each so resembles heaven as to merit being so named. Their heavenly origin is most evident since their life is centered in heaven.[62] The holy person whose gift of faith is like a moon and whose virtues are like stars, is truly a heaven. We could mean by the sun zeal for justice and fervent love and by the moon continence. Without the sun there is no brightness in the moon, and without justice and love there is no merit in continence. Hence that saying of Wisdom: "How beautiful is the chaste generation with its love."[63] And to call the stars virtues gives me no qualms, the aptness of the metaphor is so obvious. For just as the stars that shine by night are hidden by day, so true virtue that passes unnoticed in prosperity, becomes conspicuous in adversity. What prudence conceals, necessity forces into the open. So, if virtue be a star, the virtuous man is a heaven. But we are not to suppose that when God, speaking through his Prophet, said "heaven is my throne,"[64] he was referring to the wheeling heavens we see above us; no, in another text of Scripture we find what he meant more clearly expressed: "The soul of the just is the seat of wisdom."[65] If you recall the Savior's teaching that God is a spirit, to be adored in spirit,[66] you must realize that God's throne is a spiritual entity. This truth I confidently affirm, in the case of a just man no less than of an angel. My belief in its truth is

58. Mt 11:29
59. 2 Cor 5:9
60. 1 Pet 1:12
61. Eph 2:19
62. Phil 3:20

63. Wis 4:1
64. Is 66:1
65. Prov 12:23, Septuagint
66. Jn 4:24

further strengthened by the faithful promise of the Son: "I and the Father will come to him," that is, to the holy man, "and make our dwelling with him."[67] I feel too that the Prophet meant this heaven when he said: "You dwell in the holy place, the praise of Israel."[68] Finally, the Apostle says explicitly that "Christ dwells by faith in our hearts."[69]

9. No need to be surprised that the Lord Jesus should be pleased to dwell in this heaven, which he not only called into being by his word like the other creatures,[70] but fought to acquire and died to redeem. And when his passion was over the longing of his heart found echo in the words: "This is my resting-place for ever; here I will dwell, for I have desired it."[71] Happy therefore is the one to whom he says: "Come my chosen one, and I shall set up my throne within you."[72] Why are you sad now, my soul, why do you trouble me?[73] Do you not think you will find within you a place for the Lord?[74] Which of us indeed is suited for so much glory, qualified to welcome so majestic a being? Would that I were worthy to worship at his footstool![75] Who will grant me at least to walk in the footsteps of some holy soul whom he has chosen as his heritage?[76] Would that he anointed my soul with the oil of his mercy, to extend it like a curtain of skin[77] that expands when anointed, and I should be able to say: "I have run the way of your commandments, when you enlarged my heart."[78] Then perhaps I should find within me not so much a great dining-hall where he might recline with his discipline,[79] as a place where he might lay his head.[80]

67. Jn 14:23
68. Ps 21:4
69. Eph 3:17
70. Ps 32:9; Ps 148:5
71. Ps 131:14
72. Response to 10th lesson of 3rd nocturn, common of virgins.
73. Ps 41:6
74. Ps 131:5
75. Ps 131:7
76. Ps 32:12
77. Ps 103:2
78. Ps 118:32
79. Mk 14:15
80. Mt 8:20

From afar off I gaze toward the truly blessed ones, of whom is said: "I will live in them and move among them."[81]

VI. 10. What a capacity this soul has, how privileged its merits, that it is found worthy not only to receive the divine presence, but to be able to make sufficient room! What can I say of her who can provide avenues spacious enough for the God of majesty to walk in! She certainly cannot afford to be entangled in law-suits nor by worldly cares; she cannot be enslaved by gluttony and sensual pleasures, by the lust of the eyes, the ambition to rule, or by pride in the possession of power. If she is to become heaven, the dwelling-place of God, it is first of all essential that she be empty of all these defects. Otherwise how could she be still enough to know that he is God? [82] Nor may she yield in the least to hatred or envy or bitterness, "because wisdom will not enter a deceitful soul."[83] The soul must grow and expand, that it may be roomy enough for God. Its width is its love, if we accept what the Apostle says: "Widen your hearts in love."[84] The soul, being a spirit, does not admit of material expansion, but grace confers gifts on it that nature is not equipped to bestow. Its growth and expansion must be understood in a spiritual sense; it is its virtue that increases, not its substance. Even its glory is increased. And finally it grows and advances toward "mature manhood, to the measure of the stature of the fullness of Christ."[85] Eventually it becomes "a holy temple in the Lord."[86] The capacity of any man's soul is judged by the amount of love he possesses; hence he who loves much is great, he who loves a little is small, he who has no love is nothing, as Paul said: "If I have not love, I am nothing."[87] But if he begins to acquire some love however, if he tries at least to love those who love him,[88] and salutes the brethren and others who salute him,[89] I may no longer

81. 2 Cor 6:16   86. Eph 2:21
82. Ps 45:11   87. 1 Cor 13:2
83. Wis 1:4   88. Lk 6:32
84. 2 Cor 6:13   89. Mt 5:47
85. Eph 4:13

describe him as nothing because some love must be present in the give and take of social life.[90] In the words of the Lord, however, what more is he doing than others.[91] When I discover a love as mediocre as this, I cannot call such a man noble or great: he is obviously narrowminded and mean.

11. But if his love expands and continues to advance till it outgrows these narrow, servile confines, and finds itself in the open ranges where love is freely given in full liberty of spirit; when from the generous bounty of his goodwill he strives to reach out to all his neighbors, loving each of them as himself,[92] surely one may no longer query, "What more are you doing than others?" Indeed he has made himself vast. His heart is filled with a love that embraces everybody, even those to whom it is not tied by the inseparable bonds of family relationship; a love that is not allured by any hope of personal gain, that possesses nothing it is obliged to restore, that bears no burden of debt whatever, apart from that one of which it is said: "Owe no one anything, except to love one another."[93] Progressing further still, you may endeavor to take the kingdom of love by force,[94] until by this holy warfare you succeed in possessing it even to its farthest bounds. Instead of shutting off your affections from your enemies,[95] you will do good to those who hate you, you will pray for those who persecute and slander you,[96] you will strive to be peaceful even with those who hate peace.[97] Then the width, height and beauty of your soul will be the width, height and beauty of heaven itself, and you will realize how true it is that he has "stretched out the heavens like a curtain."[98] In this heaven whose width, height and beauty compel our admiration, he who is supreme and immense and glorious is not only pleased to dwell, but to wander far and wide on its pathways.

VII. 12. Do you not now see what heavens the Church possesses within her, and that she herself, in her universality,

90. Phil 4:15
91. Mt 5:47
92. Mt 19:19
93. Rom 13:8
94. Mt 11:12

95. 1 Jn 3:17
96. Mt 5:44
97. Ps 119:7
98. Ps 103:2

is an immense heaven, stretching out "from sea to sea, and from the river to the ends of the earth."[99] Consider therefore, to what you may compare her in this respect, provided you do not forget what I mentioned a short while ago concerning the heaven of heaven and heavens of heavens.[100] Just like our mother above,[101] this one, though still a pilgrim,[102] has her own heaven: spiritual men outstanding in their lives and reputations, men of genuine faith, unshaken hope, generous love, men raised to the heights of contemplation. These men rain down God's saving work like showers, reprove with a voice of thunder, shine with a splendor of miracles. They proclaim the glory of God,[103] and stretched out like curtains over all the earth,[104] make known the law of life and knowledge[105] written by God's finger into their own lives,[106] "to give knowledge of salvation to his people."[107] They show forth the gospel of peace,[108] because they are the curtain of Solomon.

13. In these curtains then we must discern the likeness of those heavenly figures whom we have just described as part of the Bridegroom's adornment.[109] We must recognize too the queen standing at his right hand, decked with ornaments similar, though not equal, to his. For although she is endowed with no small share of glory and beauty even where she sojourns as a pilgrim,[110] as well as in the day of her strength amid the splendors of the saints,[111] yet the fullness and perfection of the glory of the blessed crowns her Bridegroom in a way that is different. If I do refer to the bride as perfect and blessed, she is not wholly so. In part she resembles the tents of Kedar; but she is also beautiful, both in that part of her which already reigns in heaven, and in those illustrious men whose wisdom and virtues grace her journey through the night, like a heaven spangled with stars. Hence

99. Ps 71:8
100. See above, par. 5
101. Gal 4:26
102. 2 Cor 5:6
103. Ps 18:1
104. Ps 103:2
105. Sir 45:6
106. Ex 31:18
107. Lk 1:77
108. Eph 6:15
109. See above, par. 7
110. Ps 118:54
111. Ps 109:3

the Prophet's words: "The wise leaders shall shine like the bright vault of heaven, and those who have guided the people in the true path shall be like stars for ever and ever."[112]

14. How lowly! Yet how sublime! At the same time tent of Kedar and sanctuary of God; an earthly tent and a heavenly palace; a mud hut and a royal apartment;[113] a body doomed to death and a temple bright with light;[114] an object of contempt to the proud,[115] yet the bride of Christ. She is black but beautiful, daughters of Jerusalem:[116] for though the hardship and sorrow of prolonged exile darkens her complexion,[117] a heavenly loveliness shines through it, the curtains of Solomon enhance it. If the swarthy skin repels you, you must still admire the beauty; if you scorn what seems lowly, you must look up with esteem to what is sublime. Indeed you must note the prudence, the great wisdom, the amount of discretion and sense of fittingness generated in the bride by that controlled interplay of lowliness and exaltation according as occasion demands, so that amid the ups and downs of this world her sublime gifts sustain her lowliness lest she succumb to adversity; while her lowliness curbs her exaltation or good fortune will bring it toppling down. These poles of her life act so harmoniously. Though of their nature opposites they will work with equal effectiveness for the good of the bride.[118] They subserve her spiritual welfare.

15. So much for the likeness which the bride seems to postulate between her beauty and the curtains of Solomon. With regard to this same text however, we still have to explain that meaning to which I referred at the beginning of this discourse and for which I have given my promise:[119] the extent to which the whole similitude may be applied to her blackness only. You shall not be cheated out of that promise. But it must be postponed till the next sermon, both because the length of this one demands that we do so, and in order

112. Dan 12:3
113. Wis 9:15; Job 4:19
114. Rom 7:24
115. Ps 122:4

116. Song 1:4
117. Ps 89:10
118. Rom 8:28
119. See above, par. 1

that the customary prayers may precede all that we hope to say for the praise and glory of the Bridegroom of the Church, Jesus Christ our Lord, who is God blessed for ever. Amen.[120]

120. Rom 1:25

SERMON 28

THE BLACKNESS AND BEAUTY OF THE BRIDEGROOM AND THE BRIDE

I PRESUME YOU REMEMBER what I consider those curtains to be to which the beauty of the bride is compared, to which Solomon they belong, and how the comparison drawn from them is directed to the manifestation and praise of that beauty.[1] But if anyone thinks that it should rather be directed to the blackness, then we must call to mind those curtains with which Solomon once covered the tabernacle.[2] They were certainly black, being exposed daily to the sun and to the weathering of the rains. This was no futile arrangement; it ensured that the ornaments within would preserve their brilliance. By this example the bride does not deny her blackness but excuses it. She will never be ashamed of a condition that owes it origin to charity, that is not condemned by the judgment of truth. For who is weak with whom she does not share weakness? Who is made to stumble and she is not ablaze with indignation?[3] She accepts the blemishes consequent on works of compassion, that she may relieve or heal the sickness of passion in another. Her complexion grows dark in the zeal for moral brightness, for the prize of beauty.

2. The blackening of one makes many bright, not the blackness caused by sin, but that which results from genuine concern. "It is better," said Caiaphas, "for one man to die for the people, than for the whole nation to be destroyed."[4] It is

1. Song 1:4
2. 2 Chron 3:14

3. 2 Cor 11:29
4. Jn 11:50

better that one be blackened for the sake of all "in the likeness of sinful flesh,"[5] than for the whole of mankind to be
lost by the blackness of sin; that the splendor and image of
the substance of God[6] should be shrouded in the form of a
slave,[7] in order that a slave might live; that the brightness of
eternal light[8] should become dimned in the flesh for the
purging of the flesh; that he who surpasses all mankind in
beauty[9] should be eclipsed by the darkness of the Passion for
the enlightening of mankind; that he himself should suffer
the ignominy of the cross, grow pale in death, be totally
deprived of beauty and comeliness[10] that he might gain the
Church as a beautiful and comely bride, without stain and
fellows."[20] How then this shaggy-haired likeness to Esau?[21]
Solomon; I even embrace Solomon himself under his black
covering. For though Solomon presents this black exterior, it
is only in the curtain. Outwardly, in the skin, he is black, but
not within. In any case, "all the glory of the king's daughter
is from within."[12] Within is the brightness of divine life, the
graciousness of the virtues, the splendor of grace, the purity
of innocence. But covering it all is the abject hue that indicates infirmity, with his face as it were hidden and
despised,[13] "One who in every respect has been tempted as
we are, yet without sinning."[14] I recognize here the image of
our sin-darkened nature; I recognize the garments of skins
that clothed our sinning first parents.[15] He even brought this
blackness on himself by assuming the condition of slave, and
becoming as men are, he was seen as a man.[16] I recognize
under the kid-skin, a symbol of sin, both the hand that committed no sin and the neck through which thought of evil
never passed;[17] no word of treachery was found in his
mouth.[18] I know that you are gentle by nature, meek and

5. Rom 8:3
6. Heb 1:3
7. Phil 2:7
8. Wis 7:26
9. Ps 44:3
10. Is 53:2
11. Eph 5:27

12. Ps 44:14
13. Is 53:3
14. Heb 4:15
15. Gen 3:21
16. Phil 2:7
17. Gen 3:21
18. 1 Pet 2:22; Is 53:9

humble of heart,[19] pleasing in appearance and loveable in your ways, anointed "with the oil of gladness above your fellows."[20] How then this shaggy-haired likeness to Esau? [21] Who owns this ravaged and wrinkled face? Whose are these hairs? They are mine. These hairy hands are the sign of my likeness to sinful men.[22] These hairs are my very own: and in my hairy skin I shall see God my Savior.[23]

3. But it was not Rebekah who clothed him in this fashion, it was Mary; he received so much richer a blessing as he was born of a holier mother. And how rightly he is clothed in my likeness, because the blessing is being claimed, the inheritance requested, for me. For he had heard the words: "Ask of me and I will give you the nations, your heritage, and the ends of the earth, your possession."[24] It is from your own heritage, the speaker said, your own possession, that I will give you. How will you give it to him if it is his already? And why urge him to ask for what is his own? Or how is it his own if he has to ask for it? It must be for me, that he asks; he clothed himself in my nature for this purpose, that he might take up my cause. For "on him lies a punishment that brings us peace," as the Prophet said;[25] "and the Lord burdened him with the sins of us all."[26] "He had to be made like his brothers in every respect," as the Apostle says, "that he might become merciful."[27]

II. Accordingly, "the voice is Jacob's voice, but the hands are the hands of Esau."[28] What we hear from him is his, what we see in him is ours. The words he speaks are "spirit and life;"[29] the form we see is mortal, subject to death. We see one thing and we believe another. Our senses tell us he is black, our faith declares him fair and beautiful. If he is black it is "in the eyes of the foolish,"[30] for to the minds of the

19. Mt 11:29
20. Ps 44:8
21. Gen 27:11
22. Gen 27:23
23. Job 19:26
24. Ps 2:8

25. Is 53:5
26. Is 53:6
27. Heb 2:17
28. Gen 27:22
29. Jn 6:63
30. Wis 3:2

faithful he is wholly beautiful. He is black, then, but beautiful: black in the opinion of Herod, beautiful in the testimony of the penitent thief, in the faith of the centurion.

4. The man who cried out: "Truly this man was the Son of God! "[31] certainly perceived how great his beauty was. But where he perceived that beauty to lie is for us to ascertain. For supposing he considered only what his eyes beheld, in what way was this man beautiful, how was he the Son of God? What did the eyes of the beholders see but a man deformed and black, his hands splayed out on the cross as he hung between two criminals, an object of laughter for the wicked, of weeping for the faithful. He alone was the laughing-stock, he alone who could have stricken them with terror, who alone had a right to be honored. How then did the centurion see the beauty of the Crucified, how did he see as Son of God him "who was numbered with the transgressors"? [32] It is neither right nor necessary for me to provide an answer, for the Evangelist's observation has not allowed this to escape him. He writes: "And when the centurion, who stood facing him, saw that he thus cried out and breathed his last, he said: 'Truly this man was the Son of God!' "[33] It was the sound of his voice that inspired his belief, it was by the voice that he recognized the Son of God, and not by the face. Perhaps he was one of those sheep of whom Christ said: "My sheep hear my voice."[34]

5. The hearing succeeded where the sight failed. Appearances deceived the eye, but truth poured itself into the ear. The eye saw him to be weak, detestable, wretched, a man condemned to a most shameful death;[35] but to the ear the Son of God revealed himself, to the ear he made known his beauty, but not to that of the Jews whose ears were uncircumcised.[36] There was a certain propriety in Peter's cutting off the servant's ear,[37] to open up a way for the truth, that the truth might set him free,[38] that is, make him a freedman.

31. Mk 15:39   35. Wis 2:20
32. Is 53:12   36. Acts 7:51
33. Mk 15:39   37. Jn 18:10
34. Jn 10:27   38. Jn 8:32

The centurion was uncircumcised, but not where his ear was concerned, because at that one cry of a dying man he recognized the Lord of majesty beneath all those signs of helplessness.[39] Therefore he did not despise what he saw, because he believed in what he did not see. He did not believe, however, because of what he saw, but, without any doubt, because of what he heard, because "faith comes from hearing."[40] It would indeed have been a worthy thing if the truth had penetrated to the soul through the windows of the eyes which are a nobler power; but this, O my soul, is reserved for us till the life to come, when we shall see face to face.[41] Meantime let the remedy find entrance where the ancient malady stole a march on us; let life follow the same pathway as death, light in the wake of darkness, the antidote of truth after the poison of the serpent. And let it heal the troubled eye that it may serenely contemplate him whom the sickly eye could not see.[42] The ear was death's first gateway, let it be the first to open up to life; let the hearing restore the vision it took from us. For unless we believe we shall not understand.[43] Therefore hearing is connected with merit, sight with the reward. Hence the Prophet says: "You will give to my hearing joy and gladness,"[44] for the beatific vision is the reward of faithful hearing. We merit the beatific vision by our constancy in listening. "Blessed are the pure in heart, for they shall see God."[45] The eye that would see God must be cleansed by faith, as it is written: "He cleansed their hearts by faith."[46]

6. In the meantime then since the sense of sight is not yet ready, let us rouse up our hearing, let us exercise it and take in the truth. Happy the man of whom Truth testifies: "At the hearing of the ear he obeyed me."[47] I shall be worthy to see if before seeing I shall have been found obedient; I shall look on him with confidence if he has already received the

39. Mt 27:54
40. Rom 10:17
41. 1 Cor 13:12
42. Ps 6:8
43. Is 7:9 (Septuagint)
44. Ps 50:10
45. Mt 5:8
46. Acts 15:9
47. Ps 17:45

service of my obedience. Blessed indeed was the man who said: "The Lord God opened my ears and I did not disobey or turn back in defiance."[48] Here we find both a model of voluntary obedience and an example of perseverance. Spontaneity is found where there is no contradiction, and perseverance where there is no turning back. Both are necessary, for "God loves a cheerful giver,"[49] and "the man who perseveres to the end will be saved."[50] How I wish the Lord would open my ear, that the word of his truth would enter into my heart, cleanse my eye and make it ready for that joyful vision, so that even I could say to God: "Your ear has heard the preparation of my heart."[51] That even I, along with his other obedient followers, should hear from God: "You are clean by the word which I have spoken to you."[52] Not all who hear are cleansed, but those only who obey, the blessed ones are those who both hear and keep the word.[53] This is the hearing he asks for with the command: "Hear, O Israel;"[54] this is the hearing he offers who says: "Speak, Lord, your servant is listening;"[55] and this is the response that such a man makes: "Let me hear what God the Lord will speak within me."[56]

III.   7. To assure you that the Holy Spirit follows this order in promoting the soul's spiritual welfare, enabling it to hear before gladdening it with vision, Scripture says: "Hear, O daughter, and see."[57] So why strain with your eyes? Prepare rather to hear. Do you wish to see Christ? The first thing for you to do is to hear him, to hear about him, so that when you do see you may say: "As we have heard, so have we seen."[58] His glory is immense, the scope of the eye is meager and cannot attain to it.[59] But where the eye fails, the ear succeeds. So when God cried out: "Adam, where are

48. Is 50:5
49. 2 Cor 9:7
50. Mt 10:22
51. Ps 9:38
52. Jn 15:3
53. Lk 11:28

54. Deut 6:3
55. 1 Sam 3:10
56. Ps 84:9
57. Ps 44:11
58. Ps 47:9
59. Ps 138:6

you?"[60] I could no longer see him because I was a sinner, but I heard him. The hearing, if it be loving, alert and faithfull, will restore the sight. Faith will cleanse the eye exacerbated by godlessness; obedience will open what disobedience closed. "From your precepts," says the Psalmist, "I get understanding:"[61] the keeping of the commandments restores the intellectual light clouded over by sin. See how the faithful Isaac retained in old age a power of hearing whose vigor surpassed that of the other senses. The Patriarch's eyes grow dim, his palate is deceived, his hand lets him down, but his ear does not let him down. What wonder if the ear catches the truth, since faith comes from what is heard, and what is heard comes by the word of God,[62] and the word of God is truth?[63] "The voice," he said, "is the voice of Jacob." True! "But the hands are the hands of Esau."[64] False! You are deceived. The resemblance of the hand has led you astray. Nor is truth found in the taste, though it be pleasant. What truth has he if he thinks he is eating venison when he is dining off the flesh of domestic kids? Less still is it found in the eye that sees nothing. The eye is not dependable either for truth or wisdom, for Isaiah says: "Woe to you who are wise in your own eyes."[65] Can wisdom which is accursed be good? It is of the world, and for that reason is folly in God's sight.[66]

8. The wisdom that is good and true, as holy Job experienced it, "is drawn out of secret places."[67] Why then seek it from without, in your bodily senses? Taste resides in the palate, but wisdom in the heart. Do not look for wisdom with your eyes of flesh, because flesh and blood will not reveal it to you, but the Spirt.[68] Do not look for it in what the mouth tastes, for it is not found in the land of those who live for pleasure.[69] Do not look for it in the hand's touch, for a saintly man says: "If my mouth has kissed my hand,

60. Ps Gen 3:9
61. Ps 118:104
62. Rom 10:17
63. Jn 17:17
64. Gen 27:22

65. Is 5:21
66. 1 Cor 3:19
67. Job 28:18
68. Mt 16:17
69. Job 28:13

that is a great iniquity and a denial of God."[70] This happens, in my opinion, when the gift of God, wisdom, is ascribed not to God but to the merits of our actions. Though Isaac was wise, his senses led him astray. Only the hearing that catches the word possesses the truth. The woman whose wisdom was still carnal was rightly forbidden to touch the risen flesh of the Word, because she depended more on what she saw than on what she heard, that is, on her bodily senses rather than on God's word.[71] She did not believe that he whom she saw dead would rise again, though he himself had made this promise. Hence her eye did not rest till her sight was satisfied, because for her there was no consolation from the faith, even God's promise was not sure. Must not heaven and earth and all those things that the human eye may reach, pass away and perish, before one iota or one dot shall pass away from the words that God has spoken?[72] And yet she, who refused to be consoled by the word of the Lord, ceased her crying when she saw him, because she valued experience above faith. But experience is deceptive.

9. She is impelled, therefore, to seek the surer knowledge of faith, which discerns truths unknown to the senses, beyond the range of experience. When he said: "Do not touch me,"[73] he meant: depend no longer on this fallible sense; put your trust in the word, get used to faith.

IV.   Faith cannot be deceived. With the power to understand invisible truths, faith does not know the poverty of the senses; it transcends even the limits of human reason, the capacity of nature, the bounds of experience. Why do you ask the eye to do what it is not equipped to do? And why does the hand endeavor to examine things beyond its reach? What you may learn from these senses is of limited value. But faith will tell you of me without detracting from my greatness. Learn to

---

70. Job 31:27-28. In the context in Job this quotation refers to the worship of the heavenly bodies. The kiss was a sign of adoration.
71. Jn 20:17
72. Mt 5:18; 24:35
73. Jn 20:17

receive with greater confidence, to follow with greater security, whatever faith commends to you. "Do not touch me, for I have not yet ascended to my Father."[74] As if after he had ascended he wished to be or could be touched by her! And yet he could be touched, but by the heart, not by the hand; by desire, not by the eye; by faith, not by the senses. "Why do you want to touch me now," he says, "would you measure the glory of the resurrection by a physical touch? Do you not remember that, while I was still mortal, the eyes of the disciples could not endure for a short space the glory of my transfigured body that was destined to die?[75] I still accommodate myself to your senses by bearing this form of a servant which you are accustomed to seeing. But this glory of mine is too wonderful for you, so high that you cannot reach it.[76] Defer your judgment therefore, refrain from expressing an opinion, do not entrust the defining of so great a matter to the senses, it is for faith to pronounce on it. With its fuller comprehension, faith will define it more worthily and more surely. In its deep and mystical breast it can grasp what is the length and breath and height and depth.[77] 'What eye has not seen, nor ear heard, nor the heart of man conceived,'[78] is borne within itself by faith, as if wrapped in a covering and kept under seal.

10. "She therefore will touch me worthily who will accept me as seated with the Father, no longer in lowly guise, but in my own flesh transformed with heaven's beauty. Why wish to touch what is ugly? Have patience that you may touch the beautiful. Things will be beautiful then that are now ugly: ugly to the touch, ugly to the eye, ugly even to you in your ugliness, you who are so bound to the senses, so indifferent to faith. Become beautiful and then touch me; live by faith and you are beautiful. In your beauty you will touch my beauty all the more worthily, with greater felicity. You will touch me with the hand of faith, the finger of desire, the embrace of love; you will touch me with the mind's eye. But

74. Jn 20:17
75. Mt 17:6
76. Ps 138:6

77. Eph 3:18
78. 1 Cor 2:9

shall I still be black? God forbid! Your beloved will be fair
and ruddy, [79] strikingly beautiful, surrounded by a bloom of
roses and lilies of the valley, [80] by the choirs of martyrs and
virgins; and sitting in their midst, I, a virgin and martyr, am
alien to neither choir. Why should I not be at ease in the
white-robed choirs of virgins, virgin that I am and the Son of
a Virgin, the Bridegroom of a Virgin? Or amid the red-robed
choirs of the martyrs, I who am the motive, the strength, the
reward and the model of martyrs? Here let kind touch its
kind after the manner of its kind, and say: "My beloved is
fair and ruddy, chosen out of thousands." [81] Thousands of
thousands are with the Beloved, and ten hundred thousand
surround him but none compare with him. [82] Do you not
fear that in seeking your beloved, you may by mistake take
one of this multitude for him? But no, you will not hesitate
in making your choice. He who is a paragon among thousands, peerless in their midst, will be easy to discover. These
words will spring to your mind: "He is glorious in his apparel,
marching in the greatness of his strength." [83] No longer therefore will he appear in the swarthy skin that up to now he had
presented to the eyes of his persecutors, who would despise
him to the point of killing him or even to the eyes of his
friends after his resurrection, that they might recognize him.
No longer will he be encountered clothed in a dark skin, but
in a white robe, surpassing in beauty not only all mankind, [84] but even the angels. Why then should you wish to
touch me in this lowly condition, rigged out like a slave,
contemptible to look at? But touch me in the beauty with
which heaven endows me, crowned with glory and honor, [85]
awe-inspiring in the majesty of my divine life, yet loving and
calm with an inborn serenity."

V. 11. Here, then, we must pay tribute to the prudence of
the bride, and the profound wisdom of her words. She sought

79. Song 5:10
80. Song 2:1
81. Song 5:10
82. Dan 7:10

83. Is 63:1
84. Ps 44:3
85. Ps 8:6

her God under the image of the curtains of Solomon, that is, in the flesh. She sought life in death, the summit of glory and honor in the midst of shame, the whiteness of innocence and the splendor of the virtues under the dark vesture of the Crucified. Those curtains, black and despicable as they were, contained beneath them jewels more precious and more brilliant than a king's riches. How right not to have been put off by the blackness in the curtains, when she glimpsed the beauty beneath them. But many were put off by it, because they failed to glimpse the beauty. "For if they had known, they would not have crucified the Lord of glory."[86] Herod did not know, and therefore he despised him.[87] The Synagogue did not know, hence it taunted him with the dark weakness of his Passion: "He saved others; he cannot save himself. He is the king of Israel; let him come down now from the cross, and we will believe in him."[88] But the thief, though on the cross, recognized him from the cross, and proclaimed his total innocence: "What evil has this man done? "[89] he asked. In the same moment he bore witness to his kingly majesty, saying: "Remember me when you come into your kingdom."[90] The centurion knew him, and called him the Son of God.[91] The Church recognizes him, and strives to imitate his blackness that she may participate in his beauty. She is not ashamed to be seen as black, to be called black, for she can then say to her beloved: "The insults of those who insult you have fallen on me."[92] But make sure the blackness is that of Solomon's curtains, on the outside and not within, for my Solomon bears no blackness within. Nor does she say: "I am black like Solomon," but "as the curtains of Solomon," for the blackness of the true Peaceful One is merely external. The blackness of sin is within; sin defiles the interior before it becomes visible to the eyes. "Out of the heart come evil thoughts, theft, murder, adultery, fornication, blasphemy, and these are what defile a man;"[93] but this cannot apply to

86. 1 Cor 2:8
87. Lk 23:11
88. Mt 27:42
89. Lk 23:11

90. Lk 23:42
91. Mt 27:54
92. Ps 68:10
93. Mt 15:19

Solomon. You will never find these kinds of defilement in the true Peaceful One. For he who takes away the sins of the world has to be without sin;[94] if he is to be found fit to reconcile sinners he must duly vindicate for himself the name of Solomon.

12. But there is another blackness, that of the endurance of penance, as when a man decides to express sorrow for his sins. Solomon will not recoil if I bear such a blackness in me, if I willingly assume it because of my sins, for "you will not scorn this crushed and broken heart, O God."[95] There is also the blackness of compassion, when you condole with a brother in his suffering and his trouble fills you with gloom. This, too, our Peaceful One must not think of rejecting. Did he not himself graciously undergo it on our behalf, when he "bore our sins in his body on the tree."[96] And there is the blackness of persecution, to be regarded as a most noble adornment when endured in the cause of right and truth. For that reason "the apostles went out from the Council rejoicing that they had been found worthy to suffer indignity for the name of Jesus."[97] And "happy those who are persecuted in the cause of right."[98] I think that the Church glories especially in her free choice of this dark covering from the curtains of her Bridegroom. In any case she has been promised: "If they have persecuted me, they will also persecute you."[99]

VI. 13. Because this is so the bride goes on: "Do not gaze at me because I am swarthy, because the sun has scorched me,"[100] meaning: Do not condemn me as repulsive, because you do not find me attractive under stress of persecution, nor adorned according to worldly standards of beauty. Why reproach me for blackness caused by the heat of persecution, not by the shame of evil living? Or perhaps by the sun she means zeal for what is right, by which she is aroused and

94. Jn 1:29
95. Ps 50:19
96. 1 Pet 2:24
97. Acts 5:41
98. Mt 5:10
99. Jn 15:20
100. Song 1:5

armed against evil-doers, saying to God: "Zeal for your house has eaten me up;"[101] and "My zeal consumes me, because my foes forget your words;"[102] or again: "Hot indignation seizes me because of the wicked who forsake your law;"[103] or this: "Lord, do I not hate those who hate you, and have I not languished over your enemies? "[104] She even carefully notes those words of the Wise Man: "Do you have daughters? Do not show yourself too indulgent with them;"[105] that is when they are negligent and lax and averse to discipline, beware of greeting them with a face serenely bright; let it be severely dark. To be discolored by the sun may also mean to be on fire with fraternal love, to weep with those who weep, to rejoice with those who rejoice,[106] to be weak with those who are weak, to burn with indignation when someone is led into sin.[107] She can also say this: "Christ the Sun of Justice had made me swarthy in color,[108] because I am faint with love of him."[109] This languor drains the color from the countenance, and makes the soul swoon with desire,[110] and therefore she says: "I remembered God and was delighted, I meditated and my spirit failed me."[111] Just like a burning sun therefore, the ardor of desire darkens her complexion while still a pilgrim in the body; rebuffs make her impatient, and delay torments her love, while she sighs for the brightness of his countenance.[112] Which of us so burns with holy love that in his longing to see Christ he wearies of all the colorfulness of this world's prestige and gaiety and casts it from him, declaring as the Prophet did: "You know I have not desired man's day."[113] And with David: "My soul refused to be comforted,"[114] it scorned to be tainted with the empty joy of this world's goods. Well may she say: the sun has discolored me

101. Ps 68:10
102. Ps 118:139
103. Ps 118:53
104. Ps 138:21
105. Sir 7:26
106. Rom 12:15
107. 2 Cor 11:29
108. Mal 4:2
109. Song 2:5
110. Is 26:8
111. Ps 76:4
112. 2 Cor 5:6-8
113. Jer 17:16
114. Ps 76:3

by the contrast of its splendor; when I draw near to it I see
myself in its light to be dusky, even black, and I despise my
filthiness. But otherwise I am truly beautiful. Why do you
term swarthy one who yields only to the sun in loveliness?
The words that follow, however, seem to suggest the former
meaning, for she adds: "My mother's sons turned their anger
on me,"[115] to show that she had suffered persecution. But
here we have come to the starting-point of another sermon.
Sufficient for this occasion is all that we have received as a
gift of the Church's Bridegroom concerning his glory. He is
God, blessed for ever. Amen.[116]

115. Song 1:5
116. Rom 1:25

SERMON 29

ON DISCORD IN THE CHURCH AND IN COMMUNITIES

"MY MOTHER'S SONS turned their anger to me."[1] Annas and Caiaphas, and Judas Iscariot, were sons of the Synagogue; and from the Church's very origin these fought with great bitterness against her, daughter of the Synagogue though she was, and hanged Jesus, her Founder, on a tree.[2] In that moment God fulfilled through their agency what he had formerly foretold through the Prophet: "I will strike the shepherd, and the sheep of the flock will be scattered."[3] And perhaps it is the voice of that Church we hear in the song of Hezekiah: "My life is cut off, as by a weaver; while I was yet but beginning he cut me off."[4] It is about these and others of that same race who are known to have opposed the Christian name, that the bride complains when she says: "My mother's sons turned their anger on me." Well did she call them sons of her mother and not of her father, for they did not have God for their father but the devil; they were murderers, just as he was a murderer from the beginning.[5] Hence she does not say: "my brother," or "the sons of my father," but: "My mother's sons turned their anger on me." If she had failed to make this distinction, even the Apostle Paul would seem to be included among those of whom she complains, for he once persecuted the Church of God.[6] But because while living as an unbeliever he

1. Song 1:5
2. Acts 10:39
3. Mt 26:31; Zech 13:7
4. Is 38:12
5. Jn 8:14
6. 1 Cor 15:9

102

had acted in ignorance, he received the grace of mercy;[7] and so he exemplified that he had God for father, that he was a brother of the Church both on his Father's side and on his mother's side.

2. Take note how she accuses by name only her mother's sons as if they alone were at fault. But has she not also suffered very much from strangers? For the Prophet says: "Often since I was young have men attacked me,"[8] and "they scored my back with scourges."[9] Why then do you complain so particularly about your mother's sons, when you are so well aware that men of various races have so often assailed you? "If you take your seat at a great man's table, take careful note of what you have before you."[10] Brothers, we are seated at the table of Solomon. Who is more wealthy than Solomon? I do not refer to earthy riches, although Solomon has plenty even of these; but I want you to contemplate the table now before you that is spread with heaven's own delicacies. Refreshments both spiritual and divine are set before us here. "Take careful note, therefore," he said, "of what you have before you, knowing that you must in turn prepare a similar table." And so, with all possible care, I study what is set before me in these words of the bride, and for my own instruction and security take note that persecution by members of the household is alone mentioned by name,[11] whereas she passes over in silence numerous and grave trials which she is known to endure all over the world from every nation under heaven,[12] from pagans, from heretics and schismatics. Aware as I am of the discernment of the bride, I know it was neither by chance nor through forgetfulness that she omitted these. The truth is that she expresses her grief so openly about what hurts her so acutely, and what she thinks we must use all vigilance to avoid. And what is it that hurts her? It is domestic quarrelling, dissension within. In the Gospel you are clearly informed of this from our Savior's own mouth when he says: "A man's enemies will be

7. 1 Tim 1:13
8. Ps 128:1
9. Ps 128:3
10. Prov 23:1
11. Mt 10:36
12. Acts 2:5

those of his own household." [13] The Prophet speaks in like manner: "Even my intimate friend, who shared my table, rebels against me." [14] And again: "Were it an enemy who insulted me, I could put up with that; had a rival got the better of me, I could hide from him. But you, a man one with me, my leader and my friend, who enjoyed my meals with me," [15] that is to say: I feel more keenly, I bear more painfully, what I have to suffer from you, my guest and companion. You know who makes this complaint, and about whom.

3. You can see that the bride complains about her mother's sons with a similar sorrow and in a similar spirit when she says: "My mother's sons turned their anger on me." She repeats the sentiment on another occasion: "My friends and my neighbors drew near and stood against me." [16]

II. I ask you earnestly to keep ever far from you this abominable and detestable vice, you who have experienced and do daily experience "how good and how delightful it is for all to live together like brothers," [17] provided that the end is union and not mutual offence. Otherwise it will be neither delightful nor good, but a great misfortune, a cause of great injury. Alas for that man who disturbs the sweet bond of unity! [18] Whoever he may be he will certainly "bear his judgment." [19] Rather let me die than hear any of you justly complaining: "My mother's sons turned their anger on me." Are you not all sons of this community, like sons of the same mother, all brothers to each other? [20] What outside influence can upset you or make you sad, if you are well disposed to each other within and live in peace like brothers? "Who is there to harm you if you are zealous for what is right? " [21] Therefore, "be ambitious for the higher gifts," [22] that you may prove yourselves to be men of good zeal. The gift that

13. Mt 10:36
14. Ps 40:10
15. Ps 54:13-15
16. Ps 37:12
17. Ps 132:1

18. Mt 26:24
19. Gal 5:10
20. Mt 23:8
21. 1 Pet 3:13
22. 1 Cor 12:31

excels all others, that is clearly incomparable, is love, a truth which the heavenly Bridegroom is so often at pains to impress on his new bride. At one time he says: "By this all men will know that you are my disciples, if you have love for one another."[23] At another time: "A new commandment I give you, that you love one another;"[24] and again: "This is my commandment that you love one another,"[25] while at the same time he prays that they may be one, as he and the Father are one.[26] Does not Paul himself, who invites you to the better gifts,[27] introduce love among them as being with faith and hope surpassingly greater than knowledge? [28] And when he enumerates the many wonderful gifts of heavenly grace,[29] does he not finally direct us to that more excellent way, which he defines as no other than love? [30] In short, what may we consider comparable to this gift, which is preferred even to martyrdom and to the faith that moves mountains? [31] This therefore is what I say: May peace be yours as the fruit of your zeal, and anything that may threaten from without will not intimidate you because it will not injure you. And on the other hand, though the world outside may smile on you, the solace it offers will be in vain if, God forbid, the seed of discord sprouts in your midst.

4. Therefore my very dear brothers, preserve peace among you, and beware of offending each other,[32] whether by deed or word or any gesture whatever, lest someone, provoked and surprised by passion in a moment of weakness, should be constrained to invoke God against those who injured or saddened him,[33] and impetuously cry out this grave accusation: "My mother's sons turned their anger on me." For those who sin against a brother sin against Christ who said: "In so far as you did this to one of the least of these brothers of mine, you did it to me."[34] Nor is it enough to avoid only the more

23. Jn 13:35
24. Jn 15:12
25. Jn 17:22
26. 1 Cor 12:31
27. 1 Cor 13:13
28. Eph 3:19

29. 1 Cor 12:8-11
30. 1 Cor 12:31
31. 1 Cor 13:2-3
32. 2 Cor 13:11
33. Ps 54:9
34. Mt 25:40

serious offences, for example, public insult and abuse or the venemous slander in secret. It is not enough, I say, to guard one's tongue from these and similar kinds of nastiness; even slight offences must be avoided, if anything may be termed slight that is directed against a brother for the purpose of hurting him, since merely to be angry with one's brother makes one liable to the judgment of God.[35] And justly so. Because what you regard as slight, and therefore commit with all the more ease, will be seen in a different light by another, just as a man looking at the outward appearance and judging according to the outward appearance,[36] is prepared to think a splinter to be a plank, and a spark a blazing fire.[37] The love which believes all things is not the gift of all men.[38] A man's heart and thoughts are more prone to suspect evil than to believe good,[39] especially when the obligation of silence does not permit you, whose conduct is in question, to defend yourself, nor him who suspects you to lay bare the wound from which he suffers, that it might be healed. And so he endures the agony, grieving in his heart,[40] till he succumbs from the secret and deadly wound, totally immersed in anger and bitterness, his mind a whirl of unvoiced thoughts on the injury he has received. He cannot pray, he cannot read, nor meditate on anything holy or spiritual. And while this soul for which Christ died is cut off from the vital influence of the Spirit,[41] and goes to its death through lack of the nourishment it needs, what, I ask, are the thoughts of your own mind in the meantime? What can you find in prayer, or in any work you do, when Christ is sorrowfully crying out against you from the heart of your brother whom you have embittered, saying: "My mother's son is fighting against me, he who enjoyed my meals with me,[42] has filled me with bitterness."[43]

5. And if you say that he should not be so gravely per-

---

35. Mt 5:22
36. 1 Sam 16:7; Jn 7:24
37. Mt 7:3-5
38. 1 Cor 13:7
39. Gen 8:21
40. Rom 8:23
41. Rom 14:15
42. Ps 54:15
43. Ruth 1:20

turbed for so slight a cause, I answer: the more slight it is, the more easy for you not to have done it. Furthermore, as I have said already, I do not understand how you call slight something that is more than the feeling of anger, since you have heard from the Judge's own mouth that even this is liable to be judged.[44] Just think! And then will you call slight a gesture that offends Christ, that will bring you before the judgement seat of God, since "it is a fearful thing to fall into the hands of the living God"?[45] So when an offence is committed against you, a thing hard to avoid at times in communities like ours, do not immediately rush, as a worldly person may do, to retaliate dishonourably against your brother; nor, under the guise of administering correction, should you dare to pierce with sharp and searing words one for whom Christ was pleased to be crucified; nor make grunting, resentful noises at him, nor mutter and murmur complaints, nor adopt a sneering air, nor indulge the loud laugh of contempt, nor knit the brow in menacing anger. Let your passion die within, where it was born; a carrier of death, it must be allowed no exit or it will cause destruction, and then you can say with the Prophet: "I was troubled and I spoke not."[46]

III. 6. I understand that there are some[47] who give a more mysterious meaning to the words of our text by applying them to the devil and his angels,[48] who were once sons of that Jerusalem above which is our mother,[49] and who, since their fall, do not cease to fight against their sister, the Church. Nor will I argue with anyone who finds it more acceptable to see here a reference to those spiritual men in the Church who make war with the sword of the Spirit, which is the word of God,[50] against their impious brothers,

44. Mt 5:22
45. Heb 10:31
46. Ps 76:5
47. See Origen, *In Cant.* I, II ed. Baehrens, pp. 130-133; Gregory The Great, *Super Cant.,* I, 25,PL 79:488-489.
48. Mt 25:41
49. Gal 4:26
50. Eph 6:17

wounding them for their salvation and leading them on to spiritual things by this kind of assault. "Let a good man strike or rebuke me in kindness,"[51] wounding and healing, killing and bringing to life,[52] so that even I may dare to say: "I live, now not I, but Christ lives in me."[53] "Come to terms with your opponent," says Christ, "while you are still on the way to court with him, or he may hand you over to the judge and the judge to the torturer."[54] I shall have found a good opponent if after I have come to terms with him, there will be neither judge to speak against me nor torturer. And indeed if some of you have been saddened by me in the past for this reason, I do not regret it; the sadness was for their salvation.[55] I certainly cannot recall ever having done it without experiencing great sadness myself, such as Christ referred to when he said: "A woman in childbirth suffers."[56] But let me no longer remember my anguish, now that I enjoy the fruit of my pain, seeing Christ formed in my offspring.[57] And these, who have convalesced from their weakness[58] after and by means of many corrections, are, I know not how, bound to me by a more tender love than those who have remained strong from the beginning, without need of this kind of remedy.

7. It is in this sense that the Church, or the soul who loves God, can say that the sun has changed her color by commissioning and equipping some of her mother's sons to make salutary warfare against her, and lead her captive to his faith and love, pierced with those arrows of which Scripture says: "The warrior's arrows are sharp,"[59] and again: "Your arrows have pierced deep into me."[60] Hence she goes on to say: "There is no soundness in my flesh;"[61] but because, as a consequence, she has grown more sound and courageous in spirit, she is able to affirm: "The spirit indeed is willing but the flesh is weak."[62] Her sentiments are those of Paul: "It is

51. Ps 140:5
52. Deut 32:39
53. Gal 2:20
54. Mt 5:25
55. 2 Cor 7:8-9
56. Jn 16:21

57. Gal 4:19
58. Heb 11:34
59. Ps 119:4
60. Ps 37:3
61. Ps 37:4
62. Mt 26:41

when I am weak that I am strong."[63] Do you see how
physical infirmity can be an occasion for increasing spiritual
strength, a source of new spiritual powers. On the other hand
you know that physical strength can beget weakness of the
spirit. What wonder if the enemy's weakness makes you
stronger, unless in your madness you make friends with a
nature that ever lusts against the spirit? [64] See then, if the
Saint who, for his own good, demands to be attacked and
pierced with arrows, is not acting prudently when he says:
"Pierce my flesh with your fear."[65] How excellent that arrow
of fear that pierces and kills the desires of the flesh, that the
spirit may be saved.[66] Is it not obvious to you that he who
chastises his body and subdues it,[67] is aiding the hand that
fights against his lower nature?

IV. 8. There is another arrow: the living and active word of
God that cuts more keenly than any two-edged sword,[68] of
which our Savior said: "I have not come to send peace but
the sword."[69] "A polished arrow"[70] too is that special love of
Christ, which not only pierced Mary's soul but penetrated
through and through,[71] so that even the tiniest space in her
virginal breast was permeated by love. Thenceforth she would
love with her whole heart, her whole soul and her whole
strength,[72] and be full of grace.[73] It transpierced her thus
that it might come down even to us, and of that fullness we
might all receive.[74] She would become the mother of that
love whose father is the God who is love;[75] and when that
love was brought to birth he would place his tent in the
sun,[76] that the Scripture might be fulfilled:[77] "I will make
you the Light of the Nations, so that you may be my salvation to the ends of the earth."[78] This was fulfilled through
Mary, who brought forth in visible flesh him whom she con-

63. 2 Cor 12:10
64. Gal 5:17
65. Ps 118:120
66. 1 Cor 5:5
67. 1 Cor 9:27
68. Heb 4:12
69. Mt 10:34
70. Is 49:2

71. Lk 2:35
72. Mk 12:30
73. Lk 1:28
74. Jn 1:16
75. 1 Jn 4:8
76. Ps 18:5
77. Jn 19:24
78. Ls 49:6

ceived invisibly, neither from the flesh nor by means of the flesh. In the process she experienced through her whole being a wound of love that was mighty and sweet; and I would reckon myself happy if at rare moments I felt at least the prick of the point of that sword. Even if only bearing love's slightest wound, I could still say: "I am wounded with love."[79] How I long not only to be wounded in this manner but to be assailed again and again till the color and heat of that flesh that wars against the spirit is overcome.[80]

9. If worldly-minded maidens should taunt a person undergoing this trial, and say how unsightly she is and devoid of good color, does it not seem to you that she can reply very aptly: "Take no notice of my swarthiness, it is the sun that has burnt me."[81] And if such a person bears in mind that she has arrived at this state through the exhortations and remonstrations of God's servants who "feel a divine jealousy" for her,[82] may she not as a consequence say in truth: "My mother's sons turned their anger on me." The Church or any person inspired by true zeal will speak in this way, using this meaning, not in a mood of grief or complaint, but in joy and thanksgiving and a spirit of triumph that she has been found worthy both to become and to be called dark and unsightly for the name and love of Christ.[83] And this she attributes not to her own merits but to the grace and mercy of the God who anticipated her needs and sent her his preachers. For how could she believe without a preacher? And how can men preach unless they are sent? [84] Not with resentment but with gratitude does she recall that her mother's sons turned their anger on her. Hence what follows: "They made me look after the vineyards."[85] If this statement is examined from the spiritual viewpoint I cannot see that it bears any trace of discontent or rancor, but rather of pleasure. In order to carry out this examination however, and before presuming to attempt it—"for the place is holy"[86]—we must offer the usual

79. Song 2:5, Septuagint
80. 1 Pet 2:11
81. Song 1:5
82. 2 Cor 11:2

83. Acts 5:41
84. Rom 10:14-15
85. Song 1:5
86. Ezek 42:13

prayers to consult and win the favor of that Spirit who "searches the depths of God,"[87] and of the only-begotten Son who is in the father's bosom,[88] Jesus Christ our Lord, the Church's Bridegroom who is blessed for ever. Amen.[89]

87. 1 Cor 2:10   89. Rom 1:25
88. Jn 1:18

SERMON 30

MYSTICAL VINEYARDS AND THE PRUDENCE OF THE FLESH

"THEY MADE ME THE KEEPER of the vineyards."[1] Who are they? Do you mean those opponents to whom you recently referred? Listen and understand.[2] Perhaps she is saying that she has been given this charge by the very people who persecuted her. No need to wonder at this if she was attacked for the purpose of correcting her. Everybody knows that lots of people are frequently opposed in a well-intentioned way for their good. Every day we meet with people whose ideals are purified, who advance to perfection through the friendly corrections of their superiors. Therefore let us rather show, if we can, how her mother's sons fight against the Church with hostile purpose and with a loss that is her gain. This is matter for wonder, that they whose purpose is to harm her, do her good despite themselves. The interpretation just given covers both of these meanings, because the Church has never lacked opponents who were either well-disposed or evilly- disposed toward her. Though their motives for attacking her differed, each worked to her advantage. And if she rejoiced in what she suffered from her rivals, it is because for the one vineyard of which they seemed to deprive her, she has been compensated by being placed over many.[3] "By fighting against me and my vineyard," she says, "those who cried out: 'Raze

1. Song 1:5   3. Mt 25:21
2. Mt 15:10

112

it, raze it! down to its foundations!"[4] have given me the opportunity of exchanging one vineyard for many." This is what she implies when she says: "My own vineyard I have not kept,"[5] as if explaining why it has happened that she is no longer in charge of one but of several vineyards. This, in effect, is what the text says.

2. But if we follow the text's direct meaning, satisfied with what the words mean as they stand, we shall imagine we are reading in our holy Scripture about those material and earthly vineyards that draw daily nourishment from the dew of heaven and the fertile soil,[6] whence they produce the wine that ministers to wantonness.[7] But by doing this we shall have deduced from writings so holy and divine nothing worthy not merely of the bride of the Lord, but even of any of her companions. For what is there in common between brides and a keeper of vineyards? But if they should seem to have points in common, shall we teach as a consequence that the Church was once commissioned with a duty of this kind? Is it for vineyards that God is concerned? [8] But if, in a spiritual sense, we understand the vineyards to be the churches, to be the peoples who are believers, as the Prophet did when he said: "The vineyard of the Lord of hosts is the house of Israel,"[9] it will begin to dawn on us that it is by no means unbecoming for the bride to be made a keeper in the vineyards.

3. It seems to me that here we encounter a significant prerogative. Note in a special way how the Church extended her boundaries[10] into vineyards of this kind all over the world, from that day on which she was attacked by her mother's sons in Jerusalem, and banished from it along with her first new plantation — that company of believers who

4. Ps 136:7
5. Song 1:5
6. Gen 27:28
7. Eph 5:18

8. 1 Cor 9:9
9. Is 5:7
10. Deut 12:20

were described as "of one heart and soul."[11] This is the vineyard which she now says she has not kept, but not to her discredit. For during the persecution it had not been so uprooted that it could not be elsewhere replanted and leased "to other tenants who will deliver the produce to her when the season arrives."[12]

II.   No indeed, it did not perish, it changed to a new location; it even increased and spread further afield under the blessing of the Lord.[13] So lift up your eyes round about and see[14] if the mountains were not covered with its shade, the cedars of God with its branches;[15] if its tendrils did not extend to the sea and its offshoots all the way to the river.[16] No matter for wonder this: it is God's building, God's farm.[17] He waters it, he propagates it, prunes and cleanses it that it may bear more fruit.[18] When did he ever deprive of his care and labor that which his right hand planted? [19] There can be no question of neglect where the apostles are the branches, the Lord is the vine, and his Father is the vinedresser.[20] Planted in faith, its roots are grounded in love, dug in with the hoe of discipline, fertilized with penitential tears, watered with the words of preachers,[21] and so it abounds with the wine that inspires joy[22] rather than debauchery,[23] wine full of the pleasure that is never licentious. This is the wine that gladdens man's heart,[24] the wine that even the angels drink with gladness. In their thirst for men's salvation they rejoice in the conversion and repentance of sinners.[25] Sinners' tears are wine to them; their sorrow has the flavor of grace, the relish of pardon, the delight of reconciliation, the wholesomeness of returning innocence, the gratification of a peaceful conscience.

4. And so, from one vineyard, that seemed to have been

11. Acts 4:32
12. Mt 21:41
13. Gen 27:27
14. Is 49:18
15. Ps 79:11
16. Ps 79:12
17. 1 Cor 3:9
18. Jn 15:2

19. Ps 79:16
20. Jn 15:1
21. 1 Cor 3:6
22. Ps 103:15
23. Eph 5:18
24. Ps 103:15
25. Lk 15:10

destroyed by the storm of savage persecution, what a vast number have been propagated and flourish all over the world! And over all these the bride has been appointed keeper, that she may not be saddened for having failed to keep her first vineyard. Be consoled, daughter of Sion: if one section of Israel has become blind,[26] what is your loss? Yours is to wonder at the mystery rather than bewail the harm; let your heart be expanded to gather together the fullness of the pagans. "Say to the towns of Judah:[27] 'we had to proclaim the word of God to you first, but since you have rejected it, since you do not think yourselves worthy of eternal life, we must turn to the pagans.'"[28] God made an offer to Moses that if he were willing to abandon a people grown disloyal, and expose them to the divine vengeance, he himself would be made the father of a great nation.[29] But Moses refused. Why? Because of the all-surpassing love that bound him irresistibly to them and because he would not pursue his own interests but the honor of God,[30] nor seek his own advantage but that of many.[31] That's the sort of man Moses was.

5. The idea strikes me however, that by a secret design of Providence, this magnificent project was reserved for the bride: she, and not Moses, would beget a mighty race. It was not fitting that the friend of the Bridegroom[32] should seize in advance what was the bride's prerogative; hence not Moses but the new bride received the command: "Go into all the world, and preach the Gospel to the whole creation."[33] It was she who obviously received the mission to found a mighty race. What more could she achieve than to spread over the whole world? And the whole world readily yielded to one who was a bearer of peace, who came offering grace. But what a difference between grace and the law! What a contrast of features as they present themselves to the conscience, the one so pleasant, the other so austere! Who can

26. Rom 11:25
27. Is 40:9
28. Acts 13:46
29. Ex 32:10-13

30. 1 Cor 13:5
31. 1 Cor 10:33
32. Jn 3:29
33. Mk 16:15

look with equal regard on one who condemns and one who counsels, one who holds to account and one who pardons, one who punishes and one who embraces? One does not welcome with equal ardor the darkness and the light, anger and peace, judgment and mercy, the shadow and the substance, the rod and the reward, the curb and the kiss. The hands of Moses were heavy, as Aaron and Hur well knew;[34] the yoke of the law was heavy, as witnessed by the Apostles themselves who proclaimed that neither they nor their ancestors could carry it;[35] the yoke was heavy, the reward paltry: the land was but a thing of promise.[36] Moses, therefore, was not destined to produce a mighty race. But you, the Church who is our mother, holding out the reward of life here and now and of the future life as well,[37] will find ready welcome everywhere because of the twofold grace you bring: a yoke that is easy to bear,[38] a kingdom that is sublime. Expelled from Jerusalem, you are received all over the world, wherever your promises attract men so that your laws do not alarm them. Why then still lament the loss of one vineyard when you have been so abundantly compensated? "No longer will you be deserted, a wife hated and unvisited; I will make you an eternal pride and a never-ending joy. You shall suck the milk of nations, and be suckled at the breasts of kings. So you shall know that I the Lord am your deliverer, your ransomer the mighty one of Jacob."[39] This then is what the bride means when she says she was made keeper of the vineyards, and that she had failed to keep her own.

III. 6. I scarcely ever read these words without finding fault with myself for having undertaken the care of souls, I who am not fit to take care of my own soul: here I speak of souls as vineyards. If you approve of this interpretation may we not consequently and appropriately call faith the vine, the virtues the branches, good works the cluster of grapes, and devotion the wine. Without the vine there is no wine; without

---

34. Ex 17:12
35. Acts 15:10
36. Deut 4:1; 8:1

37. 1 Tim 4:8
38. Mt 11:30
39. Is 60:15-16

faith there is no virtue. "Without faith it is impossible to please God,"[40] perhaps one cannot help but displease him, for "whatever does not proceed from faith is sin."[41] Those people therefore who made me keeper of the vineyards should have taken into account how I had kept my own. For how long a time was it uncultivated and abandoned, reduced to a wilderness! It had failed completely to produce wine, its branches withered without the fruit of virtue because its faith was sterile.[42] Faith was there but it was dead. Without good works how could it be otherwise? That was my life as a layman. On my conversion to the Lord I began to improve, though very little, not as much as I should have. But then, what man is fit to do this? Certainly not the holy Prophet who said: "Unless the Lord keeps watch over a city, in vain the watchman stands on guard."[43] What attacks I remember being exposed to from him who shoots arrows at the innocent from cover! [44] O my vineyard, what an amount of produce was robbed from me by subtle trickery, at the very time when I was growing more vigilant in my care of you! How many and how precious the clusters of good works either blighted by anger, or snatched away by boasting, or defiled by vainglory! What temptations did I not endure from gluttony, from mental slothfulness, from pusillanimity of spirit and the storm of passion! [45] Such was my state; and yet they made me the keeper of the vineyards, failing to consider what I was doing or had done with my own; nor listening to the voice of the teacher who said: "If a man does not know how to manage his own household, how can he care for God's Church? "[46]

7. What amazes me is the audacity of those who seem to harvest only brambles and thistles from their own vineyards,[47] and yet are not afraid to intrude themselves on the vineyards of the Lord. These are not keepers and vinedressers but thieves and robbers.[48] Enough said. But woe to me even

40. Heb 11:6
41. Rom 14:23
42. Jas 2:20
43. Ps 126:1
44. Ps 63:5

45. Ps 54:9
46. 1 Tim 3:5
47. Gen 3:18; Mt 7:16
48. Jn 10:8

now because of the danger to my own vineyard, and now
more than ever, when I am involved in so many concerns and
forced to be less attentive to the one, less careful about it. I
have no opportunity to fence it round or dig a winepress
there.[49] Alas! its wall is broken down,[50] and every passer-by
can pluck its fruit! There is nothing to shelter it from sorrow; anger and impatience make it their thoroughfare. Press-
ing needs like little foxes steadily destroy it;[51] anxieties,
suspicions, cares, charge in from all sides; rare is the hour
when bickering groups with their tiresome quarrels are miss-
ing from my door. I have no power to prevent them, no
means of evading them, not even time for prayer. Will a flood
of tears be enough to fertilize the barrenness of my soul?[52] I
meant to say "of my vineyard," but quoted the Psalm
through habit; it means the same thing. I do not regret a
mistake that draws attention to the metaphor, for the sermon
concerns the soul, not a vineyard. So when vineyard is mentioned let the soul be remembered: its barrenness deplored
under the former's figure and name. Hence I ask what
amount of tears will irrigate the barrenness of my vineyard.
All its boughs have withered through neglect:[53] they remain
fruitless because they have no moisture.[54] O good Jesus, well
you know how they are gathered in bundles of twigs and
consumed daily in your sacrifice by the burning fire of sorrow in my heart. Let the broken spirit, I implore, be a sacrifice to you: "You will not scorn this crushed and broken
heart, O God."[55]

IV. 8. On account of my imperfection then, I apply the
present text in this way to myself. But a man who is perfect[56] will be able to give another meaning to the words: "My
own vineyard I have not kept,"[57] the meaning intended by
the Savior when he said in the Gospel: "Anyone who loses
his life for my sake will find it."[58] It is clear that a man is fit

49. Mt 21:33
50. Ps 79:13
51. Song 2:15
52. Ps 34:12
53. Ps 87:10

54. Lk 8:6
55. Ps 50:19
56. Lk 6:40
57. Song 1:5
58. Mt 10:39

and worthy to be in charge of vineyards when he can pains-
takingly apply himself to the care of the ones committed to
him without let or hindrance in caring for his own, provided
he does not concentrate on selfish interest,[59] nor on what is
profitable to himself, but to others. Hence Peter was made
keeper of so many vineyards that were of the circumcision,[60]
because he was ready to go to prison and to death;[61] love of
his own vineyard, of his own life that is, prevented him in no
way from concentrating on the care of those committed to
him. Paul too was rightly entrusted with a vast forest of
vineyards, because so little was he worried by concern for his
own vineyard that he was ready not only to be put in bonds
but even to die in Jerusalem for the name of our Lord Jesus
Christ.[62] "I dread none of these things," he said, "nor do I
account my life more precious than myself."[63] How excellent
a discernment of values, when he judges that nothing he owns
is to be preferred to himself.

9. Yet how many have preferred to their own salvation a
pittance of worthless money. Paul preferred not even his life.
"I do not account my life more precious than myself," he
said. Do you make a distinction between yourself and your
life, then? You do well in seeing more worth in your self
than in anything you possess. But how is it that your life is
not your self? I feel that because Paul was then guided by
the Spirit,[64] and had a self that acknowledges that the Law is
good,[65] he thought it more becoming to designate this self as
the principal and supreme entity in himself, rather than anything else that was his. The remaining part of his soul being
clearly of an inferior nature, and therefore belonging to a
lower and baser form of being, namely the body, not only
because its function is to impart life and feeling to it but
also to preserve and nourish it: this sensual and carnal
thing is regarded by the spiritual man as unworthy to
be called self. He judged it better to see it as something
belonging to him rather than as adequately equipped to re-

59. 1 Cor 13:5
60. Col 4:11
61. Lk 22:33
62. Acts 21:13

63. Acts 20:24
64. Gal 5:16, 25
65. Rom 7:16

present his personality. "When I say me," he said, "understand it to mean what is most excellent in me, that in which I exist by favor of God, my mind and reason. When I speak of my soul, think of that lower principle whose purpose as you see is to animate the body, and even share in its concupiscence. I once lived at that level, but not now, because I no longer walk according to the flesh, but according to the Spirit.[66] 'I live, now not I, but Christ lives in me.'[67] Not in the flesh but in this spirit is my true self to be found. What if the soul still experiences carnal lusts? 'The thing behaving that way is not my true self but sin living in me.'[68] And therefore I do not regard this carnal instinct as my real self, but as something possessed by my self: in other words, my sensitive soul." To express carnal love is a function of that soul, as is the life it communicates to the body. This is the life that Paul spurned for the sake of his true self, being ready not only to be put in bonds but even to die in Jerusalem[69] on behalf of the Lord, and in this manner to lose his life as the Lord had counseled.[70]

10. You too, if you abandon your own will, if you fully renounce the pleasures of the body, if you crucify your lower nature with its passions and desires,[71] and if you "put to death those parts of you which belong to the earth,"[72] will be truly doing as Paul did, since you will not account your life as more precious than yourself;[73] by this loss that saves, you will prove yourself a follower of Christ. It is wiser to lose it in order to save it, than by saving it to lose it. "For anyone who wants to save his life, will lose it."[74]

V. What have you to say to this, you who are so particular about your food, so unconcerned about your behavior? Hippocrates and his followers teach us to save our lives in this world, Christ and his followers teach us to lose them. Which

66. Rom 8:4
67. Gal 2:20
68. Rom 7:17
69. Acts 21:13
70. Mt 10:39; 16:25

71. Gal 5:24
72. Col 3:5
73. Acts 20:24
74. Mt 16:25

of the two do you choose as master? But the man who
complains: "This is bad for my eyes, that gives me headache,
this affects my heart, that upsets my stomach"—he shows
clearly who his master is. Each of us holds forth in the style
of the master he has learned from. It was not from the
Gospel, nor from the prophets, nor from the letters of the
apostles, that you learned to pick and choose like this. It was
flesh and blood, not the Spirit of the Father, that revealed
this wisdom to you,[75] for it is the wisdom of the flesh. But
listen to what our physicians think of this kind of wisdom:
"To set one's mind on the flesh," they say, "is death;"[76] and
"the mind that is set on the flesh is hostile to God."[77] Would
you have me preach to you the doctrine of Hippocrates or
Galenus, or even of the school of Epicurus? But I, a follower
of Christ, am speaking to Christ's followers: if I should introduce strange doctrines here, I should be in sin. The ideal
of Epicurus was the body's sensual pleasure, of Hippocrates
to promote its good health, but my Master preaches contempt of these two pursuits. What each of those philosophers
seeks, and teaches us to seek with all diligence—in one case
how to sustain the body's life, in the other how to pander to
its enjoyment—the Savior advises us to lose.[78]

11. Is not this the message that pounded in your ears from
the school of Christ when just now it was proclaimed: "He
who loves his life loses it"?[79] He loses it, he said, either by
dying as a martyr or by chastising himself as a penitent.
Certainly, it is a kind of martyrdom to put to death the deeds
of the body by the power of the Spirit,[80] less horrifying
indeed than that in which the limbs are severed by the sword,
but more gruelling because more prolonged. Do you not see
how these words of my Master condemn that wisdom of the
flesh,[81] whereby a man either abandons himself to sensual
indulgence or pays excessive attention to the body's health?
You have heard from the Sage that true wisdom does not

75. Mt 16:17
76. Rom 8:6
77. Rom 8:7
78. Mt 10:39

79. Jn 12:25
80. Rom 8:13
81. Rom 8:7

dissipate itself by living voluptuously; it is not found in the land of those who live for pleasure.[82] But the one who does find it can say: "I loved wisdom more than health or beauty."[83] If more than health or beauty, far more still than sensuality and debauchery. But why should a man bother to abstain from sensual pleasures if he spends so much time every day probing into the mysteries of the human constitution and devising ways of procuring variety in foods? "Beans," he says, "produce flatulency, cheese causes dyspepsia, milk gives me headache, water is bad for my heart, cabbages bring on melancholy, I feel choleric after onions, fish from the pond or from muddy water does not agree with my constitution." Are you not actually saying that food to your taste is not available in all the rivers, the fields, the gardens and the cellars?

12. I earnestly request that you remember you are a monk, not a physician, and that you will be judged not on the quality of your constitution but on your profession. I beg of you to be concerned first of all for your own peace, then for the hardship you cause to those who serve you; beware of being a burden on the community, and take conscience into account. I do not mean your conscience but your neighbor's; that of the man who because of you, while he sits and eats what is placed before him, murmurs about your strange fasting. For he is scandalized by either your unwarrantable superstition or what seems the hard-heartedness of the person whose duty it is to provide for you. Your brother, I repeat, is scandalized by your strange behavior, this insistence on getting special foods that to him seems superstitious; or he will accuse me of harshness for not endeavouring to supply the nourishment you need.[84] There are some who flatter themselves, but to no purpose, that they may follow the example of Paul who advised his disciple to give up drinking only water, and to take a little wine for the sake of his digestion and frequent bouts of illness.[85] These ought to remember

82. Job 28:13
83. Wis 7:10

84. Prov 30:8
85. 1 Tim 5:23

first of all that the Apostle did not prescribe such a drink for himself, and that his disciple did not ask for it. In the second place, this advice was given, not to a monk but to a bishop whose life was very necessary to the Church in its tender infancy. This was Timothy. Give me another Timothy and if it should please you I will offer him gold to eat and balsam to drink. But it is self-pity that makes you arrange for your own diet. Making your own arrangements like this seems to me suspect, I fear it is worldly wisdom masquerading in the dress and name of discretion.[86] But let me at least remind you that if you decide to drink wine on the authority of the Apostle, you should not overlook the word "little" with which he qualified it. And so enough on that subject. But let us return to the bride and learn from her how to lose our own vineyards to our benefit, especially we who seem to be appointed keepers in the vineyards of the Bridegroom of the Church, our Lord Jesus Christ, who is blessed for ever. Amen.[87]

---

86. Rom 8:6   87. Rom 1:25

SERMON 31

THE VARIOUS WAYS OF SEEING GOD

"TELL ME, you whom my soul loves, where you pasture your flock, where you make it lie down at noon?"[1] The Word, who is the Bridegroom, often makes himself known under more than one form to those who are fervent. Why so? Doubtless because he cannot be seen yet as he is.[2] That vision is unchanging, because the form in which he will then be seen is unchanging; for he is, and can suffer no change determined by present, past or future. Eliminate past and future, and where then is alteration or any shadow of a change?[3] For whatever evolves out of the past and does not cease to move toward future development, passes through the instant that is the present, but one cannot say: it is. How can one say: it is, when it never remains in the same state?[4] That alone truly is, which is neither altered from its past mode of being nor blotted out by a future mode, but "is" alone is predicated of it impregnably and unchangeably, and it remains what it is. No reference to the past can deny that it is from all eternity, nor any reference to the future that it is for all eternity. In this way it proves that it truly is, that is, it is uncreated, interminable, immutable. When he therefore who exists in this manner — who, furthermore, cannot be one moment in this form, another in that — is seen just as he is, that vision

1. Song 1:6
2. 1 Jn 3:2

3. Jas 1:17
4. Job 14:2

124

endures, as I have said, since no alteration interrupts it. This is the moment when that one denarius mentioned in the Gospel is given in the one vision that is offered to everyone who sees.[5] For as he who is seen is immutable in himself, he is present immutably to all who contemplate him; to these there is nothing more desirable that they wish to see, nothing more enticing that they could see. Can their eager appetite, then, ever grow weary, or that sweetness ebb away, or that truth prove deceptive, or that eternity come to a close? And if both the ability and will to contemplate are prolonged eternally, what is lacking to total happiness? Those who contemplate him without ceasing are short of nothing, those whose wills are fixed on him have nothing more to desire.

2. But this vision is not for the present life; it is reserved for the next, at least for those who can say: "We know that when he appears we shall be like him, for we shall see him as he is."[6] Even now he appears to whom he pleases, but as he pleases, not as he is. Neither sage nor saint nor prophet can or could ever see him as he is, while still in this mortal body; but whoever is found worthy will be able to do so when the body becomes immortal. Hence, though he is seen here below, it is in the form that seems good to him, not as he is. For example, take that mighty source of light, I speak of that sun which you see day after day; yet you do not see it as it is, but according as it lights up the air, or a mountain, or a wall. Nor could you see even to this extent if the light of your body, the eye,[7] because of its natural steadiness and clearness, did not bear some degree of likeness to that light in the heavens. Since all the other members of the body lack this likeness, they are incapable of seeing the light. Even the eye itself, when troubled, cannot approach the light, because it has lost that likeness. Just as the troubled eye, then, cannot gaze on the peaceful sun because of its unlikeness, so the peaceful eye can behold it with some efficacy because of a certain likeness. If indeed it were wholly equal to it in purity, with a

5. Mt 20:9-10   7. Mt 6:22
6. 1 Jn 3:2

completely clear vision it would see it as it is, because of the complete likeness. And so when you are enlightened you can see even now the Sun of Justice[8] that "enlightens every man who comes into this world,"[9] according to the degree of the light he gives, by which you are made somehow like him; but see him as he is you cannot, because not yet perfectly like him. That is why the Psalmist says: "Come to him and be enlightened, and your faces shall never be ashamed."[10] That is very true, provided we are enlightened as much as we need, so that "with our unveiled faces contemplating the glory of God, all grow brighter and brighter as we are turned into the same image, as by the spirit of the Lord."[11]

3. Note that we must approach gently, not intrude ourselves upon him, lest the irreverent searcher of majesty be overwhelmed by glory.[12] This approach is not a movement from place to place but from brightness to brightness, not in the body but in the spirit, as by the Spirit of the Lord; evidently by the spirit of the Lord, not by ours, although in ours. The brighter one becomes, the nearer is the end; and to be absolutely bright is to have arrived. For those thus arrived in his presence, to see him as he is means to be as he is, and not to be put to shame by any form of unlikeness. But, as I have said, this is for the next life.

II. In the meantime this immense variety of forms, these countless species of creatures, what are they but rays emanating from the Godhead, showing that he from whom they come truly is, but not fully explaining what he is. Hence what you see is what emanates from him, not himself. Nevertheless, though not seeing himself but what comes from him, you are made aware beyond all doubt that he exists, and that you must seek him. Grace will not be wanting to the seeker, nor ignorance excuse the negligent. All have access to this kind of vision. According to the Apostle Paul, it is common to everyone who has the use of reason: "The invisible attri-

8. Mal 4:2   11. 2 Cor 3:18
9. Jn 1:9   12. Prov 25:27
10. Ps 33:6

butes of God have been clearly perceived in the things that have been made."[13]

4. Another kind of vision is that by which in former times the Fathers were often graciously admitted to sweet communion with God, who became present to them, though they did not see him as he is but only in the form he thought fitting to assume. Nor does he appear to all in a similar manner, but as the Apostle says: "in many and various ways,"[14] still remaining one in himself, in accord with his word to Israel: "The Lord your God is one God."[15] This manifestation, though not apparent to everybody, took place exteriorly, and consisted of images or the spoken word. But there is another form of divine contemplation, very different from the former because it takes place in the interior, when God himself is pleased to visit the soul that seeks him,[16] provided it is committed to seeking him with all its desire and love. We are told what the sign of such a visit is by one who experienced it. "Fire goes before him and burns up his adversaries round about."[17] The fire of holy desire ought to precede his advent to every soul whom he will visit, to burn up the rust of bad habits and so prepare a place for the Lord. The soul will know that the Lord is near[18] when it perceives itself to be aflame with that fire, and can say as the Prophet did: "He has sent a fire from on high down into my bones, and enlightened me;"[19] and again: "My heart became hot within me and in my meditation fire burst forth."[20]

5. When the Beloved who is thus sought for pays a visit in his merciful love to the soul that is filled with longing, that prays often, even without intermission,[21] that humiliates itself in the ardor of its desire, that soul may fittingly say with St Jeremiah: "You are good, O Lord, to those who hope in you, to the soul that seeks you."[22] And that soul's angel, one

13. Rom 1:20
14. Heb 1:1
15. Deut 6:4
16. Lam 3:25
17. Ps 96:3

18. Ps 33:19
19. Lam 1:13
20. Ps 38:4
21. 1 Thess 5:17
22. Lam 3:25

of the friends of the Bridegroom,[23] and by him commissioned to be the minister and witness of that secret and
mutual exchange — that angel, I say, must be dancing with
joy! Does he not participate in their gladness and bliss, and
turning to the Lord, say: "I thank you, Lord of majesty,
because 'you have granted him his heart's desire, not denied
him what his lips entreated' "? [24] He is everywhere the soul's
tireless attendant, never ceasing to lure it on and guide it with
constant inspirations, as he whispers: "Take delight in the
Lord, and he will give you the desire of your heart;"[25] and
again: "Wait for the Lord and keep his way."[26] Or: "If he
seems slow, wait for him; he will surely come, he will not
delay."[27] Turning to the Lord, he says: " 'As a hart longs for
flowing streams, so that soul longs for you, O God'.[28] It has
yearned for you in the night, and your Spirit within it watched for you from morning onwards."[29] And again: "All the
day this soul reaches out to you;[30] grant what it wants because it is shouting after you;[31] relent a little and show your
mercy.[32] Look down from heaven and see, and visit this
desolate spirit."[33] This loyal groomsman, watching without
envy over this interchange of love, seeks the Lord's glory
rather than his own;[34] he is the go-between for the lover and
his beloved, making known the desires of one, bearing the
gifts of the other. He quickens the soul's affections, he con-
ciliates the Bridegroom. Sometimes too, though rarely, he
brings them into each other's presence, either snatching her
up to him, or leading him down to her: for he is a member of
the household, a familiar figure in the palace, one who has no
fear of being rebuffed, who daily sees the face of the
Father.[35]

6. Be careful, however, not to conclude that I see something corporeal or perceptible to the senses in this union

23. Song 1:6
24. Ps 20:3
25. Ps 36:4
26. Ps 36:34
27. Hab 2:3
28. Ps 41:2
29. Is 26:9

30. Ps 87:10
31. Mt 15:23
32. Ps 89:13
33. Ps 79:15
34. Jn 7:18
35. Mt 18:10

between the Word and the soul. My opinion is that of the Apostle, who said that "he who is united to the Lord becomes one spirit with him."[36] I try to express with the most suitable words I can muster the ecstatic ascent of the purified mind to God, and the loving descent of God into the soul, submitting spiritual truths to spiritual men.[37] Therefore let this union be in the spirit, because "God is a spirit,"[38] who is lovingly drawn by the beauty of that soul[39] whom he perceives to be guided by the Spirit,[40] and devoid of any desire to submit to the ways of the flesh, especially if he sees that it burns with love for himself.

III. One who is so disposed and so beloved will by no means be content either with that manifestation of the Bridegroom given to the many in the world of creatures,[41] or to the few in visions and dreams. By a special privilege she wants to welcome him down from heaven into her inmost heart, into her deepest love; she wants to have the one she desires present to her not in bodily form but by inward infusion, not by appearing externally but by laying hold of her within. It is beyond question that the vision is all the more delightful the more inward it is, and not external. It is the Word, who penetrates without sound; who is effective though not pronounced, who wins the affections without striking on the ears. His face, though without form, is the source of form, it does not dazzle the eyes of the body but gladdens the watchful heart; its pleasure is in the gift of love and not in the color of the lover.

7. Not yet have I come round to saying that he has appeared as he is, although in this inward vision he does not reveal himself as altogether different from what he is. Neither does he make his presence continuously felt, not even to his most ardent lovers, nor in the same way to all. For the various desires of the soul it is essential that the taste of God's presence be varied too, and that the infused flavor of divine

---

36. 1 Cor 6:17
37. 1 Cor 2:13
38. Jn 4:24

39. Ps 44:12
40. Gal 5:16
41. Rom 1:20

delight should titillate in manifold ways the palate of the soul that seeks him. You must already have noticed how often he changes his countenance in the course of this love-song, how he delights in transforming himself from one charming guise to another in the beloved's presence: at one moment like a bashful bridegroom manoeuvring for the hidden embraces of his holy lover, for the bliss of her kisses; at another coming along like a physician with oil and ointments, because weak and tender souls still need remedies and medicines of this kind, which is why they are rather daintily described as maidens. Should anybody find fault with this, let him be told that "it is not the healthy who need the doctor, but the sick."[42] Sometimes, too, he joins up as a traveller with the bride and the maidens who accompany her on the road, and lightens the hardships of the journey for the whole company by his fascinating conversation, so that when he has parted from them they ask: "Did not our hearts burn within us as he talked to us on the road? "[43] A silver-tongued companion who, by the spell of his words and manners, persuades everyone, as if in a sweet-smelling cloud arising from the ointments, to follow him. Hence they say: "We will run after you in the odor of your ointments."[44] At another time he comes to meet them as a wealthy father of a family "with bread enough and to spare" in his house;[45] or again like a magnificent and powerful king, giving courage to his timid and poverty-stricken bride, stirring up her desire by showing her the ornaments of his glory, the riches of his wine-presses and storehouse, the produce of his gardens and fields, and finally introducing her into his private apartments.[46] For "her husband's heart has confidence in her,"[47] and among all his possessions there is nothing that he thinks should be hidden from her whom he redeemed from indigence, whose fidelity he has proved, whose attractiveness wins his embraces. And so he never ceases, in one way or another, to reveal himself to the inward eye of those who seek him, thus fulfilling the

---

42. Mt 9:12
43. Lk 24:32
44. Song 1:3

45. Lk 15:17
46. Song 1:3
47. Prov 31:11

promise that he made: "Be assured I am with you always, to the end of time."[48]

8. On all these occasions he is kind and gentle, full of merciful love.[49] In his kisses he shows that he is both loving and charming; with the oil and the ointments that he is boundlessly considerate and compassionate and forgiving; on the journey he is gay, courteous, ever gracious and ready to help; in the display of his riches and possessions he reveals a kingly liberality, a munificent generosity in the bestowal of rewards. Through the whole context of this song you will find images of this nature to delineate the Word. Hence I feel that the Prophet was thinking on these lines when he said: "Christ the Lord is a spirit before our face; under his shadow we shall live among the nations,"[50] because now we see in a mirror dimly and not yet face to face.[51] So it will be while we live among the nations; among the angels it will be otherwise. For then we shall enjoy the very same happiness as they; even we shall see him as he is,[52] in the form of God,[53] no longer in shadow.

IV. Just as we say that our ancestors possessed only shadows and images, whereas the truth itself shines on us by the grace of Christ present in the flesh, so also no one will deny that in relation to the world to come, we still live in the shadow of the truth, unless he wishes to deny what the apostle asserts: "our knowledge is imperfect and our prophecy is imperfect;"[54] or when he says: "I do not reckon myself to have got hold of it yet."[55] Why should there not be a distinction between him who walks by faith and him who walks by sight?[56] Hence the just man lives by faith,[57] the blessed rejoices in the vision; the holy person here below lives in the shadow of Christ,[58] the holy angel above is glorified in the splendor of his shining countenance.

48. Mt 28:20
49. Ps 85:5
50. Lam 4:20
51. 1 Cor 13:12
52. 1 Jn 3:2
53. Phil 2:6
54. 1 Cor 13:9
55. Phil 3:13
56. 2 Cor 5:7
57. Hab 2:4; Rom 1:17
58. Lam 4:20

9. That the faith is shadowy is a blessing, it tempers the light to the eye's weakness and prepares the eye for the light; for it is written: "He cleansed their hearts by faith."[59] Faith therefore does not quench the light but protects it. Whatever it may be that the angel sees, is preserved for me by the shadow of faith, stored up in its trusty breast, until it be revealed in due time. If you cannot yet grasp the naked truth is it not worthwhile to possess it wrapped in a veil? Our Lord's Mother herself lived in the shadow of faith, for she was told: "Blessed are you who believed."[60] Even the body of Christ was a shadow for her, as implied in the words: "The power of the Most High will cover you with its shadow."[61] That is no mean shadow which is formed by the power of the Most High. Assuredly there was power in the flesh of Christ that overshadowed the Virgin, since by means of the envelope of his vivifying body she was able to bear his majestic presence, and endure the unapproachable light,[62] a thing impossible to mortal woman. That was power indeed by which every opposing might was overcome. Both the power and the shadow put the demons to flight and became a shelter for men: an invigorating power surely, a shadow radiating coolness.

10. We therefore who walk by faith[63] live in the shadow of Christ; we are fed with his flesh as the source of our life. For Christ's flesh is real food.[64] And perhaps for that reason he is now described here as appearing in the guise of a shepherd, when the bride addresses him as though one of the shepherds: "Tell me where you pasture your flock, where you make it lie down at noon."[65] The Good Shepherd who lays down his life for his sheep! [66] He gives them his life, he gives them his flesh; his life their ransom, his flesh their food. How wonderful! He is their shepherd, their food, their redemption. But this sermon is getting too long, the subject is extensive and contains great truths that cannot be explained in

59. Acts 15:9
60. Lk 1:45
61. Lk 1:35
62. 1 Tim 6:16

63. 2 Cor 5:7
64. Jn 6:56
65. Song 1:7
66. Jn 10:11

a few words. This necessitates that we break off rather than finish off. Since the matter is merely suspended we must keep it alive in our memories, so as to resume soon again where we have left off, and continue it with the aid of our Lord Jesus Christ, the Church's Bridegroom, who is God blessed for ever. Amen.[67]

67. Rom 1:25

SERMON 32

HOW CHRIST ADAPTS HIS GRACES TO PERSONAL NEEDS

"TELL ME WHERE you pasture your flock, where you make it lie down at noon."[1] This is where we are, from here we proceed. But before I begin to treat of these words and the vision they imply, I think we should summarize briefly the other visions that preceded it, and see how they can be applied spiritually to us according to each one's desires and merits. If we receive the grace to understand these, we shall more easily find light on the matter we are about to discuss. For we are faced with a difficult task. The words that describe these visions or images seem to refer to bodies or bodily substances, yet they are means of conveying spiritual truths to us, and hence there must be a spiritual character to our enquiry into their causes and meaning. And who is qualified to investigate and comprehend those countless affective movements of the soul caused by the presence of the Bridegroom dispensing his multiform graces?[2] Yet if we turn our gaze to our interior, and if the Holy Spirit will be pleased to give us his light to see the fruits that by his action he constantly produces within us, I think we shall not remain entirely devoid of understanding about these mysteries. For I trust that "we have not received the spirit of the world but the Spirit which is from God, that we might understand the gifts bestowed on us by God."[3]

1. Song 1:6
2. I Pet 4:10

3. I Cor 2:12

134

2. If then, any of us, like the holy Prophet, finds that it is good to cling close to God,[4] and—that I may make my meaning more clear—if any of us is so filled with desire[5] that he wants to depart and to be with Christ,[6] with a desire that is intense, a thirst ever burning, an application that never flags, he will certainly meet the Word in the guise of a Bridegroom on whatever day he comes.[7] At such an hour he will find himself locked in the arms of Wisdom; he will experience how sweet divine love is as it flows into his heart. His heart's desire will be given to him,[8] even while still a pilgrim on earth,[9] though not in its fullness and only for a time, a short time. For when after vigils and prayers and a great shower of tears he who was sought presents himself, suddenly he is gone again, just when we think we hold him fast. But he will present himself anew to the soul that pursues him with tears, he will allow himself to be taken hold of but not detained, for suddenly a second time he flees from between our hands. And if the fervent soul persists with prayers and tears, he will return each time and not defraud him of his express desire,[10] but only to disappear soon again and not to return unless he is sought for with all one's heart. And so, even in this body we can often enjoy the happiness of the Bridegroom's presence, but it is a happiness that is never complete because the joy of the visit is followed by the pain at his departure. The beloved has no choice but to endure this state until the hour when she lays down the body's weary weight, and raised aloft on the wings of desire, freely traverses the meadows of contemplation, and in spirit follows the One she loves without restraint wherever he goes.[11]

3. Nevertheless, he will not reveal himself in this way to every person, even momentarily, but only to the one who is proved to be a worthy bride by intense devotion, vehement desire and the sweetest affection. And the Word who comes

4. Ps 72:28
5. Dan 9:23
6. Phil 1:23
7. I Pet 5:6

8. Ps 20:3
9. 2 Cor 5:6
10. Ps 20:3
11. Rev 14:4

to visit will be clothed in beauty,[12] in every aspect a Bridegroom.

II. But the person who has not yet been raised to this state, who smarts at the remembrance of past deeds and says to God in bitterness of soul:[13] "Do not condemn me,"[14] or who may still be caught up in the snare of his own evil propensities, still perilously tempted,[15] this person needs a physician, not a bridegroom; hence kisses and embraces are not for him, but only oil and ointments, remedies for his wounds. Is not this how we too often feel? Is not this our experience at prayer, we who are tempted daily by our passions and filled with remorse for our past sins? O good Jesus, from what great bitterness have you not freed me by your coming, time after time? When distress has made me weep, when untold sobs and groans have shaken me, have you not anointed my wounded conscience with the ointment of your mercy and poured in the oil of gladness?[16] How often has not prayer raised me from the brink of despair and made me feel happy in the hope of pardon? All who have had these experiences know well that the Lord Jesus is a physician indeed, "who heals the broken-hearted and binds up their wounds."[17] And those who cannot lay claim to experience must for that very reason put their trust in him when he says: "The Spirit of the Lord has anointed me, he has sent me to bring good news to the humble, to bind up the broken-hearted."[18] And if they should still be in doubt, let them draw near and put it to the test and so learn by inward experience what this means: "I desire mercy and not sacrifice."[19] But let us pursue the subject.

4. When men grow weary of studying spiritual doctrine and become lukewarm, when their spiritual energies are drained away, then they walk in sadness along the ways of the Lord.[20] They fulfill the tasks enjoined on them with hearts

12. Ps 92:1
13. Job 10:1
14. Job 10:2
15. Jas 1:14
16. Ps 44:8

17. Ps 146:3
18. Is 61:1
19. Mt 9:13
20. Lk 24:17

that are tired and arid, they grumble without ceasing, they complain of the long days and the long nights in words like those of Job: "When I lie down I say: 'When shall I arise?' And then I shall be waiting for evening."[21] If when we are subject to these moods, the compassionate Lord draws near to us on the way we are traveling,[22] and being from heaven begins to talk to us about heavenly truths,[23] sings our favourite air from among the songs of Sion,[24] discourses on the city of God, on the peace of that city, on the eternity of that peace and on the life that is eternal, I assure you that this happy discourse will bear along as in a carriage the man who has grown tired and listless; it drives all trace of aversion from the hearer's mind and weariness from his body. Does it not seem that this is what was felt, this is what was asked for by the man who said: "My soul has slumbered through weariness, strengthen me according to your word"?[25] And when he obtains his request will he not cry out: "O how I love your law! It is my study all day long"?[26] For our meditations on the Word who is the Bridegroom, on his glory, his elegance, power and majesty, become in a sense his way of speaking to us. And not only that, but when with eager minds we examine his rulings, the decrees from his own mouth;[27] when we meditate on his law day and night,[28] let us be assured that the Bridegroom is present, and that he speaks his message of happiness to us lest our trials should prove more than we can bear.

5. When you find yourself caught up in this kind of thinking, beware of seeing the thoughts as your own; you must rather acknowledge that he is present who said to the prophet: "It is I, announcing righteousness."[29]

III. Our own thoughts bear a very close resemblance to the words Truth speaks within us; no one can easily differentiate between what springs from the heart and what he hears from

21. Job 7:4
22. Lk 24:17
23. Jn 3:31
24. Ps 136:3
25. Ps 118:28

26. Ps 118:97
27. Ps 118:13
28. Ps 1:2
29. Is 63:1

without unless he attends carefully to what the Lord says in the Gospel: "Out of the heart come evil thoughts;"[30] or that question: "Why do you think evil in your hearts?"[31] And again: "When he (the devil) lies, he speaks according to his own nature."[32] The Apostle says: "Not that we are sufficient of ourselves to think of anything as coming from us," meaning here anything good, "but our sufficiency is from God."[33] So when we yield our hearts to wicked thoughts, the thoughts are our own; if we think on good things, it is God's word. Our hearts produce the evil thoughts, they listen for those that are good. "Let me hear," the heart says, "what God the Lord will speak, for he will speak peace to his people."[34] God accordingly utters words of peace, of goodness, of righteousness within us; we do not think these things of ourselves, we hear them in our interior. On the other hand, murders, adulteries, robberies, blasphemies and similar evils come forth from the heart;[35] we do not hear them, we produce them. For "the fool says in his heart: 'there is no God.'"[36] And hence, "The wicked has provoked God, for he has said in his heart: 'He will not call to account.'"[37] But there is still another kind of thought that is perceived indeed in the heart but not uttered by it. It does not come forth from the heart as our thought does, nor is it that word which we have said is directed to the heart, namely, the word of the Word, because it is evil. It is produced within us by hostile powers, like the images that come to us from bad angels,[38] such as we read the devil put into the heart of Judas, son of Simon the Iscariot, to betray the Lord.[39]

6. For who can keep watch over his inward thoughts so closely and so assiduously, whether they merely occur to him or whether he is their author, as to be able to decide clearly which of the heart's illicit desires are the fruit of his own frailty, which an insinuation of the devil? I believe this is

30. Mt 15:19
31. Mt 9:4
32. Jn 8:44
33. 2 Cor 3:5
34. Ps 84:9

35. Mt 15:19
36. Ps 13:1
37. Ps 9:34
38. Ps 77:49
39. Jn 13:2

more than mortals can achieve, unless by the light of the Holy Spirit they receive that special gift which the Apostle lists with the other charisms under the name of discernment of spirits.[40] According to Solomon, no matter how vigilantly a man may guard his heart[41] and watch with the closest scrutiny every movement of his inward being, he will not be able to diagnose or judge exactly between the evil that is inborn and the evil implanted from without, even after prolonged study and frequent experience of these matters. For "who can understand sins?"[42] It is of little consequence to us to know the source of the evil within us, provided we know it is there; no matter what its source we must watch and pray that we may not consent to it.[43] The Prophet prays against both these evils: "Cleanse me from my secret sins, O Lord, and spare your servant from those others."[44] As for me, I cannot hand on to you what I have not received.[45] And I certainly have not received the power to distinguish with certitude between what springs from the heart and what is sown there by the enemy. Both are evil, both have an evil source; both are in the heart, though both do not originate there. I am fully certain that I bear them within, but by no means certain which to attribute to the heart, which to the enemy. But this problem, as I have said, entails no danger.

7. But where the error is dangerous, even fatal, there we are provided with a rule that is certain: not to attribute to ourselves what comes from God within us, thinking that the visit of the Word is no more than a thought of our own. The distance of good from evil is the distance between these two things: for just as evil cannot proceed from the Word, neither can good proceed from the heart unless it has been previously inspired by the Word, because "a sound tree cannot bear evil fruit, nor can a bad tree bear good fruit."[46] But I think enough has been said to clarify which movements of the heart are from God and which from ourselves. And this, I

---

40. 1 Cor 12:10
41. Prov 4:23
42. Ps 18:13
43. Mt 26:41

44. Ps 18:13
45. 1 Cor 15:3
46. Mt 7:18

feel, had to be done in order that the enemies of grace[47] may
know that without grace man's heart is incapable of thinking
good thoughts, that its capacity to do so comes from God:[48]
the good thought is God's inspiration, not the heart's offspring. You therefore, if you hear his voice, will no longer be
ignorant of whence it comes or whither it goes,[49] because
you will know it proceeds from God and goes to the heart.
But make sure that the word which goes forth from the
mouth of God does not return to him empty, see that it
prospers and accomplishes all those things for which he sent
it,[50] so that you too will be able to say: "The grace of God in
me has not been fruitless."[51] Happy the man who has the
Word for an inseparable companion who is always accessible,
whose delightful conversation is an unceasing pleasure that
frees him at all times from the flesh's bothersome vices, and
enables him to use his time profitably in a wicked age.[52] He
shall be neither wearied nor troubled, since, according to
Scripture, no matter what happens to the righteous man, it
will not make him sad.[53]

IV. 8. It seems to me that he appears in the guise of a
mighty Father of a family or sovereign ruler to those whose
hearts are high as they approach him,[54] who, filled with
magnanimous courage because of greater liberty of spirit and
purity of conscience, love to dare what is above the common
measure. These are restless men, eager to penetrate the deeper mysteries, to grasp sublimer truths, to strive for what is
more perfect, not so much in the physical as in the spiritual
order. Because of the grandeur of their faith these are considered worthy of experiencing all fullness; in all the treas-
ure-houses of wisdom there is nothing from which the Lord,
the God who knows all things,[55] would think of turning these

47. An allusion to Abelard and his followers whom Bernard compares to
Pelagius in his letter "On the Errors of Abelard." Ep 9:23f; Trans Bruno S.
James, *Letters* (Burns Oates: London, 1953), Letter 240.

48. 2 Cor 3:5   52. Eph 5:16
49. Jn 3:8   53. Prov 12:21
50. Is 55:11   54. Ps 63:7
51. 1 Cor 15:10   55. 1 Sam 2:3

men away; avid for truth as they are, and their motives free
of vanity. Moses was such a man, and he dared to say to God:
"If I have found favor in your sight show me yourself."[56]
Such was Philip, who begged that the Father be shown to
him and his fellow-disciples.[57] Thomas, too, was such a man,
for he refused to believe unless he touched with his hand the
spear-wound in Christ's side.[58] This meant indeed a lack of
faith, but it was a superb consequence of his greatness of
soul. Again there was David, who said to God: "My heart has
said to you: 'I have been searching for you;' Lord, I do seek
your face."[59] Men of this kind undertake great deeds because
they are themselves great; and what they undertake they
achieve, in accord with the promise which runs: "Every place
on which the sole of your foot treads shall be yours."[60] Great
faith deserves great rewards; and if you step out with trust
where the good things of the Lord are to be found, you will
possess them.

9. God spoke to Moses face to face;[61] not by riddles and
images was he privileged to see the Lord, but openly; whereas
the Lord points out that he appears to other prophets only in
vision, and speaks to them in dreams. Philip too received his
heart's desire[62] when shown the Father in the Son, in that
immediate reply of Christ: "Philip, he who has seen me, has
seen the Father;"[63] and, "I am in the Father and the Father
is in me."[64] Thomas, according to his heart's desire[65] and the
protestation he had made, was permitted to touch him.[66]
And what of David? Does he not show that he has not been
entirely deprived of his wish when he says that he will not
give sleep to his eyes nor slumber to his eyelids until he finds
a place for the Lord? [67] To great men like these the Bridegroom will come in his greatness; he will perform mighty
deeds with them,[68] sending out his light and his truth,[69] lead-

56. Ex 33:13
57. Jn 14:8
58. Jn 20:25
59. Ps 26:8
60. Deut 11:24
61. Num 12:8
62. Ps 36:4

63. Jn 14:9
64. Jn 14:10
65. Ps 20:3
66. Jn 20:27
67. Ps 131:4-5
68. Ps 125:2
69. Ps 42:3

ing them on and directing them to his holy mountain and the tent where he dwells. Any one of these men can say: "He who is mighty has done great things for me."[70] His eyes will see the king in his beauty[71] going before him into the beautiful places of the desert, to the flowering roses and the lilies of the valley,[72] to gardens where delights abound and streams run from the fountains, where storerooms are filled with delightful things and the odors of perfume, till last of all he makes his way to the privacy of the bedchamber.

10. There you have the treasures of wisdom and knowledge hidden where the Bridegroom dwells,[73] and there the pastures of life, prepared for the nourishment of men seeking holiness. "Blessed is the man who has fulfilled his desire from them."[74] But let him be given at least this warning: not to wish to possess for himself alone goods that can suffice for the many. And perhaps for this reason after all these things the Bridegroom is described as appearing in a shepherd's guise, to provide a guideline to the man who has received the task of feeding a flock that contains so many of the ordinary people who are unable to understand those truths by their own efforts, just as sheep will not attempt to go out to the fields unless led by a shepherd. The bride thoughtfully takes note of this, and asks to be shown where he eats, where he rests in the midday heat,[75] being ready, as may be gathered from her remark, both to be fed and to give food, as his helper and under his direction. She does not think it safe for the flock to wander far from their chief Shepherd because of wolves on the prowl, especially those who come to us in the clothing of sheep;[76] and hence her endeavor to eat in the same pastures with him and rest in the same shady places. And she gives the reason: "Lest I begin to wander after the flocks of your companions."[77] These are they who want to appear to be friends of the Bridegroom, but are not; and though their concern is to feed their own flocks rather than

70. Lk 1:49
71. Is 33:17
72. Song 2:1
73. Col 2:3
74. Ps 126:5
75. Song 1:6
76. Mt 7:15
77. Song 1:6

his, they cunningly spread the rumor: "Look, here is the Christ, look, he is there,"[78] and so seduce many people whom they lead away from the flocks of Christ and join to their own. So far I have been dealing with the obvious meaning of the words. But for the spiritual meaning that lies hidden beneath, you must await a new sermon. This will depend on whatever our Lord Jesus Christ, the Church's Bridegroom, will be pleased to impart to me in his mercy and through your prayers. He is God, blessed for ever. Amen.[79]

---

78. Mt 24:5; Mk 13:21   79. Rom 1:25

SERMON 33

ENDS TO BE PURSUED—THE MYSTICAL NOONTIDE—
TEMPTATIONS TO BE AVOIDED

"TELL ME, YOU WHOM MY SOUL LOVES, where you pasture your flock, where you make it to lie down at noon."[1] But another voice, that of Job, says: "Tell me why you judge me like this? "[2] This man does not complain of the judgement, he merely queries its cause, seeking to gain knowledge from his afflictions rather than be destroyed by them. Still another man made a similar request: "Make your ways known to me, O Lord, teach me your paths."[3] What he means by paths he reveals in another text: "He leads me in the path of righteousness."[4] Therefore the man who longs for God does not cease to seek these three things, righteousness, judgment, and the place where the Bridegroom dwells in glory:[5] the path in which he walks,[6] the wariness with which he walks, and the home to which he walks. About this home the Prophet says: "One thing have I asked of the Lord, that will I seek after: that I may dwell in the house of the Lord;"[7] and again: "O Lord, I love the beauty of your house, and the place where your glory dwells."[8] Of the remaining two he says: "Righteousness and judgment are the preparation of your throne."[9] The man who is in earnest rightly seeks these three things, since they are

1. Song 1:6
2. Job 10:2
3. Ps 24:4
4. Ps 22:3
5. Ps 25:8

6. Ps 142:8
7. Ps 26:4
8. Ps 25:8
9. Ps 88:15

the throne of God and the preparation of his throne. By a special privilege of the bride, all these gifts beautifully and equally concur in the crowning of her virtues: she receives loveliness from the habit of righteousness, prudence from her knowledge of judgments, and chastity from her desire for the presence or glory of her Bridegroom. Such are the gifts that are fitting for a bride of the Lord: beauty, knowledge and chastity. Therefore the petition which I have placed last concerns the Bridegrooms's dwelling-place. She asks him whom her soul loves to reveal to her where he pastures his flock, where he makes it lie down at noon.

2. But take note in the first place how exquisitely she distinguishes spiritual love from carnal desire, when, in her wish to draw her Beloved's attention by her affection rather than by his name, she does not say simply, "whom I love," but "O you whom my soul loves," thereby indicating that her love is spiritual.

II. Consider carefully then, what it is that gives her so much pleasure in the place of pasture. Nor must you overlook the reference to the hour of noon, nor above all that she looks for a place where he who feeds the flock also lies down, a sign of great security. It would seem that the expression "lie down" is used to indicate that in this place there is no need to stand and keep watch for the safety of the flock, since the flock freely wanders in the meadows while the shepherd lies down and rests in the shade. Happy the place in which the sheep move to and fro at will,[10] and no one to frighten them! [11] Who will grant that you and I together may be fed on the mountains, along with the ninety-nine sheep who, we read, were left there when their shepherd went down for the one who had strayed? [12] It was because he had left them in a safe place that he was able to undertake a long journey without hesitation, and hence he could afford to lie down securely. What can the bride do but yearn for that place of rest, of security, of exultation, of wonder, of overwhelming joy. But

10. Jn 10:9
11. Nahum 2:11

12. Mt 18:12

alas! unhappy me, far from it as I am, and saluting it from afar, the very memory of it causes me to weep with the affection expressed by those exiles: "By the waters of Babylon, there we sat down and wept, when we remembered Zion."[13] Let me cry out both with the bride and with the Prophet: "Praise your God, O Zion! for he strengthened the bars of your gates; he blesses your sons within you."[14] Who would not be filled with vehement longing to be fed in that place, on account of its peace, on account of its richness, on account of its super-abundance? There one experiences neither fear not distaste, nor any want. Paradise is a safe dwelling-place, the Word is sweet nourishment, eternity is wealth beyond calculation.

3. I too have the Word, but the Word made flesh; and the Truth is set before me, but in the sacrament. An angel is nourished with the richness of the wheat,[15] is satiated with the pure grain; but in this life I have to be content with the husk, as it were, of the sacrament, with the bran of the flesh, with the chaff of the letter, with the veil of the faith. And these are the kind of things whose taste brings death[16] unless they are seasoned in some degree with the first fruits of the Spirit.[17] I shall surely find death in the pot if it be not sweetened with the meal of the Prophet.[18] For without the Spirit the sacrament is received as a judgment,[19] the flesh is of no avail,[20] the letter kills,[21] and faith is dead.[22] It is the Spirit who must give these things life if I am to find life in them.[23] But no matter how great the effusion of the Spirit that enriches these,[24] the husk of the sacrament is not received with the same pleasure as the fat of the wheat, nor is faith the equivalent of vision,[25] nor memory of presence, nor time of eternity, nor a face of its reflection, nor the image of God[26] of a slave's condition.[27] As far as all these are concern-

13. Ps 136:1
14. Ps 147:1-2
15. Ps 80:17
16. Job 6:6 (Douai)
17. Rom 8:23
18. 2 Kings 4:40-41
19. 1 Cor 11:29
20. Jn 6:64

21. 2 Cor 3:6
22. Jas 2:20
23. Jn 6:64
24. Ps 147:14
25. 2 Cor 5:7
26. Col 1:15
27. Phil 2:7

ed, faith is the source of my riches, my intellect is a pauper. Can there indeed be equal pleasure in understanding and in faith, when the latter is the source of merit, the former the reward? You see then that the foods are as different as the places where they are eaten are distant from each other; and as the heavens are raised far above the earth,[28] so those who dwell there enjoy an abundance of greater gifts.

4. Let us make haste then my sons, let us make haste to a place that is safer, to a pasture that is sweeter, to a land that is richer and more fertile. Let us make haste to a place where we may dwell without fear, where we may abound and never want, where we may feast and never weary. For while passing judgment tranquilly on all things,[29] O Lord of hosts, you feed in security and with fairness all who dwell in that place, you who are at the same time the Lord of armies and shepherd of sheep.

III. You feed your flock therefore, and at the same time make them rest, but not here below. For you were standing that time you looked down from heaven at one of your little sheep, Stephen, when he was surrounded by wolves here on earth.[30] And so I beseech you, "show me where you pasture your flock, where you make it lie down at noon,"[31] that is, the whole day long: for that noon is a day that knows no evening. Consequently, "a day in your courts is better than a thousand elsewhere,"[32] because its sun never sets. But perhaps it had a sunrise, when that sanctified day first dawned upon us through the tender mercy of our God, in which the Rising Sun visited us from heaven.[33] Truly then "we received your mercy, O God, in the midst of your temple,"[34] when, as you rose out of the shadow of death,[35] the morning light shone over us,[36] and in the dawn we saw the glory of God.[37] How many prophets and kings desired to see this, and did not see it! [38] Why should this have been

28. Is 55:9
29. Wis 12:18
30. Acts 7:55
31. Song 1:6
32. Ps 83:11
33. Lk 1:78

34. Ps 47:10
35. Ps 22:4
36. Is 9:2
37. Ex 16:7
38. Lk 10:24

unless because it was night, and that long-awaited dawn on which mercy had been promised had not yet come? Hence that prayer of the Psalmist: "Let me hear in the morning of your mercy, for in you I put my trust."[39]

5. The dawning of this day began when the Sun of righteousness was announced to the earth by the Archangel Gabriel; when the Virgin conceived God in her womb by the power of the Holy Spirit, and still remaining a virgin gave birth to him;[40] and it continued as long as he was seen on earth and lived among men.[41] For during all that time only a feeble light, just like the dusk of dawn, was visible, so that almost the whole world failed to realize that day-time for mankind had come. For "if they had known, they would never have crucified the Lord of glory."[42] Even the small group of disciples had been told: "up to now you have but little light,"[43] because it was still only the dawn, and the beginning, or rather a token light of the coming day, for the Sun concealed his rays rather than shed them over the earth. Paul too said that "the night is far gone, the day is at hand,"[44] signifying that the light was as yet so dim that he preferred to say the day was approaching than that it had come. But when did he say this? He said it when the Sun, after its return from beneath the earth, had ascended to the heights of heaven. With what greater reason might he have said it when "the likeness of sinful flesh"[45] still covered that dawn like a dense cloud, since his body resembled ours in its liability to all manner of suffering, to which neither the bitterness of death nor the shame of the cross was wanting? With what greater reason, I insist, might he have said it when the light was so minimal, so meagre, that it seemed a reflection of the dawning rather than of the Sun itself.

39. Ps 142:8
40. Lk 1:26-38
41. Bar 3:38
42. 1 Cor 2:8
43. Jn 12:35. St Bernard treats the word *modicum* as an adjective in this text. It is normally treated as an adverb.
44. Rom 13:12
45. Rom 8:3

6. The dawn, then, and a quite clouded one at that, was the whole life of Christ upon earth, which remained obscure until he died and rose again, to put the dawn to flight by the clearer light of his glorious presence. With the coming of sunrise, night was swallowed up in victory.[46] And so we are told that "very early on the Sunday morning, just after sunrise, they came to the tomb."[47] Surely it was morning when the sun had risen? But the resurrection endowed it with a new beauty, with a more serene light than usual, because "even though we once knew him according to the flesh, we know him thus no longer."[48] The Prophet wrote: "He is robed in majesty; the Lord is robed, he is girded with strength,"[49] because he shook off the flesh's frailties like cloudlets and put on the robe of glory.[50] Since then the Sun is risen indeed, and has gradually poured down its rays over the earth;[51] its light has begun to appear increasingly clearer, its warmth to be more perceptible.

IV. However, even though it increases in warmth and strength, though it multiplies and extends its rays over the whole course of our mortal lives — for it will be with us even to the end of the world[52] — it will not attain to its noontide splendor, nor be seen here below in that fullness which it will exhibit hereafter, at least to those who are destined for the privilege of this vision. O true noontide, fullness of warmth and light, trysting-place of the sun; noontide that blots out shadows, that dries up marshes, that banishes evil odors! O perpetual solstice, day that will never decline to evening! [53] O noontide light, with your springtime freshness, your summer-like gracefulness, your autumnal fruitfulness and — let me not seem to omit it — your winter of quiescence and leisure! Although, if you prefer it, winter alone of these is over and gone.[54] Show me this place, she said, where there is

46. 1 Cor 15:54
47. Mk 16:2
48. 2 Cor 5:16
49. Ps 92:1
50. Sir 45:9

51. Hab 3:11 — according to an old version
52. Mt 28:20
53. Lk 24:29
54. Song 2:11

so much brightness and peace and fullness, so that, just as Jacob while still in this life saw the Lord face to face and his soul was saved;[55] or as Moses saw him, not by means of images and obscure sayings or through dreams like some of the other Prophets, but in a manner unrivalled and beyond the experience of all others, known only to himself and God;[56] or as Isaiah, after the eyes of his heart had been opened, saw him seated on a high and exalted throne;[57] or just as Paul, rapt into Paradise, heard words that he could not explain and saw his Lord Jesus Christ,[58] so may I too merit the ecstatic grace of contemplating you in your light[59] and beauty,[60] as you generously feed your flock and make them rest securely.

7. Here on earth too, you feed your sheep but not to their full satisfaction; nor is it possible for you to rest, you must stand and keep watch because of the terrors of the night.[61] Alas! there is neither clear light, nor a full repast, nor a safe place to stay; and therefore. "Tell me where you pasture your flock, where you make it lie down at noon." You call me blessed when I hunger and thirst for righteousness.[62] But what is this in comparison with the happiness of those who are filled with the good things of your house,[63] who feast and rejoice in the sight of their Lord, who are jubilant with joy? [64] But if I do suffer for the sake of righteousness you nevertheless declare me blessed.[65] To eat is pleasurable, but one does not eat in security if fear be present. To suffer and feast simultaneously is surely a bitter pleasure? All things here below fall short of perfection, many are beyond the reach of my desires, and nothing is safe. When will you fill me with the joy of your presence? [66] Lord, I do seek your face.[67] Your face is the noontide. "Tell me where you pasture your flock, where you make it lie down at noon." I

55. Gen 32:30
56. Num 12:9
57. Is 6:1
58. 2 Cor 12:4
59. Is 33:17
60. Ps 35:10
61. Song 3:8

62. Mt 5:6
63. Ps 64:5
64. Ps 67:4
65. 1 Pet 3:14
66. Ps 15:11
67. Ps 26:8

know well enough where you pasture it without lying down; tell me where you pasture it and make it lie down. I am not unaware of your accustomed pasturage at other times; but I do wish to know where that pasturage is at noon. For during my time in this life, in this my place of pilgrimage,[68] I am accustomed to feed and be fed under your protection, in the Law and the Prophets and the Psalms, in the meadows of the Gospels;[69] I have found rest too in the company of the apostles; and often I have done my utmost to beg food for myself and those belonging to me from the doings of the saints, from their words and writings. More often, however, because this was closer to hand, I have eaten the bread of pain[70] and drunk the wine of sorrow,[71] "my tears have been my food day and night, while men say to me continually: 'Where is your God?' "[72] My one hope is your table — "for you have prepared a table before me against them that afflict me"[73] — from which I receive by favor of your mercy all that I need for refreshment when I feel sad and inwardly disturbed. This is the pasture that I have known and frequented in following you as my shepherd;[74] but tell me also about those secret places that I do not know.

V. 8. There are too, those other shepherds who say they are companions of yours but are not,[75] shepherds whose flocks feed on lands filled with a deadly food; there they are fed neither with you nor by you, and I have not entered their fields nor even approached them. These are the men who say: "Look, here is the Christ," or, "Look, he is there,"[76] as they make promises of pastures more rich in wisdom and knowledge; people believe them and multitudes flock to them, to be made twice as fit for hell as they themselves are.[77] Why this, if not because they have neither noontide nor light clear enough to see the truth in its purity? They easily accept

68. Ps 118:54
69. Lk 24:44
70. Ps 126:2
71. Ps 59:5
72. Ps 41:4

73. Ps 22:5
74. Jer 17:16 (Vulgate)
75. Rev 2:2
76. Mk 13:21
77. Mt 23:15

what is false because of its likeness to the truth, since in the dusk it is far from easy to distinguish it from the truth, especially as "stolen waters are sweet and bread tastes better when eaten in secret."[78] Hence my request that you tell me "where you pasture your flock, where you make it lie down at noon," that is, in the clear light, lest I be seduced and begin to wander after the flocks of your companions, because they are wanderers, devoid of the certain truth that gives stability. Though always learning, they never attain to knowledge of the truth.[79] Such are the comments of the bride on the varied and vain doctrines of the philosophers and heretics.

9. I feel, however, that not alone because of these, but because of the deceits of invisible powers, spirits whose work is seduction, who lie in ambush,[80] "fitting their arrows to the the string to shoot in the dark at the upright in heart,"[81] because of these, I say emphatically, I feel that we also must yearn for that noontide, so that in its clear light we may detect the tricks of the devil, and be able to distinguish with ease between our angel and that angel of Satan[82] who "disguises himself as an angel of light."[83] For we cannot defend ourselves from the attack of the noontide devil[84] except with the aid of noontide light. I believe that he is styled the noontide devil because some of those wicked spirits, who, because of their obstinate and darkened wills are like the night, even perpetual night, yet, for the purpose of deceiving men, can become bright as day, even as noon. In this they follow their prince, who, not content with being equal to God,[85] opposes and exalts himself above everything that is called or worshipped as a god.[86] Hence when this kind of noontide devil sets out to tempt a man, there is no chance whatever of parrying him; he will tempt and overthrow his victim by suggesting what appears to be good, by persuading him, un-

78. Prov 9:17
79. 2 Tim 3:7
80. Ps 9:29
81. Ps 10:3
82. 2 Cor 12:7

83. 2 Cor 11:14
84. Ps 90:6
85. Phil 2:6
86. 2 Thess 2:4

suspecting and unprepared as he is, to commit evil under the guise of good, unless the Sun from heaven[87] shines into his heart with noontide brightness. The tempter really appears like noon, clothed in a certain splendor, when he comes with the suggestion of an apparently greater good.

10. How often, for example, does he not persuade a monk to anticipate the hour of rising, and mock at him as he sleeps in choir while his brothers pray! How often does he not suggest that fasts be prolonged, until a man is so weak that he is useless for the service of God! How often, in envy of a man's fervor in community life, does he not persuade him to live as a hermit in order to achieve greater perfection, until the unhappy man finally discovers how true that saying is which he had read to no purpose: "Woe to him who is alone, for when he falls he has none to lift him up! "[88] How often has he not inspired a man to work harder than necessary at manual labor, until exhaustion makes him unfit for the other regular observances! How many has he not won over to indiscreet indulgence in physical exercises which the Apostle considers of little value,[89] and sapped their spiritual stamina! And lastly, you yourselves will know how some—to their shame I say it[90]—were at first so filled with ardor in all they undertook that they could not be restrained, but who in the end became so indolent as to merit the reproach of the Apostle: "Having begun with the Spirit, are you now ending with the flesh? "[91] What a degrading alliance they have made with those bodies on which they had previously waged a cruel warfare! For shame! those who once stubbornly refused what was necessary now insistently demand what is superfluous! And if they remain so invincibly obstinate, troubling with their indiscreet fasts and erratic behavior those with whom they are bound to dwell harmoniously in the home,[92] I fail to see how they think they can maintain a loving union with them. They seem to me to have made this possibility more remote. Wise in their own eyes,[93] and determined to

87. Lk 1:78
88. Eccles 4:10
89. 1 Tim 4:8
90. 1 Cor 6:5

91. Gal 3:3
92. Ps 67:7
93. Is 5:21

accept neither advice nor command, let them reflect on what answer they shall give, not to me but to him who says: "Rebellion is as the sin of witchcraft, and stubbornness like the crime of idolatry."[94] Just before this he had said that "to obey is better than sacrifice, and to listen better than to offer the fat of rams,"[95] the offering of self-willed abstinence. Hence the Lord says through the Prophet: "Do I eat the flesh of bulls, or drink the blood of goats? "[96] to show that he will not accept fasting from the proud and the unclean.

11. My fear at the moment is, that while condemning these erring monks I may seem to encourage the gluttonous, that what I speak as a remedy for the former may be interpreted by the latter to their peril.

VI.   Therefore let both sides know that there are four kinds of temptation, described by the Prophet as follows: "His truth will surround you with a shield: you will not fear the terror of the night, nor the arrow that flies by day, nor the pestilence that stalks in the darkness, nor invasion, nor the noonday devil."[97] You others should pay attention too, because I trust that this will be of profit to everyone. All of us who have been converted to the Lord have felt and still feel the truth of what Scripture says: "My son, if you come forward to serve the Lord, stand in fear, and prepare your soul for temptation."[98] Our common experience tells us that it is fear which disturbs us at the beginning of our conversion, fear of that dismaying picture we form for ourselves of the strict life and unwonted austerities we are about to embrace. This is called a nocturnal fear,[99] either because in scripture adversity is usually represented by darkness, or because the reward for which we are prepared to suffer adversity is not yet revealed to us. For if we could see the dawn of that day in whose light we should perceive the rewards as well as the trials, our desire of the rewards would entirely obliterate fear, since in the clear light it would be apparent that "the suffer-

94. 1 Sam 15:23
95. 1 Sam 15:22
96. Ps 49:13

97. Ps 90:5-6
98. Sir 2:1
99. Song 3:8; Ps 90:5

ings we now endure bear no comparison with the splendor, as yet unrevealed, which is in store for us."[100] But since this is now hidden from our eyes,[101] and darkness reigns about us, we are subjected to "the terror of the night," and face with dread the endurance of present evils in place of the blessings we do not see. Beginners on the way to God, therefore, must in particular watch and pray against this first temptation,[102] or they will be suddenly overcome by pusillanimity of spirit as by a storm,[103] and unfortunately recoil from the good work they have begun.

12. But when this temptation has been conquered, let us take up arms against the praises of men, who find matter for their compliments in the praiseworthy life we lead. Otherwise we shall be exposed to wounds from "the arrow that flies by day,"[104] which is vainglory. For fame is said to fly, and that by day, because it springs from works done in the light. But if this temptation is blown away like the empty air, we shall be confronted with a stronger one, with an offer of the riches and honors of the world, for the man who despises praise may hanker for position. Our Lord himself experienced this order of temptation: after the suggestion that he pitch himself from the temple for the sake of mere vanity, all kingdoms of the world were shown to him and offered to him.[105] And you, following the Lord's example, must refuse what is offered. If not, you will become victims of "the pestilence that stalks about in the darkness,"[106] which is hypocrisy. For this has its source in ambition, its dwelling in darkness: for it conceals what it really is and pretends to be what it is not. Active at all times, it retains the appearance of piety as a mask to hide behind,[107] and barters it virtue to purchase honors.

13. The last temptation is that of the noontide devil, whose task is to lay ambushes for the perfect, those persons of tried virtue who have survived all other temptations: pleasures,

100. Rom 8:18
101. Lk 19:42
102. Mt 26:41
103. Ps 54:9
104. Ps 90:6
105. Mt 4:8
106. Ps 90:6
107. 2 Tim 3:5

applause, honors. What further weapons has the tempter with which to fight openly against men of this kind? But what he does not dare openly he will attempt in disguise; and when he is aware that a man will abominate what he sees to be patently evil, he tries to seduce him by means of a counterfeit good. Those who can say with the Apostle: "We are not ignorant of his designs,"[108] will be all the more careful to avoid that trap the more they advance. This is why Mary was perturbed by the angel's greeting:[109] unless I am mistaken she suspected some deceit; nor would Joshua receive the angel as a friend until he was sure he was a friend.[110] For, like a man with experience of the plotting of the noontide devil, he enquires whether he is for him or for his enemies. Wearied at the oars, with a hostile wind lashing their ship, the apostles too cried out with fear when they saw the Lord walking over the sea, and took him for a ghost.[111] Was not this cry of fear a sign that they clearly thought him to be the noontide devil? And you recall how Scripture says: "About the fourth watch of the night he came to them, walking on the sea."[112] In the fourth or final stage, then, let us beware of this temptation. The greater the perfection a man may seem to have attained,[113] the more he must be convinced of the need to watch vigilantly for the noontide devil. He who was the true noontide made himself known to the disciples with the words: "It is I, have no fear,"[114] and their mistrust of this strange phenomenon was dispelled. And whenever this painted falsehood tries to take us unawares, may the true Noontide, shining from the heavens, send forth his light and his truth even to us;[115] let him divide the light from the darkness,[116] lest we be numbered by the Prophet among those "who put darkness for light and light for darkness."[117]

VII. 14. If you are not worn out by the length of this sermon, I shall try to apply these four temptations in due

108. 2 Cor 2:11
109. Lk 2:29
110. Josh 5:13ff.
111. Mk 6:48-49
112. Mk 6:48

113. 1 Cor 10:12
114. Mk 6:50
115. Ps 42:3
116. Gen 1:4
117. Is 5:20

order to the Church, and Body of Christ.[118] I shall try to be as brief as possible. Consider the Church of the early centuries: was she not most bitterly afflicted by "the terror of the night"? For it was surely night when anyone who killed the saints thought he was doing a service to God.[119] When this temptation had been overcome and the tempest stilled, she became illustrious, and in accord with the promise made to her, soon occupied a position of pre-eminence in the world.[120] Disappointed by this frustration, the enemy craftily changed his tactics from "the terror of the night" to "the arrow that flies by day,"by which he would now wound the Church's members.[121] Vain and ambitious men came into power, intent on making a name for themselves;[122] they abandoned the Church, their mother, and for long afflicted her with diverse and perverse doctrines. This scourge was in turn repelled by the wisdom of the saints, as the first had been by the endurance of the martyrs.

15. The times in which we live are, by the mercy of God, free from these two evils, but are obviously contaminated by "the pestilence that stalks in darkness." Woe to this generation because of the "yeast of the Pharisees — that is, their hypocrisy,"[123] if that can be called hypocrisy which is so prevalent that it cannot be hidden, and so impudent that it does not want to be! Today a foul corruption permeates the whole body of the Church, all the more incurable the more widespread it becomes, all the more dangerous the more it penetrates inwardly. For if a heretic were to rebel in public, he would be cast out to wither;[124] if an enemy were to attack her violently, she could perhaps take refuge from him.[125] But as things stand, whom will she cast out, or from whom will she hide herself? Everyone is a friend, everyone an enemy; everyone is indispensable, everyone an adversary; everyone is a member of the household, but not one is peace-loving; all are neighbors to each other, but all insist on their own way.[126] Called to be ministers of Christ, they are servants of

118. Col 1:24
119. Jn 16:2
120. Is 60:14-16
121. Acts 12:1
122. Gen 11:4

123. Lk 12:1; Mt 16:6
124. Jn 15:6
125. Ps 54:13
126. 1 Cor 13:5

Antichrist. Promoted to honors over the possessions of the Lord, they pay the Lord no honor. Hence that bogus splendor that you see every day, that theatrical apparel, that regal pomp. Hence the gold embossments on their bridles, on their saddles, on their spurs: spurs that carry more costly adornment than their altars. Hence the banquet-laden tables with their glittering glass-ware; the carousing and drunkenness;[127] the music of harp and lyre and flute; the vats overflowing with wine, storehouses crammed to the doors, and a surplus to be stowed elsewhere.[128] Hence the painted casks, the packed money-bags. Such is the goal they aim at when they seek a prelacy in the Church, to be deans or archdeacons, bishops or archbishops. Nor do these come to them by way of merit, but through this agency that works in the darkness.

16. Long ago the following prophecy was made, and now we see its fulfilment: "See how in peace my bitterness is most bitter."[129] It was bitter at first in the slaying of the martyrs, more bitter in later times in the struggle with the heretics, but now most bitter of all in the corrupt morals of the members of the household. She cannot drive them away nor fly from them, so strong have they grown, so numerous beyond counting.[130] This sickness of the Church is deeply rooted and incurable,[131] which is why that during peace her bitterness is most bitter. But what is the nature of this peace? It is a peace that is not peace.[132] She has peace from the pagans, peace from the heretics, but not from her own sons. And so today we hear her grief-laden words: "Sons have I reared and brought up, but they have rebelled against me."[133] They have rebelled, they have dishonored me, by their shameful lives, their shameful gains, their shameful trafficking, by all the intrigue that is perpetuated in the darkness. Nothing remains but for the noontide devil to appear in our midst, to seduce those who still abide in Christ, who remain faithful to his truth.[134] For he has already swallowed up the

127. Rom 13:13
128. Ps 143:13
129. Is 38:17
130. Ps 39:6

131. Jer 30:12
132. Jer 6:14
133. Is 1:2
134. Job 2:9

rivers of the wise and the streams of the powerful; he is even confident that Jordan will flow into his mouth,[135] that he will devour the humble and the simple who are still in the Church. For he is Antichrist, who pretends that he is not only the day but the very noon, who "exalts himself against every so-called god or object of worship,"[136] whom "the Lord Jesus will slay with the breath of his mouth,"[137] whom he will destroy with the light of his coming, because he is the true and eternal Noontide, the Bridegroom and defender of the Church; he is God, blessed for ever. Amen.[138]

135. Job 40:21-23
136. 2 Thess 2:4

137. 2 Thess 2:8
138. Rom 1:25

SERMON 34

TRUE HUMILITY

"IF YOU DO NOT KNOW, O fairest among women, go forth and follow the flocks of your companions and pasture your kids beside the shepherds' tents."[1] Of old, taking advantage of the familiar friendship that had developed between him and God, that holy man Moses so longed for the great favor of seeing him that he said to God: "If I have found favor in your sight, show yourself to me."[2] Instead of that he received a vision of an inferior kind, but one which nevertheless would help him to attain eventually to the one for which he longed. Following the guileless urging of their hearts, the sons of Zebedee also dared to ask for a great favor, but they too were directed back to the way by which they must ascend to higher things.[3] In similar fashion now, when the bride seems to demand a very special concession, she is rebuffed with an answer that, though harsh, is meant to be helpful and trustworthy. Anyone who strives forward toward the spiritual heights must have a lowly opinion of himself; because when he is raised above himself he may lose his grip on himself, unless through true humility, he has a firm hold on himself. It is only when humility warrants it that great graces can be obtained, hence the one to be enriched by them is first humbled by correction that by his humility he may merit them. And so when you perceive that

1. Song 1:7
2. Ex 33:13

3. Mt 20:21

160

you are being humiliated, look on it as the sign of a sure guarantee that grace is on the way.[4] Just as the heart is puffed up with pride before its destruction, so it is humiliated before being honored.[5] You read in Scripture of these two modes of acting, how the Lord resists the proud and gives his grace to the humble.[6] Did he not decide to reward his servant Job with generous blessings after the outstanding victory in which his great patience was put to the severest test? He was prepared for blessings by the many searching trials that humbled him.[7]

II. 2. But it matters little if we willingly accept the humiliation which comes from God himself, if we do not maintain a similar attitude when he humiliates us by means of another. And I want you to take note of a wonderful instance of this in St David, that time when he was cursed by a servant and paid no heed to the repeated insults, so sensitive was he to the influence of grace. He merely said: "What has this to do with me and you, O sons of Zeruiah?"[8] Truly a man after God's own heart,[9] who decided to be angry with the one who would avenge him rather than with the one who reviled him. Hence he could say with an easy conscience: "If I have repaid with evils those who offended me, let me rightly fall helpless before my enemies."[10] He would not allow them to silence this evil-spoken scoundrel; to him the curses were gain. He even added: "The Lord has sent him to curse David."[11] A man altogether after God's own heart, since the judgment he passed was from the heart of God. While the wicked tongue raged against him, his mind was intent on discovering the hidden purpose of God. The voice of the reviler sounded in his ears, but in his heart he disposed himself for blessings. Was God in the mouth of the blasphemer? God forbid! But he made use of it to humiliate David. And this was not hidden from the Prophet, to whom God had

4. Ps 85:17
5. Prov 16:18
6. Jas 4:6
7. Job 1:8; 2:3

8. 2 Sam 16:10
9. Acts 13:22
10. Ps 7:5
11. 2 Sam 16:10

manifested the unpredictable secrets of his wisdom.[12] Hence he says: "It was good for me that you humiliated me, that I might learn your statutes."[13]

3. Do you see that humility makes us righteous? I say humility and not humiliation. How many are humiliated who are not humble! There are some who meet humiliation with rancor, some with patience, some again with cheerfulness. The first kind are culpable, the second are innocent, the last just. Innocence is indeed a part of justice, but only the humble possess it perfectly. He who can say: "It was good for me that you humiliated me," is truly humble. The man who endures it unwillingly cannot say this; still less the man who murmurs. To neither of these do I promise grace on the grounds of being humiliated, although the two are vastly different from each other, since the one possesses his own soul in his patience,[14] while the other perishes in his murmuring. For even if only one of them does merit anger, neither of them merits grace, because it is not to the humiliated but to the humble that God gives grace.[15] But he is humble who turns humiliation into humility, and he is the one who says to God: "It was good for me that you humiliated me." What is merely endured with patience is good for nobody, it is an obvious embarrassment. On the other hand we know that "God loves a cheerful giver."[16] Hence even when we fast we are told to anoint our head with oil and wash our face,[17] that our good work might be seasoned with spiritual joy and our holocaust made fat.[18] For it is the possession of a joyful and genuine humility that alone enables us to receive grace. But the humility that is due to necessity or constraint, that we find in the patient man who keeps his self-possession,[19] cannot win God's favor because of the accompanying sadness, although it will preserve his life because of patience. Since he does not accept humiliation spontaneously or willingly, one cannot apply to such a person the scriptural com-

12. Ps 50:8
13. Ps 118:71
14. Lk 21:19
15. Jas 4:6

16. 2 Cor 9:7
17. Mt 6:17
18. Ps 19:4
19. Lk 21:19

mendation that the humble man may glory in his exaltation.[20]

III.   4. If you wish for an example of a humble man glorying with all due propriety, and truly worthy of glory, take Paul when he says that gladly will he glory in his weaknesses that the power of Christ may dwell within him.[21] He does not say that he will bear his weaknesses patiently, but he will even glory in them, and that willingly, thus proving that to him it is good that he is humiliated,[22] and that it is not sufficient that one keep his self-possession by patience when he is humbled; to receive grace one must embrace humiliation willingly. You may take as a general rule that everyone who humbles himself will be exalted.[23] It is significant that not every kind of humility is to be exalted, but that which the will embraces; it must be free of compulsion or sadness.[24] Nor on the contrary must everyone who is exalted be humiliated, but only he who exalts himself, who pursues a course of vain display. Therefore it is not the one who is humiliated who will be exalted, but he who voluntarily humiliates himself; it is merited by this attitude of will. Even suppose that the occasion of humiliation is supplied by another, by means of insults, damages or sufferings, the victim who determines to accept all these for God's sake with a quiet, joyful conscience, cannot properly be said to be humiliated by anyone but himself.

5. But where does this take me? I feel that your endurance of this protracted discussion on humility and patience is an exercise in patience; but let us return to the place from which we digressed. All that I have said developed from the answer in which the Bridegroom decided that the bride's aspiration toward lofty experiences should be restrained, not in order to confound her, but to provide an occasion for more solid, more deep humility, by which her capacity and worthiness for the sublimer experiences she desired would be increased.

20. Jas 1:9
21. 2 Cor 12:9
22. Ps 118:71
23. Lk 14:11
24. 2 Cor 9:7

However, we are but at the beginning of this present verse, so with your permission, I shall postpone discussion of it to another sermon, lest the Bridegroom's words be recounted or heard with weariness. May our Lord Jesus Christ, who is blessed for ever,[25] avert this from his servants. Amen.

25. Rom 1:25

SERMON 35

THE BRIDEGROOM REPROVES THE BRIDE—TWO KINDS OF IGNORANCE

"IF YOU DO NOT KNOW yourself, go forth."[1] What a hard and bitter reproof: "Go forth." This is the kind of language that slaves hear from masters smarting with anger, or slave-girls from mistresses they have gravely offended: "Get out of here, get away from me, clear out of my sight, away from this house." And this kind of harsh and bitter expression,[2] extremely reproachful, is now used by the Bridegroom against his beloved, but with this condition: if she does not know herself. Nothing he could say was more warranted to frighten her than the threat that she should go forth. And you can see this if you think well on the place she is to go forth from and where she is told to go. From where and to where, if not from the spirit to the flesh, from things that are the soul's delight to desire of earthy pleasures,[3] from the inward repose of the mind to the world's clattering bustle where worry allows no peace; in all of which there is nothing but toil and sorrow[4] and spiritual suffering.[5] The soul has been taught by the Lord and received the power to enter into itself, to long for the presence of God in its inmost depths, to seek his face continually — for God is a spirit,[6] and those who seek him ought to walk by the promptings of the Spirit rather than of the flesh,[7] lest

1. Song 1:7
2. Ps 90:3
3. Tit 2:12
4. Ps 89:10

5. Eccles 1:14, 17
6. Jn 4:24
7. Gal 5:16; Rom 8:12

they live according to the flesh. Would that soul regard a temporary experience of hell as more horrible, more punitive, than having once tasted the sweetness of this spiritual desire, to have to go out again to the allurements or rather the irksome demands of the flesh, and be involved as before in the insatiable prurience of the body's senses? Ecclesiastes says: "The eye is not satisfied with seeing, nor the ear filled with hearing."[8] Listen to a man who has experienced the things I speak of: "The Lord is good to those who wait for him, to the soul that seeks him."[9] To attempt to turn this holy man away from that good, would cause him to feel as if driven out of Paradise, from the very gateway to glory. Listen to another man with a similar experience: "My heart says to you: 'My face has sought you;' your face, O Lord, I shall seek."[10] Whence he said: "It is good for me to adhere to God;"[11] and he addresses his soul with the words: "Return, O my soul, to your rest; for the Lord has dealt bountifully with you."[12] Therefore I say to you: There is nothing so feared by a man who has once received this favor, than, abandoned by grace, to have to go out again to the fleshly consolations, which are really desolations, and to endure once more the tumult of physical desire.

2. "Go forth and pasture your kids:"[13] it is a terrible, an awe-inspiring threat. As much as to say: know yourself unworthy of that familiar and sweet contemplation of things heavenly, things of the spirit, divine things. Therefore go forth from that heart of yours which has been my sanctuary, where it was your custom to drink sweet draughts from the secret, holy teachings of truth and wisdom; be like a woman of the world,[14] become entangled in pandering to the nourishment and delights of your flesh. Since through them sin enters the soul like death through the windows,[15] he calls the restless, wanton senses of the body kids, which signifies sin — at the judgment they are to be placed on the left.[16] The

---

8. Eccles 1:8
9. Lam 3:25
10. Ps 26:8
11. Ps 72:28
12. Ps 114:7

13. Song 1:7
14. Job 2:10
15. Jer 9:21
16. Mt 25:33

words that follow in the text, "beside the shepherds' tents,"[17] agree suitably with this interpretation. For unlike lambs, kids are fed not above but beside the shepherds' tents. Even though during the days of their service here below[18] they dwell in tents set upon the earth and made of earth, namely, their own bodies, shepherds who are worthy of the name are accustomed to feed the flocks of the Lord with food from the heavenly pastures, not from the earth; it is the Lord's will that they preach, not their own.[19] The kids however, the bodily senses, do not need heavenly things, but staying beside the shepherds' tents, they choose their foods from all the material goods of this world, which is the body's sphere; but desire, far from being satisfied, is but stimulated by these foods.

3. What a shameful change of occupation! Her previous occupation was to nourish her exiled pilgrim soul with holy meditations, feeding on heavenly truths, to seek after God's good-pleasure and the mysteries of his will, to penetrate the heavens by the power of her love and wander in thought through the abodes of the blessed, to pay homage to the patriarchs and apostles and throngs of prophets, to admire the triumphs of the martyrs and be lost in wonder at the superb beauty of the angel choirs. Now she has to abandon all these, and subject herself to the shameful task of serving the body, of obeying the flesh; she must satisfy stomach and palate, and beg throughout the world, this world whose form is passing away,[20] for the means to gratify in some degree her perpetually ravenous curiosity. My tears flow like streams for a soul in this plight:[21] she who once fed so delicately now lies grovelling on the dunghill.[22] One may say with the blessed Job that she fed the barren, childless woman and did no good to the widow.[23]

II. It is worth noting that he did not simply tell her to go forth, but to go after the flocks of her companions and to

17. Song 1:8
18. Job 14:14
19. Jn 4:34
20. 1 Cor 7:31

21. Ps 118:136
22. Lam 4:5
23. Job 24:21

feed her kids.[24] It seems to me that here he is warning us of
something very important. What is that? Alas! that one who
was so excellent, at one time a member of the flock and now
in wretched decline from bad to worse, is not permitted to
remain with the flocks but commanded to go behind them.
You ask what I mean. You yourselves can read: "When man
was being honored, he did not understand; and now he is
compared to senseless beasts and becomes like them."[25] That
is how one so excellent is made one of the flock. And the
brutes, if they could speak, would surely say: "See, Adam
has become like one of us."[26] He who was being honored!
"How honored? " you ask. His dwelling was in Paradise, he
spent his days in the midst of delights.[27] His food the sweet-
smelling apples, his bed the flowered banks,[28] he was crowned with glory and honor,[29] made keeper of the things his
Creator had made, and knew neither trouble nor want. A gift
still more sublime was the divine likeness he bore, that destined him for companionship with the angel hosts, with the
multitudes of heaven's armies.[30]

4. But he "exchanged the glory of God for the image of an
ox that eats grass."[31] That is why the bread of angels[32] became like grass in the manger,[33] set before us for the beasts
that we are. For the Word was made flesh, and according to
the Prophet, all flesh is grass. But the grass of the Word has
not been withered nor has its bloom turned pale,[34] because
the Spirit of the Lord has rested upon him.[35] And even
though the grass may wither and the flower fade, the Word of
the Lord remains forever.[36] Therefore if the grass is the
Word, and the Word remains forever, the grass too of necessity remains forever. How could it bestow eternal life if it did
not itself remain forever?

5. Let us ponder together on the voice of the Son addres-

24. Song 1:7
25. Ps 48:13
26. Gen 3:22
27. Gen 2:8
28. Song 2:5
29. Ps 8:6
30. Lk 2:13

31. Ps 105:20
32. Ps 77:25
33. Lk 2:12
34. Is 40:6, 8
35. Is 11:2
36. Is 40:8

sing the Father in the words of the Psalm. "You will not allow your Holy One to see corruption."[37] He is obviously speaking of the body that lay lifeless in the tomb. This is that same Holy One of whom the angel spoke when he announced to the Virgin Mary: "The Holy One to be born of you will be called the Son of God."[38] How could it be possible for that holy grass to see corruption,[39] sprouting as it was in the springlike meadows, perpetually green, of an incorruptible womb? It can even hold fast the eager eyes of the angels in a joy that will never grow weary. The grass will lose its freshness only if Mary will lose her virginity. And so he who is food for man has changed himself into fodder for beasts, because man has been changed into a beast. Alas! a sad and pitiable change, that man, a native of Paradise, lord of the earth, citizen of heaven, member of the household of the Lord of hosts,[40] a brother of the blessed spirits and co-heir of the heavenly powers, finds himself lying in a stable by a sudden transformation due to his own weakness, in need of grass because of his animal likeness, and tied to the manger because of his untamed roughness. As it is written: "Curbed by bit and bridle, the jaws of those who will not stay close to you."[41] Acknowledge, O ox, your owner and you, ass, your Lord's crib,[42] that God's Prophets may be found trustworthy in their foretelling of these wonderful works of God.[43] Acknowledge, Beast, him whom in your human condition you did not acknowledge; adore in the stable him from whom you fled in Paradise; pay honor now to the crib of one whose rule you scorned; eat now as grass him for whom as bread, the Bread of angels, you lost all taste.

III. 6. You ask: "What is the cause of this debasement?" Simply that when man was in honor he lacked understanding.[44] What did he not understand? The Psalmist does not explain, but let me explain. Placed in a position of honor,

---

37. Ps 15:10
38. Lk 1:35
39. Ps 15:10
40. Eph 2:19
41. Ps 31:9
42. Is 1:3
43. Sir 36:18
44. Ps 48:13

he was so intrigued by the dignity of his rank that he did not understand that he was but clay, and soon experienced in himself what a member of the captive race both wisely noted and truly expressed at a much later date: "If anyone thinks he is something, when he is nothing, he deceives himself."[45] Woe to that first unhappy man that no one was then present who could say to him: "Dust and ashes, why are you proud?"[46] From then on this fairest of creatures was reduced to the level of the herd; from then on the likeness of God was changed to the likeness of a beast; from then on association with the animals took the place of fellowship with the angels. You see how careful we must be to shun this ignorance that has brought evils by the thousands on the whole human race! For the Psalmist compares man to the senseless beasts,[47] for the reason that he lacked understanding. We must avoid ignorance at any cost, or if we are found to be still without understanding[48] even after chastisement, more serious evils than the former will multiply upon us and it will be said of us: "We tried to cure Babylon; she has gotten no better."[49] And rightly so, if the chastisement has failed to make us understand what we have heard.

7. And see if perhaps it was not for this reason that the Bridegroom, in order to fill his beloved with a fear of this ignorance by the thunder of his threatening, did not say "Go forth with the flocks," or "go forth to the flocks," but "Go forth after the flocks of your companions." Why does he speak in this manner? Surely for the purpose of showing that the second ignorance was more to be feared, to be ashamed of, than the first, for the first brought man to a level with the beasts, the latter made him lower. Because men, unaccepted or reprobated on account of their ignorance, have to stand before the dreaded judgment seat and be committed to the unquenchable fire, but not so the beasts. Men of this type will fare worse in relation to the beasts than if they did not exist at all. "It would have been better for that man," he

45. Gal 6:3
46. Sir 10:9
47. Ps 48:13
48. Mt 15:16
49. Jer 51:9

said, "if he had not been born."[50] He does not mean if he
had not been born at all, but if he had not been born a man;
better to have been a beast or any other irrational creature,
which, since it lacks the faculty of judging, will not be
brought to judgment, nor through this to punishment. The
rational soul then, that is ashamed of its first ignorance,
should remember that though it has beasts for companions in
the enjoyment of earthly goods, it will not have their company in its endurance of hell's torments; that it will ultimately be banished with shame even from the flocks of its bestial companions; that it will not travel with them but plainly
after them; for when they shall have ceased to feel any evil, it
will be exposed to evils of all kinds from which it will never
be set free, if indeed it has added the second ignorance to the
first. Accordingly man goes forth and walks alone after the
flocks of his companions, since he alone is thrust into the pit
of hell.[51] Does he not seem to you to hold the last place[52]
who is bound hands and feet and thrown out into the dark?
The last state of that man will obviously be worse than the
former,[53] for then he was on terms of equality with the
beasts, now he is reduced to a lower condition.

IV. 8. If you pay close attention, I think you will decide
that even in this life man has a lower position than the beasts.
Do you not think that man endowed with reason but failing
to live reasonably is more of a beast than the beasts themselves? For if the beast does not control himself by reason he
has an excuse based on his very nature, for that gift was
totally denied to him; but man has no excuse, because reason
is a special prerogative of his nature. A man then in this
condition is rightly judged to go forth from the company of
other living creatures and drop to a lower level, since he is the
only creature who violates the laws of his nature by a degen-
erate way of life. Gifted with reason, he imitates those who
lack it in what he does and in what he loves. It is demon-

50. Mt 26:24   52. Mt 22:13
51. Ps 85:13   53. Mt 12:45

strably clear therefore, that man is inferior to the herds, in this life by the depravity of his nature, in the next by the severity of the punishment.

9. That is how a man becomes accursed when he is found to be ignorant of God. Or should I say ignorant of self? I must include both: the two kinds of ignorance are damnable, either is enough to incur damnation. And do you want to know why? It should be perfectly obvious about ignorance of God if you can see that there is only one eternal life: to acknowledge the Father as true God, and Jesus Christ whom he has sent.[54] Therefore hear the Bridegroom plainly and openly condemning the soul's ignorance of itself. For what does he say? Not "if you do not know God," but "if you do not know yourself." It is clear therefore that he who does not know will not be known,[55] whether the ignorance refers to himself or to God. If God gives us help, it will be to our profit to speak again about this twofold ignorance. But not now: you are tired, we have not prefaced it with the customary prayers, and either I shall treat so important a matter carelessly, or you will listen with less attention to truths that should be absorbed with ardent desire. If you try to take a meal when already full and without appetite, not only is it useless but very harmful. All the more so if the food of the soul is taken with disrelish: instead of increasing knowledge it will merely trouble the mind. May Jesus Christ, the Church's Bridegroom, who is blessed for ever,[56] preserve us from this. Amen.

54. Jn 17:3
55. 1 Cor 14:38

56. Rom 1:25

SERMON 36

THE ACQUIRING OF KNOWLEDGE

HERE I AM AS I PROMISED; here I am, both in compliance with your request and to give to God the service I owe him. Three reasons therefore compel me to speak to you: fidelity to my promise, brotherly love, and the fear of the Lord. If I refuse to speak, my own mouth condemns me.[1] But what if I do speak? Then I dread a similar judgment, that my mouth will condemn me as one who speaks but fails to accomplish. Help me therefore with your prayers that I may always speak as I ought, and act in accord with my words.[2] You are aware that I propose to speak today of ignorance, or rather of different kinds of ignorance. You remember I mentioned two kinds, one with regard to ourselves, the other with regard to God. And I warned that we must beware of these two, because both are reprehensible. It remains for me now to expound this more clearly and at greater length. But first I think we must try to discover if all ignorance is reprehensible. It seems to me that this is not true—nor does all ignorance occasion loss—since there are various and countless things of which one may know nothing without detriment to salvation. If you are ignorant of the craftsman's art, for example that of the carpenter or mason, or any other craft practiced by men for the purposes of the present life, does this prevent your being

1. Job 16:7; 9:20   2. 1 Tim 5:13

saved? But while unacquainted with any of the liberal arts —
though not denying that they may be learned and practiced
for honorable and useful ends — how many people are saved
by living well and doing good, those whom the Apostle
mentions in the Epistle to the Hebrews,[3] men who were dear
to God not because of knowledge of literature but because of
a good conscience and a sincere faith?[4] They all pleased God
in their lives by the merits of their lives, not by their knowledge. Peter and Andrew and the sons of Zebedee, and all the
other disciples, were not chosen from a school of rhetoric or
philosophy; and yet through them the Savior made his salvation effective throughout the world.[5] Unlike a certain holy
man who made this claim for himself,[6] it was not because
their wisdom surpassed that of all other living men, but because of their faith and meekness,[7] that he made them his
friends, sanctified them, and appointed them teachers. And
when they revealed to the world the paths of life,[8] it was not
with sublime language or the polished words of human
wisdom.[9] Rather it pleased God, since the world in its
wisdom did not recognize him, that through the foolishness
of their preaching believers should be saved.[10]

II. 2. Perhaps you think that I have sullied too much the
good name of knowledge, that I have cast aspersions on the
learned and proscribed the study of letters. God forbid! I am
not unmindful of the benefits its scholars conferred, and still
confer, on the Church, both by refuting her opponents and
instructing the simple.[11] And I have read the text: "As you
have rejected knowledge, so do I reject you from my priest-
hood;"[12] read that the learned will shine as brightly as the
vault of heaven, and those who have instructed many in
virtue as bright as stars for all eternity.[13] But I recall reading
too that knowledge puffs up,[14] and "the more the knowl-

---

3. Heb 11
4. 1 Tim 1:5
5. Ps 73:12
6. Eccles 1:16
7. Sir 45:4
8. Ps 15:11

9. 1 Cor 2:1
10. 1 Cor 1:21; Jn 1:10
11. Tit 2:8
12. Hos 4:6
13. Dan 12:3
14. 1 Cor 8:1

edge, the more the sorrow."[15] There are then different kinds of knowledge, one contributing to self-importance, the other to sadness. Which of the two do you think is more useful or necessary to salvation, the one that makes you vain or the one that makes you weep? I feel sure you would prefer the latter to the former, for vanity but pretends to health whereas pain expresses a need. Anyone who thus demands is on the way to being saved, because the one who asks receives. [16] Furthermore, Paul tells us that he who heals the brokenhearted[17] abhors the proud: "God opposes the proud but gives grace to the humble."[18] Paul also said, "By the grace given to me I bid every one among you not to think more than he ought to think, but to think with sober judgment." [19] He does not forbid thinking, but inordinate thinking. And what is meant by thinking with sober judgment? It means taking the utmost care to discover what are the essential and primary truths, for the time is short.[20] All knowledge is good in itself, provided it be founded on the truth; but since because of the brevity of time you are in a hurry to work out your salvation in fear and trembling,[21] take care to learn, principally and primarily, the doctrines on which your salvation is more intimately dependent. Do not doctors of medicine hold that part of the work of healing depends on a right choice in the taking of food, what to take first, what next, and the amount of each kind to be eaten? For although it is clear that all the foods God made are good, if you fail to take the right amount in due order, you obviously take them to the detriment of your health. And what I say about foods I want you to apply to the various kinds of knowledge.

3. I prefer though to let you consult the Master. The doctrine I have preached is not really mine but his; though mine as well insofar as it is the word of him who is Truth. For Paul said: "If anyone imagines that he knows something, he does not yet know as he ought to know."[22] He does not approve

15. Eccles 1:18
16. Lk 11:10
17. Ps 146:3
18. Jas 4:6; 1 Pet 5:5
19. Rom 12:3
20. 1 Cor 7:29
21. Phil 2:12
22. 1 Cor 8:2

of the well-read man who observes no scale of values in the knowledge he possesses. See how the fruit and usefulness of knowledge is determined by the manner in which one knows. And what does that manner imply? It implies the order, the application, and the sense of purpose with which one approaches the object of study. The order implies that we give precedence to all that aids spiritual progress; the application, that we pursue more eagerly all that strengthens love more; and the purpose, that we pursue it not through vain-glory or inquisitiveness or any base motive, but for the welfare of oneself or one's neighbor.

III.   For there are some who long to know for the sole purpose of knowing, and that is shameful curiosity; others who long to know in order to become known, and that is shameful vanity. To such as these we may apply the words of the Satirist: "Your knowledge counts for nothing unless your friends know you have it."[23] There are others still who long for knowledge in order to sell its fruits for money or honors, and this is shameful profiteering; others again who long to know in order to be of service, and this is charity. Finally there are those who long to know in order to benefit themselves, and this is prudence.

4. Of all these categories, only the last two avoid the abuse of knowledge, because they desire to know for the purpose of doing good.[24] People with sound judgment act in this way.[25] Let all others heed the warning: he who knows what he ought to do and fails to do it, commits sin;[26] just as food eaten but not digested is injurious to one's health. Food that is badly cooked and indigestible induces physical disorders and damages the body instead of nourishing it. In the same way if a glut of knowledge stuffed in the memory, that stomach of the mind, has not been cooked on the fire of love, and transfused and digested by certain skills of the soul, its habits and actions — since, as life and conduct bear witness,

23. Persius, *Satires*, 1:27   25. Ps 110:10
24. Ps 35:4   26. Jas 4:17

the mind is rendered good through its knowledge of good —
will not that knowledge be reckoned sinful,[27] like the food
that produces irregular and harmful humors? Is not sin a
humor of evil? Are not bad habits humors of evil? Will
not a man in this condition suffer in his conscience in-
flammations and torments, since he does not act as he
knows he should? And will he not find within himself
the threat of death[28] and damnation as often as he calls
to mind the saying of God, that the man who knows
what his Lord wants, but fails to respond as he should, will
receive many strokes of the lash? [29] Perhaps the Prophet was
lamenting in the guise of such a man when he said: "There is
an anguish within me, anguish within! "[30] Or perhaps the
repetition of the woes hint at a different meaning that I
ought to follow up. It is possible that the Prophet spoke
these words in his own person when, filled with a knowledge
and overflowing with a love that he longed with all his soul to
communicate, he found no one who wanted to listen; the
knowledge that he could not impart became a burden on his
mind. This holy teacher of the Church therefore, bewails
both those who scorn to learn how to live, and those who,
knowing the truth, yet live evil lives. This could explain the
prophet's repetition of those words.

5. Do you not see then, how truly the Apostle perceived
that knowledge puffs up? [31]

IV. I wish therefore that before everything else a man
should know himself, because not only usefulness but right
order demand this. Right order, since what we are is our first
concern; and usefulness, because this knowledge gives humility rather than self-importance, it provides a basis on which to
build. For unless there is a durable foundation of humility,[32]
the spiritual edifice has no hope of standing.[33] And there is
nothing more effective, more adapted to the acquiring of

27. Deut 23:21   31. 1 Cor 8:1
28. 2 Cor 1:9   32. 1 Cor 3:12
29. Lk 12:47   33. Mk 3:25
30. Jer 4:19

humility, than to find out the truth about oneself. There must be no dissimulation, no attempt at self-deception, but a facing up to one's real self without flinching and turning aside. When a man thus takes stock of himself in the clear light of truth, he will discover that he lives in a region where likeness to God has been forfeited,[34] and groaning from the depths of a misery to which he can no longer remain blind, will he not cry out to the Lord as the Prophet did: "In your truth you have humbled me"?[35] How can he escape being genuinely humbled on acquiring this true self-knowledge, on seeing the burden of sin that he carries,[36] the oppressive weight of his mortal body, the complexities of earthly cares, the corrupting influence of sensual desires; on seeing his blindness, his worldliness, his weakness, his embroilment in repeated errors; on seeing himself exposed to a thousand dangers, trembling amid a thousand fears, confused by a thousand difficulties, defenceless before a thousand suspicions, worried by a thousand needs; one to whom vice is welcome, virtue repugnant? Can this man afford the haughty eyes, the proud lift of the head?[37] With the thorns of his misery pricking him, will he not rather be changed for the better?[38] Let him be changed and weep, changed to mourn-

---

34. *Regio dissimilitudinis* This is an expression which is very commonly used by the Cistercian Fathers. See e.g., William of St Thierry: *Exposition on the Song of Songs* 65 (CF 6:52); *Meditations* 4:6 (CF 3:113); Aelred of Rievaulx: *Jesus at the Age of Twelve* (CF 2:6); *Sermons on Isaiah* 8 (PL 195:391); Isaac of Stella: *Second Sermon for the Feast of All Saints* 13 (SCh 130:106); and elsewhere in Bernard: *On Grace and Free Choice* 28 (OB 3:185), 32 (OB 3:188); *Occasional Sermons* 40:4 (OB 6-1:237), 42:2-3 (OB 6-1:256-257); *Letters* 8:2 (BSJ, Ep 9, p. 39). Originating with Plato and Plotinus the idea of a land or region of unlikeness was adopted by Christian writers such as Eusebius, St Athanasius and St Augustine (e.g., see *Confessions* vii, 10), until it is found to be of almost universal use in the Middle Ages. Most of the Cistercian authors associate the land of unlikeness with that far-away country in Luke 15:13 and thus the emphasis is on the notion of sin; however, sometimes, especially in the case of St Bernard, it is merely a question of the soul being an alien on earth, an exile in a land that is not its true country. See also, J. M. Déchanet, "Introduction," CF 3:xlvii; A. Hallier, *The Monastic Theology of Aelred of Rievaulx*, CS 2 (Spencer, 1969), p. 12; and F. Vandenbrouke, *Why Monks?*, CS 17 (Washington, 1972), pp. 25-26.
35. Ps 118:75
36. 2 Tim 3:6
37. Sir 23:5
38. Ps 31:4

ing and sighing, changed to acceptance of the Lord, to whom in his lowliness he will say: "Heal me because I have sinned against you."[39] He will certainly find consolation in this turning to the Lord, because he is "the Father of mercies and the God of all comfort."[40]

6. As for me, as long as I look at myself, my eye is filled with bitterness.[41] But if I look up and fix my eyes on the aid of the divine mercy, this happy vision of God soon tempers the bitter vision of myself, and I say to him: "I am disturbed within so I will call you to mind from the land of the Jordan."[42] This vision of God is not a little thing. It reveals him to us as listening compassionately to our prayers, as truly kind and merciful, as one who will not indulge his resentment.[43] His very nature is to be good, to show mercy always and to spare. By this kind of experience, and in this way, God makes himself known to us for our good. When a man first discovers that he is in difficulties, he will cry out to the Lord who will hear him[44] and say: "I will deliver you and you shall glorify me."[45] In this way your self-knowledge will be a step to the knowledge of God; he will become visible to you according as his image is being renewed within you.[46] And you, gazing confidently on the glory of the Lord with unveiled face, will be transformed into that same image with ever increasing brightness, by the work of the Spirit of the Lord.[47]

7. You can see now how each of these kinds of knowledge is so necessary for your salvation, that you cannot be saved if you lack either of them. If you lack self-knowledge you will possess neither the fear of God nor humility. And whether you may presume to be saved without the fear of God and humility, is for you to judge. The murmuring that I hear among you shows me quite clearly that this is not your idea of wisdom, or rather not your way of being foolish, so we need not linger over what is obvious. But there are other

39. Ps 40:5
40. 2 Cor 1:3
41. Job 17:2
42. Ps 41:7
43. Joel 2:13

44. Ps 90:15
45. Ps 49:15
46. Col 3:10
47. 2 Cor 3:18

things to attend to, or should we come to an end for the sake of those who are asleep down there? I thought that with one sermon I should fulfill my promise about the two kinds of ignorance, and I would have, but it is already too long for those who are tired of it. Some, I can see, are yawning, and some are asleep. And no wonder, for last night's vigils were prolonged; that excuses them. But what shall I say to those who were asleep then, and now sleep again? I am not now going to add to their shame, it is enough to have mentioned it. But for the future they must be on the alert, or they will have to endure the sting of further reproach. With this hope in view I pass over the matter for the moment; and though reason demands that I continue the sermon, out of charity for them I shall postpone it to another time, making an end where there is no end. And they, because of the mercy shown them, must give glory along with us to the Church's Bridegroom, our Lord, who is God blessed for ever. Amen.[48]

48. Rom 1:25

SERMON 37

KNOWLEDGE AND IGNORANCE OF GOD AND OF SELF

I PRESUME THERE IS NO NEED TODAY to remind you to stay awake, because I feel that the remarks I made as recently as yesterday, friendly remarks, will be enough to keep those concerned on the alert. You remember that you have agreed with me that no one is saved without self-knowledge, since it is the source of that humility on which salvation depends, and of the fear of the Lord that is as much the beginning of salvation as of wisdom.[1] No one, I repeat, is saved without that knowledge, provided he is old enough and sane enough to possess it. I say this because of children and mental defectives, to whom a different principle applies. But what if you have no knowledge of God? Is hope of salvation compatible with ignorance about God? Surely not. For you cannot love what you do not know, nor possess what you do not love. Know yourself and you will have a wholesome fear of God; know him and you will also love him. In the first, wisdom has its beginning, in the second its crown, for "the fear of the Lord is the beginning of wisdom,"[2] and "love is the fulfilling of the law."[3] You must avoid both kinds of ignorance, because without fear and love salvation is not possible. Other matters are irrelevant in this context: to know them does not guarantee salvation, nor does ignorance of them mean damnation.

1. Ps 110:10; Sir 1:16   3. Rom 13:10
2. Ibid.

181

2. I am far from saying however, that knowledge of literature is to be despised, for it provides culture and skill, and
enables a man to instruct others. But knowledge of God and
of self are basic and must come first, for as I have already
shown, they are essential for salvation. This was the viewpoint of the Prophet, this was the order of precedence he
inculcated when he said: "Sow for yourselves righteousness,
and reap the hope of life." and then: "Set alight for yourselves the light of knowledge."[4] He puts knowledge in the
last place, because, like a picture that cannot stand on the air,
it requires that the solid structure of the other two precede
and support it. I may safely pursue studies if my hope of
eternal life has first been rendered secure. You therefore have
sown righteousness for yourself if by means of true self-
knowledge you have learned to fear God, to humble yourself,
to shed tears, to distribute alms and participate in other
works of charity; if you have disciplined your body with
fastings and prayers, if you have wearied your heart with acts
of penance and heaven with your petitions. This is what it
means to sow righteousness. The seeds are our good works,
our good desires, our tears, for the Psalmist says: "They wept
as they went forth, sowing their seeds."[5] But why? Shall
they always weep? God forbid! "They shall come home
with shouts of joy, carrying their sheaves."[6] And so rightly
do they shout for joy, since they bring back sheaves of glory.
But you say: "That is for the resurrection on the last day;[7] a
long time to wait! "

II. Do not permit your will to be broken, do not yield to
pusillanimity;[8] you have in the meantime the first-fruits of
the Spirit,[9] which even now you may reap with joy. "Sow
for yourselves righteousness, and reap the hope of life."[10]
These words do not postpone your triumph till the last day,
when the object of your desire will be possessed, not hoped
for; they refer to the time now at your disposal. But when

4. Hos 10:12
5. Ps 125:6
6. Ibid.
7. Jn 11:24

8. Ps 54:9
9. Rom 8:23
10. Hos 10:12

eternal life does come, what great gladness there will be, what joy beyond imagining!

3. And can the hope of this great happiness be without happiness? The Apostle speaks of rejoicing in hope.[11] David, when he expressed the hope of entering the house of God, said that it gave him happiness now, not in the future.[12] Eternal life was not yet his, but his hope reached out to it; so that in his heart he experienced the Scriptural truth that the just man finds joy not only in the reward but even in the expectation of it.[13] The assurance of pardon for sins begets this joy in the heart where the seeds of righteousness are sown, if that assurance is corroborated by a holier life inspired by the efficacy of the grace received. Everyone among you who enjoys this experience understands what the Spirit says, for his voice never contradicts his activity. This is why one understands what is said; what one hears from without he feels within. For one and the same Spirit both speaks to us and works within you,[14] distributing gifts to each individual at will,[15] giving to some the power to speak what is good, to others the power to do it.[16]

4. Anyone therefore who has the happiness of being borne aloft on the wings of grace and of breathing freely in the hope of consolation after the early period of conversion with its bitterness and tears, already in this life gathers the fruit of his tears; he has had a vision of God and heard the voice that says: "Give him a share of the fruits of his hands."[17] If he has tasted and seen that the Lord is sweet, has he not seen God:[18] Lord Jesus, how pleasant and sweet must you be to him whom you have not merely blessed with forgiveness of sins but endowed too with the gift of holiness;[19] and along with that, added to the treasury of his goods, the promise of eternal life. Happy the man with all this for a harvest, who now has the fruits of holiness and at the end eternal life.[20] It was but right that he who wept when faced with the truth

11. Rom 12:12
12. Ps 121:1
13. Peov 10:28
14. 1 Thess 2:13
15. 1 Cor 12:11

16. 1 Cor 12:8-10
17. Prov 31:31
18. Ps 33:9
19. Col 2:13
20. Rom 6:22

about himself,[21] should rejoice on seeing the Lord,[22] whose all-merciful eyes gave him strength to carry those precious sheaves: forgiveness, sanctification, and the hope of eternal life. It bears out the truth in the Prophet's words: "Those who sow in tears shall reap in jubilation! "[23] We find the two kinds of knowledge within these words: that of ourselves in the sowing in tears; and that of God, in the reaping in joy.

III.   5. If we have first made sure of this two-fold knowledge, we are less likely to become conceited by any other learning we may add to it. The earthly gain or honor it may confer on us is far beneath the hope conceived and the deeply rooted joy in the soul that springs from this hope does not disappoint us, because God's love has been poured into our hearts by the Holy Spirit, who has been given to us.[24] It does not disappoint because love fills us with assurance. Through it the Holy Spirit bears witness to our spirit that we are sons of God.[25] What advantage can we derive from any amount of our learning that is not less than the glory of being numbered among God's sons? Small indeed; nor can the earth itself with its fullness[26] be compared to it, even if one of us gained possession of it all. But if we are ignorant of God how can we hope in one we do not know? If ignorant about ourselves, how can we be humble, thinking ourselves to be something when we are really nothing? [27] And we know that neither the proud nor the hopeless have part or companionship in the inheritance of the saints.[28]

6. Let us consider therefore with what extreme care we ought to banish from our minds these two kinds of ignorance. One is responsible for the beginning, the other for the consummation of every sin, just as in the case of the two kinds of knowledge where one begets the fear of God and is the beginning of wisdom and the other begets the love that is its crown. These roles of knowledge have already been ex-

21. Lk 22:62
22. Jn 20:20
23. Ps 125:5
24. Rom 5:5

25. Rom 8:16
26. Ps 23:1
27. Gal 6:3
28. Col 1:12

plained, now let us examine the roles of ignorance. Just as the fear of the Lord is the beginning of wisdom,[29] so pride is the beginning of all sin;[30] and just as the love of God is the way to the perfection of wisdom, so despair leads to the committing of every sin. And as the fear of God springs up within you from knowledge of self and love of God from the knowledge of God, so on the contrary, pride comes from want of self-knowledge and despair from want of knowledge of God. Ignorance of what you are contributes to your pride, because your deluded and deluding thoughts lie to you, telling you you are better than you are. For this is pride, this is how all sin originates—that you are greater in your own eyes than you are before God, than you are in truth. Hence it has been said of him who first committed a grave sin of this kind—I mean the devil—that he did not abide in the truth, but was a liar from the beginning,[31] since what he was in his own mind was not what he was in truth. But what would be the consequences if his departure from truth consisted in thinking himself less important than he was? His genuine ignorance would excuse him and no one would call him proud; rather than his error exposing him to scorn,[32] we should have humility leading him to grace.[33] For if each of us could clearly see the truth of our condition in God's sight, it would be our duty to depart neither upwards nor downwards from that level, but to conform to the truth in all things.[34] Since God's judgment however, is now in darkness[35] and his word is hidden from us,[36] so that no man knows whether he deserves to be loved or hated,[37] it is certainly the better thing, the safer thing, to follow the advice of him who is truth, and choose for ourselves the last place.[38] Afterwards we may be promoted from there with honor, rather than cede to another, to our shame, the higher seat we had usurped.

29. Ps 110:10; Sir 1:16
30. Sir 10:15
31. Jn 8:44
32. Ps 35:3
33. Jas 4:6; 1 Pet 5:5
34. Rom 2:8
35. Ps 17:12
36. Lk 18:34
37. Eccles 9:1
38. Lk 14:10

IV.   7. You run no risk therefore, no matter how much you lower yourself, no matter how much your self-esteem falls short of what you are, that is, of what Truth thinks of you. But the evil is great and the risk frightening if you exalt yourself even a little above what you are, if in your thoughts you consider yourself of more worth than even one person whom Truth may judge your equal or your better. To make myself clearer: if you pass through a low doorway you suffer no hurt however much you bend, but if you raise your head higher than the doorway, even by a finger's breadth, you will dash it against the lintel and injure yourself. So also a man has no need to fear any humiliation, but he should quake with fear before rashly yielding to even the least degree of self-exaltation. So then, beware of comparing yourself with your betters or your inferiors, with a particular few or with even one. For how do you know but that this one person, whom you perhaps regard as the vilest and most wretched of all, whose life you recoil from and spurn as more befouled and wicked, not merely than yours, for you trust you are a sober-living man and just and religious,[39] but even than all other wicked men; how do you know, I say, but that in time to come, with the aid of the right hand of the Most High,[40] he will not surpass both you and them if he has not done so already in God's sight? That is why God wished us to choose neither a middle seat nor the last but one, nor even one of the lowest rank; for he said, "Sit down in the lowest place,"[41] that you may sit alone, last of all, and not dare to compare yourself, still less to prefer yourself, to anyone. See how great the evil that springs from our want of self-knowledge; nothing less than the devil's sin and the beginning of every sin, pride.[42] What ignorance of God leads to, we shall see on another occasion. We have been late in coming together here today and the shortness of the time does not permit it now. For the present it suffices that each one has been warned about want of self-knowledge, not only by means of my sermon but also by the goodness of the Bridegroom of the Church, our Lord Jesus Christ, who is God, blessed for ever. Amen.[43]

39. Tit 2:12
40. Ps 76:11
41. Lk 14:10

42. Sir 10:15
43. Rom 1:25

SERMON 38

IGNORANCE OF GOD LEADS TO DESPAIR
THE BEAUTY OF THE BRIDE

TO WHAT THEN does ignorance of God lead? We must begin here, for this is where, as you will recall, we finished yesterday. What does it lead to? I have already told you: despair. Now I shall explain how. Imagine a man who decides to take stock of his way of life, who, unhappy in his sinful conduct, wants to reform and abandon his evil and carnal ways.[1] If he does not know how good God is,[2] how kind and gentle,[3] how willing to pardon,[4] will not his sensually-inspired reason argue with him and say: "What are you doing? Do you want to lose this life and the next? Your sins are too grave and too many; nothing that you do, even to stripping the skin from your flesh, can make satisfaction for them. Your constitution is delicate, you have lived softly, a lifetime's habits are not easily conquered." Dismayed by these and similar arguments, the unhappy man quits the struggle, not knowing how easily God's omnipotent goodness could overthrow all these obstacles, since he wills that no man should perish.[5] Instead there is final impenitence, the greatest crime of all, an unforgivable blasphemy.[6] In his agitation he is either swallowed up by excessive sadness[7] and lost in a deep depression from which he will never have the consolation of emerging, in accord with Scripture's

---

1. Ps 118:101
2. Ps 72:1
3. Ps 85:5
4. Is 55:7

5. 2 Pet 3:9
6. Mt 12:31-32
7. 2 Cor 2:7

187

saying that the wicked man shows only contempt when caught in the midst of evils;[8] or he will dissimulate, flatter himself with false reasonings and, as far as in him lies, surrender irrevocably to the world, to find his pleasure and delight in what advantages it offers. But just when he believes that he has peace and security, misfortunes of all kinds will overwhelm him and he will not escape.[9] Thus despair, the greatest evil of all, follows on ignorance of God.

II. 2. The Apostle says that there are some who have no knowledge of God.[10] My opinion is that all those who lack knowledge of God are those who refuse to turn to him. I am certain that they refuse because they imagine this kindly disposed God to be harsh and severe, this merciful God to be callous and inflexible, this lovable God to be cruel and oppressive. So it is that wickedness plays false to itself,[11] setting up for itself an image that does not represent him. What are you afraid of, you men of little faith?[12] That he will not pardon your sins? But with his own hands he has nailed them to the cross.[13] That you are used to soft living and your tastes are fastidious? But he is aware of our weakness.[14] That a prolonged habit of sinning binds you like a chain? But the Lord loosens the shackles of prisoners.[15] Or perhaps angered by the enormity and frequency of your sins he is slow to extend a helping hand? But where sin abounded, grace became superabundant.[16] Are you worried about clothing and food and other bodily necessities so that you hesitate to give up your possessions?[17] But he knows that you need all these things. What more can you wish? What else is there to hold you back from the way of salvation? This is what I say: you do not know God, yet you will not believe what we have heard.[18] I should like you to believe those whom experience

8. Prov 18:3
9. 1 Thess 5:3
10. 1 Cor 15:34
11. Ps 26:12
12. Mt 8:26
13. Col 2:14
14. Ps 102:14
15. Ps 145:7
16. Rom 5:20
17. Mt 6:25-32
18. Is 53:1

has taught, for "if you do not believe you will not under-stand."[19] Not everyone however, has faith.[20]

3. God forbid that we should think the bride has been admonished on the grounds of ignorance of God, for she has been gifted not merely with great knowledge of him who is both her Bridegroom and God, but with his friendship and familiar intercourse. She has enjoyed his frequent colloquys and kisses, and with a daring born of this intimacy can say to him: "Tell me where you pasture your flock, where you make it lie down at noon".[21] It is not he that she demands to be shown, but the place where his glory dwells,[22] although his domicile and his glory are no other than himself. But he thinks fit to reprove her on account of her presumption, and hints that she lacks self-knowledge by judging herself ready for a vision so great: in her excitement she may have over-looked that she was still living on this earth, or hoped against hope that even while still in this earthy body she could draw near to his inaccessible brightness. Hence he at once recalls her to her senses, proves her ignorance to her, and reprimands her boldness: "If you do not know yourself," he told her, "go forth."[23] Here the Bridegroom speaks to his beloved not as a bridegroom, but with the awesome tones of a master. He is not venting his anger; his intention is to inspire the fear that purifies, that by this purification she may be made ready for the vision she longs for. It is a vision reserved for the pure of heart.[24]

III. 4. How aptly he describes her as beautiful, not in every sense, but beautiful among women;[25] a qualification meant to restrain her, to enable her to know her limitations.[26] I believe that by women he means people who are sensual and worldly, people devoid of manliness, whose conduct lacks both fortitude and constancy, people who are entirely super-ficial, soft and effeminate in their lives and behavior. But the

19. Is 7:9 (Septuagint)
20. 2 Thess 3:2
21. Song 1:6
22. Ps 25:8

23. Song 1:7
24. Mt 5:8
25. Song 1:7
26. Ps 38:5

person who is spiritual, although enjoying a beauty that comes from following the ways of the Spirit rather than the ways of the flesh,[27] will still fall short of perfect beauty by the fact of living in the body. Hence the bride is not beautiful from every aspect, but beautiful among women, among people whose ideals are worldly, people who, unlike herself, are not spiritual; but not among the angels in their bliss, not among the Virtues, the Powers, the Dominations. And just as one of the Fathers was said to be a man of integrity among his contemporaries,[28] surpassing all of his time and generation, and Thamar is shown to be righteous when compared with Judah,[29] that is, more righteous than he, and the tax collector in the Gospel is said to have gone down from the temple at rights with God rather than the pharisee,[30] and even as the great John was once magnificently acclaimed as having no rival for greatness, but only among those born of women,[31] not among the blessed choirs of heavenly spirits, so the bride is declared beautiful now, but, for the time being, among women, and not among the blessed spirits of heaven.

5. Therefore as long as she is on earth she must cease from searching too curiously into the nature of the things of heaven, lest by intruding on God's majesty she be overwhelmed by glory.[32] As long as she lives among women she must refrain from prying into the truths that are proper to the citizens of heaven, truths that are visible to them alone, lawful for them alone; heaven's realities are for its citizens. "The vision that you ask for, Bride of mine, is above your capacity,[33] you are as yet unable to gaze upon that sublime noontide brightness that is my dwelling place. You have asked where I pasture my flocks, the place where I rest at noon.[34] But to be drawn up through the clouds, to penetrate to where light is total, to plunge through seas of splendor and make your home where light is unapproachable,[35] that is beyond

27. Rom 8:1
28. Noah Gen 7:1
29. Gen 38:26
30. Lk 18:14
31. Lk 7:28

32. Prov 25:27
33. Ps 138:6
34. Song 1:6
35. 1 Tim 6:16

the scope of an earthly life or an earthly body. That is reserved for you at the end of all things, when I shall take you, all glorious, to myself, without spot or wrinkle or any such thing.[36] Do you not know that as long as you live in the body you are exiled from the light? [37] With your beauty still incomplete[38] how can you consider yourself fit to gaze on beauty in its totality? And why should you want to see me in my splendor, while you still do not know yourself? Because if you had a better knowledge of yourself you would know that, burdened with a perishable body,[39] you cannot possibly lift up your eyes and fix them on this radiant light that the angels long to contemplate.[40] The time will come when I shall reveal myself, and your beauty will be complete, just as my beauty is complete; you will be so like me that you will see me as I am.[41] Then you will be told: "You are all fair my love, there is no flaw in you."[42] But for now, though there is some resemblance, there is also some want of resemblance, and you must be content with an imperfect knowledge.[43] Be aware of what you are, do not hanker after truths that are too high for you,[44] nor for experiences beyond your power to bear. Otherwise, you do not know yourself, o beautiful among women—for ever I give you the title beautiful, but beautiful among women, with a beauty that is imperfect. When the perfect comes, the imperfect will pass away.[45] Therefore, "If you do not know yourself. . . ." But the words that follow have been dealt with, and there is no need to deal with them again. I promised to put some helpful thoughts before you about the two kinds of ignorance; if I have failed to satisfy you fully, give me credit for my good-will. For I certainly have the will to do it, but the means to accomplish it I do not have,[46] except in so far as the Church's Bridegroom, the Lord Jesus Christ, enables me by his kindness to work for your well-being. May he be blessed for ever. Amen.[47]

36. Eph 5:27
37. 2 Cor 5:6
38. Song 4:7
39. Wis 9:15
40. 1 Pet 1:12
41. 1 Jn 3:2
42. Song 4:7
43. 1 Cor 13:9
44. Sir 3:22
45. 1 Cor 13:10
46. Rom 7:18
47. Rom 1:25

SERMON 39

THE DEVIL AND HIS ARMY

"TO MY COMPANY OF HORSEMEN amid Pharaoh's chariots have I likened you, o my love."[1] For a start we are free to infer from these words that the Fathers prefigured the Church, and that the mysteries of our salvation were foreshown to them. The grace of baptism that both saves men and washes sins away, is clearly expressed in the exodus of Israel from Egypt,[2] when the sea performed that twofold marvel of service in providing a passage for the people and taking vengeance on their enemies. "Our fathers were all under the cloud," said St Paul, "and all were baptized into Moses in the cloud and in the sea."[3] But as usual I must show the sequence of the words, the connection between the present text and those we have already dealt with, and draw from them as well as I can some consoling doctrine to improve our lives. So when the bride is harshly rebuked for her presumption, lest she succumb to sadness, she is reminded of the favors she has already received and promised that others are to come. He even acknowledges again her beauty and calls her his love. "My love," he says, "if I have spoken to you harshly, do not suspect me of hating you or of being spiteful, for the very gifts with which I have honored and adorned you are clear signs of my love for you. Far from intending to withdraw them I shall add still more."

1. Song 1:8
2. Ps 113:1

3. 1 Cor 10:1-2

192

Or he could say it this way: "My love, do not be disappointed that your request is not being answered now; you have already received quite a lot from me, and even greater favors will be yours if you follow my directions and persevere in my love."[4] The text may thus be linked up with the previous ones.

2. Now let us see what those gifts are that he says he has bestowed on her. The first is that he has compared her to his horsemen amid Pharaoh's chariots: by putting to death all the flesh's sinful tendencies[5] he has freed her from the bondage of sin, just as his people were freed from the slavery of Egypt when the chariots of Pharaoh were overturned and swallowed up in the sea.[6] That is surely a very great mercy, and I shall not be foolish if I wish to glory in having received it. I speak only the truth.[7] I declare and will go on declarings: "If the Lord had not been my help, my soul would soon have found its dwelling in hell."[8] I am neither ungrateful nor forgetful, I will sing of the mercies of the Lord forever.[9] But this is as far as I compare myself with the bride. As for the rest, by a unique privilege after her deliverance she has been accepted as his beloved and adorned with a splendor befitting the Lord's own bride, but for the present time only on the cheeks and neck. She has been promised necklaces for ornamentation, made of costly gold, inlaid with beautiful silver.[10] Can anyone not be entirely pleased with such an endowment? Firstly his mercy sets her free, secondly he favors her with his love, thirdly he makes her clean and pure, and finally he promises to enrich her with gems of rarest quality.

3. I have no doubt that some of you understand what I am saying from your own experience, which enables you even to anticipate my words. But running through my mind is the verse: "The unfolding of your words gives light; it imparts understanding to the simple,"[11] and because of these I feel that a little more extensive treatment is justified. For wisdom

4. 1 Kings 6:12
5. Rom 8:13
6. Ex 14:28
7. 2 Cor 12:6

8. Ps 93:17
9. Ps 88:1
10. Song 1:9-10
11. Ps 118:130

is a kindly spirit[12] that is pleased with a teacher who is kind and diligent, who, despite his anxiety to gratify his intelligent students, does not hesitate to adapt himself to the backward ones. Wisdom herself says that they who explain her shall have life everlasting,[13] a reward I would by no means be deprived of. For even those matters whose meaning seems obvious have certain aspects that can be obscure, and time is not wasted in discussing them in more detail with capacious and quick-witted minds.

II.   4. But now let us take a look at the comparison drawn from Pharaoh and his army and the horsemen of the Lord. The comparison is not between the two armies, they are merely the basis of it. For light and darkness have nothing in common, the faithful no partnership with the unfaithful.[14] But there is a clear comparison between the person who is holy and spiritual and the horsemen of the Lord, and between Pharaoh and the devil and both their armies. And do not be surprised that one person is compared to a company of horsemen, for if that one person is holy an army of virtues is at hand: well-ordered affections, disciplined habits, prayers like burnished weapons, actions charged with energy, awesome zeal, and finally unrelenting conflicts with the enemy and repeated victories. Hence in later texts we read: "Terrible as an army set in array,"[15] and "What shall you see in the Shulamite but the companies of the camps?"[16] If this explanation fails to satisfy you, then recall that the spiritual person is never without a company of angels who display a divine jealousy in guarding her for her husband, to present her to Christ as a pure bride.[17] And do not say to yourself: "Where are they? Who has seen them? " The prophet Elisha saw them and obtained by his prayers that Gehazi should see them, too.[18] You do not see them because you are neither a prophet nor the son of a prophet. The patriarch Jacob saw

---

12. Wis 1:6
13. Sir 24:31
14. 2 Cor 6:14-15
15. Song 6:3

16. Song 7:1
17. 2 Cor 11:2
18. 2 Kings 6:17

them and exclaimed: "This is God's camp."[19] The Teacher of the Nations saw them and said: "Are they not all ministering spirits sent forth to serve for the sake of those who are to obtain salvation? "[20]

5. The bride therefore, progressing on her course with the support of ministering angels, with the aid of the heavenly host, does resemble the horsemen of the Lord that by a stupendous miracle of divine power once triumphed over the chariots of Pharaoh.[21] If you pay careful attention, the wonder aroused in you by the magnificent achievements in the Red Sea can still be aroused by the achievements of today. Rather her victories today are even more magnificent, for the physical exploits of that occasion find spiritual fulfillment now. Surely you see that greater courage is shown and greater glory achieved in overthrowing the devil rather than Pharaoh, in conquering spiritual powers rather than Pharaoh's chariots? There the battle was waged against flesh and blood; here it is waged against sovereignties and powers, against the forces that control this world's darkness, the spiritual army of evil in the heavens.[22] Let us examine together the details of this comparison. There you have a people rescued from Egypt, here man is rescued from the world; there Pharaoh is vanquished, here the devil; there Pharaoh's chariots are overturned, here the passions of the flesh that attack the soul are being undermined;[23] there it was the waves that triumphed, here our tears; the former with the sea's might, the latter in bitterness. If the demons encounter a soul of this quality I can hear them now crying out: "Let us flee from before Israel, for the Lord is fighting for him."[24]

III. Would you wish me to designate some of Pharaoh's captain's by their proper names, and describe his chariots for you, so that you may discover for yourselves if there be any others like them: One mighty captain of the spiritual and invisible king of Egypt is Malice, another is Sensuality, an-

19. Gen 32:2
20. Heb 1:14
21. Ex 14:18

22. Eph 6:12
23. 1 Pet 2:11
24. Ex 14:25

other Avarice. Each of them possesses, under his king, the
territory assigned to him. Malice therefore is in command
wherever the wicked commit their crimes, Sensuality presides
over shameful rites of lust, while thievery and fraud are within the domain of Avarice.

6. And now let us look at the chariots prepared by Pharaoh
for his princes to persecute the people of God. Malice has a
chariot with four wheels named Cruelty, Impatience, Recklessness and Impudence. This chariot's swift sorties mean the
shedding of blood,[25] nor can it be stopped by innocence, nor
delayed by patience, nor checked by fear nor inhibited by
shame. It is drawn by two vicious horses ready to destroy as
they go, earthly Power and worldly Pomp. They are the
source of its dazzling speed, for Power gallops where evil
beckons, and Pomp courts popular favor in pursuit of dishonest ends. Hence the Psalmist says that the sinner is praised
for his evil desires and the dishonest man gets a blessing;[26]
hence, too, the other words: "This is your hour and the
power of darkness."[27] And these two horses are driven by
two coachmen called Arrogance and Envy; Arrogance drives
Pomp, Envy urges on Power. The former is borne rapidly
along by a diabolical love of vain display that fills his heart.
But the man with genuine self-possession, who is prudently
circumspect, seriously concerned about modesty, firmly established in humility, wholesomely chaste, will never be lightly carried away by this empty wind. In like manner the beast
of earthly Power is driven by Envy, urged on by jealousy's
spurs, by worry about possible failure and the fear of being
surpassed. One spur is the haunting fear of being supplanted,
the other the fear of a rival. These are the goads by which
earthly Power is ever disquieted. This is what one finds in the
chariot of Malice.

7. The chariot of Sensuality also rolls along with four vices
for wheels: Gluttony, Lust, Seductive Dress and Enervation,
that is, the offspring of sloth and inertia. And it is drawn by

25. Ps 13:3   27. Lk 22:53
26. Ps 9:23

two horses, Prosperous Life and Abundance of Goods. The two coachmen are Lazy Languor and False Security, for wealth is the ruin of the slothful and Scripture says that the prosperity of fools destroys them,[28] not because they are successful but because it gives them false security. "When people say, 'there is peace and security,' then sudden destruction will come upon them."[29] These coachmen have neither spurs nor whips nor any instrument of this kind; instead they carry a canopy for shade and a fan to freshen the air. The canopy's name is Dissimulation, and its purpose to provide a shade to ward off the heat of human cares. A person used to soft, effeminate ways will dissemble even when faced with necessary cares, and rather than experience life's perplexing troubles he will conceal himself in the thickets of dissimulation. The fan is Permissiveness, that stirs up flattery like a breeze. For voluptuaries have liberal hands and buy with their gold the flattery of the sycophant. I shall say no more on this subject.

8. Avarice, too, has vices for its four wheels: Pusillanimity, Inhumanity, Contempt of God, Forgetfulness of Death. The beasts to which it is yoked are Obstinacy and Rapacity, and one coachman drives them whose name is Greed for Gain. Avarice is a solitary vice that cannot endure many retainers; one servant suffices. But he is a prompt and tireless executor of the task in hand, lashing his horses onward with cruel whips called Craving to Acquire and Fear of Loss.

IV. 9. The ruler of Egypt has still other captains whose chariots are used in their lord's service, for example Pride, who is one of the more important captains, along with that enemy of the faith, Impiety, whose position is so influential in Pharaoh's palace and kingdom. Besides these, Pharaoh's army contains many officers and nobles of inferior rank whose number is almost countless. What their names are and their duties, their armor and equipment, I leave to you yourselves to pursue as a project of study. But trusting in the

28. Prov 1:32   29. 1 Thess 5:3

prowess of these captains and their chariots, the invisible
Pharaoh rushes to and fro, inspired by a tyrannical rage, as he
directs his attacks with all the power he can muster against
the entire family of God. Even in these very days he is per-
secuting the people of Israel as they escape from Egypt.[30]
And these, neither supported by chariots nor clad in armor,
but strengthened solely by the hand of God,[31] sing out with
confidence: "I will sing to the Lord for he has gloriously
triumphed; horse and rider he has thrown into the sea."[32]
"Some boast of chariots and some of horses, but we boast of
the name of the Lord our God."[33] Now you have heard what
I wished to say on the suggested comparison between the
horsemen of the Lord and the chariots of Pharaoh.

10. In this text he calls her his love. He was her lover even
before she was freed from sin, for if he had not loved her he
would not have set her free; it was through this gift of freedom that she was won over to become his love. St John's
words explain it: "It was not that we loved him, but first he
loved us."[34] Recall the story of Moses and the Ethiopian
woman and see that even then there was a foreshadowing of
the union between the Word and the sinner.[35] Try to identify
too if you can, what you savor most in pondering on this
sweetest of mysteries: the most benign gesture of the Word,
or the unfathomable glory of the soul, or the unpredictable
confidence of the sinner. Moses could not change the color of
his Ethiopian wife,[36] but Christ could. For the text continues: "Your cheeks are beautiful as the turtle dove's."[37]
But this must wait for another sermon, so that always eagerly
partaking of the food provided for us on the Bridegroom's
table,[38] we may continue to praise and glorify him, Jesus
Christ our Lord, who is God blessed for ever. Amen.[39]

30. Ps 113:1
31. Ezra 7:28
32. Ex 15:1
33. Ps 19:8
34. 1 Jn 4:10

35. Ex 2:21; Num 12:1
36. Jer 13:23
37. Song 1:9
38. Lk 10:8
39. Rom 1:25

SERMON 40

THE FACE OF THE BRIDE

"**Y**OUR CHEEKS ARE BEAUTIFUL as the turtle dove's."[1] The bride's modesty is a delicate thing; and I feel that at the Bridegroom's reproof a warm flush suffused her face, so heightening her beauty that she immediately was greeted with: "Your cheeks are beautiful as the turtle dove's." You must not give an earthbound meaning to this coloring of the corruptible flesh, to this gathering of bood-red liquid that spreads evenly beneath the surface of her pearly skin, quietly mingling with it to enhance her physical beauty by the pink and white loveliness of her cheeks. For the substance of the soul is incorporeal and invisible, possessing neither bodily limbs not any visible coloring. Try then as best you can to grasp the nature of this spiritual entity by means of a spiritual insight; and to conserve the fittingness of the proposed comparison take note that the mind's intention is the soul's face. The quality of work is evaluated from the intention, just as the body's beauty from the face. We may see in this flush on the cheek an unassuming disposition in which virtue and beauty thrive and grace increases. "Your cheeks then are beautiful as the turtle dove's." When describing her beauty he referred as is customary to her face, for when a person's beauty is praised the normal thing to say is that she has a beautiful or comely face;[2] though I cannot see what was the purpose of speaking

1. Song 1:9   2. Gen 29:17; 39:6; Esther 2:7

199

of cheeks in the plural except that it cannot have been without a purpose. For the one who speaks is the Spirit of Wisdom, who performs no action, not even the smallest, in vain, nor speaks except according to his nature. Whatever it be, there is a reason why he prefers to speak of cheeks in the plural than of face in the singular. And unless you can offer something better, I shall give you my view of the reason.

II.　2. The intention which we have referred to as the face of the soul must have two elements: matter and purpose, what you intend and why. It is from these two that we judge the beauty or deformity of the soul, and hence the person in whom they are found correct and pure may justly and truly be told: "Your cheeks are beautiful as the turtle dove's." But she who lacks one of these cannot be complimented that her cheeks are beautiful as the turtle dove's, because of her partial deformity. Much less can it be suitably said to one who possesses neither of these qualities. But all this will become more clear by giving examples. If, for instance, a person makes up his mind to pursue the truth, and that solely from a love of truth, is it not obvious that for him both matter and motive are equally correct and that he had achieved the right to be told that his cheeks are beautiful as the turtle dove's, since on neither cheek does an unbecoming blemish appear? But if his reason for pursuing the truth is self-glorification or the attainment of some worldly advantage,[3] then even though one of his cheeks should seem perfectly formed, I feel you would not hesitate to consider him partially deformed because of the baseness of the motive that disfigures the other cheek. But if you discover a man who has no good motives, who is entangled in the net of sensual desire, a glutton and voluptuary like those whose god is the belly, who glory in their shame, whose minds are set on earthly things:[4] what of him? If his intention is vitiated both in matter and motive will you not judge him to be totally repellent?

　　3. Therefore to direct one's mind completely to worldly

<hr>

3. Gal 5:26; Phil 2:3　　　　　　　　4. Phil 3:19

pursuits rather than toward God is the sign of a worldly person whose cheeks are totally devoid of beauty. To direct one's mind as it were toward God but not for the sake of God, betrays the attitude of the hypocrite, one of whose cheeks may seem attractive because of a vaunted concern for God, but whose pretence nullifies every form of attractiveness and contaminates the whole with its ugliness. Again, if one directs one's mind to God solely or chiefly because of the necessities of the present life, I cannot say that it stinks with the dregs of hypocrisy, but it is so befogged by pettiness of spirit that it cannot merit acceptance. On the contrary, to give one's attention to something other than God, although for God's sake, means to embark on Martha's busy life rather than Mary's way of contemplation. I do not say that this soul is deformed, but it has not attained to perfect beauty, for it worries and frets about so many things,[5] and is bound to be stained to some degree with the grime of worldly affairs. This however is quickly and easily cleansed at the hour of a death made holy by the grace of a pure intention and a good conscience. And therefore, to seek God for his own sake alone, this is to possess two cheeks made most beautiful by the two elements of intention. This is the bride's own special gift, the source of that unique prerogative by which she may be told with all propriety: "Your cheeks are beautiful as the turtle dove's."

III. 4. But why as the turtle dove's? This is a chaste little bird that leads a retired life, content to live with one mate; if it loses this mate it does not seek another but lives alone thenceforward. In order that you who hear me may not hear in vain the doctrines that were written for your sake,[6] that now for your sake are being examined and discussed: you I say who are moved by the urgings of the Holy Spirit and long to perform all that is required of one who would be the bride of God, strive to ensure that both elements of your intention are like two beautiful cheeks; then, in imitation of that most

5. Lk 10:38-42   6. 1 Cor 9:10

chaste of birds, and following the advice of the Prophet, abide
in solitude because you have raised yourself above yourself.[7]
You are well above yourself when espoused to the Lord of
angels; surely you are above yourself when joined to the Lord
and become one spirit with him? [8] Live alone therefore like
the turtle dove. Avoid the crowds, avoid the places where
men assemble; forget even your people and your father's
house and the king will desire your beauty.[9] O holy soul,
remain alone, so that you might keep yourself for him alone
whom you have chosen for yourself out of all that exist.
Avoid going abroad, avoid even the members of your household; withdraw from friends and those you love, not
excepting the man who provides for your needs. Can you not
see how shy your Love is, that he will never come to you
when others are present? Therefore you must withdraw,
mentally rather than physically, in your intention, in your
devotion, in your spirit. For Christ the Lord is a spirit before
your face,[10] and he demands solitude of the spirit more than
of the body, although physical withdrawal can be of benefit
when the opportunity offers, especially in time of prayer. To
do this is to follow the advice and example of the Bridegroom, that when you want to pray you should go into your
room, shut the door and then pray.[11] And what he said he
did. He spent nights alone in prayer,[12] not merely hiding
from the crowds[13] but even from his disciples and familiar
friends. He did indeed take three of his friends with him
when the hour of his death was approaching;[14] but the urge
to pray drew him apart even from them. You too must act
like this[15] when you wish to pray.

5. Apart from that the only solitude prescribed for you is
that of the mind and spirit. You enjoy this solitude if you
refuse to share in the common gossip, if you shun involvement in the problems of the hour and set no store by the

7. Lam 3:28
8. 1 Cor 6:17
9. Ps 44:11-12
10. Lam 4:20
11. Mt 6:6

12. Lk 6:12; 9:18
13. Jn 12:36
14. Mt 26:37
15. Lk 10:37; 22:41

fancies that attract the masses; if you reject what everybody covets, avoid disputes, make light of losses, and pay no heed to injuries.[16] Otherwise you are not alone even when alone. Do you not see that you can be alone when in company and in company when alone? However great the crowds that surround you, you can enjoy the benefits of solitude if you refrain from curiosity about other people's conduct and shun rash judgment. Even if you should see your neighbor doing what is wrong, refuse to pass judgment on him, excuse him instead. Excuse his intention even if you cannot excuse the act, which may be the fruit of ignorance or surprise or chance. Even if you are so certain that to dissemble is impossible, you must still endeavor to convince yourself by saying: "It was an overwhelming temptation; what should become of me if it attacked me with the same force? " Remember too that all this time I have been speaking to the bride, not to the friend of the Bridegroom, who has another reason for keeping careful watch to prevent his charge from sinning, to examine if sin has been committed, and to administer correction when it has. The bride is free from this kind of obligation, she lives alone for the love of him who is her Bridegroom and Lord, who is God blessed for ever. Amen.[17]

16. 2 Sam 19:19   17. Rom 1:25

SERMON 41

THE INTELLECT, FAITH AND CONTEMPLATION

"YOUR NECK AS JEWELS."[1] Normally the neck is adorned with jewels, not compared to them. For those who wear jewelry have no beauty of their own, and must go to another source to beg its outward show that they might make it deceptively their own. But the neck of the bride is so beautiful in itself, so exquisitely formed by nature, that any external adornment is superfluous. Why load it with a pretentious coloring of strange baubles when its own native loveliness is so complete, more than equal to the splendor of any jewels that could be found to enrich it? This is what the Bridegroom wished to convey, for he did not say, as one would expect, that the jewels were suspended round her neck, but that it was "as jewels." Here we must call upon the Holy Spirit, that just as his love enabled us to discover the spiritual cheeks of the bride, so it may also reveal to us the spiritual mystery of the neck. And to my mind, for I can only say what I think, nothing seems more credible or probable than that the word neck signifies the soul's intellect. I feel that you too will support this interpretation when you examine the reason for the comparison. Do you not see that the function of the neck somehow resembles that of the intellect, by which your soul receives its vital spiritual nourishment, and communicates it to the inward faculties of the will and the affections? And so when this neck of the bride, understood as the pure and simple intellect, is radiant through and through with the clear and naked truth,[2] it has no need of

1. Song 1:9   2. Heb 4:13

embellishment; on the contrary it is itself a precious jewel that becomingly adorns the soul, which is why it is portrayed as resembling jewels. The truth is a jewel of great excellence, so are purity and candor, and especially the power to make a sober estimate of oneself.[3] The intellect of rationalists and heretics is not endowed with this radiance of purity and truth; hence they spend time and energy in primping and festooning it with the tinsel of words and tricks of sophistry, lest it be seen for what it is, and the shame of its falseness be revealed as well.

II.   2. The text continues: "We will make you ornaments of gold, studded with silver."[4] If it were "I will make" in the singular and not "we will make" in the plural I should declare unconditionally and unhesitatingly that the Bridegroom was the speaker here too. But perhaps it would be more appropriate to assign it to his companions, who try to console the bride with the promise that until she can see in the beatific vision him for whom she longs so ardently, they will make her beautiful and costly pendants for her ears. The reason for this I think is that faith comes by hearing:[5] as long as she walks by faith and not by sight[6] she must put more reliance on the ear than on the eye. It is pointless for her to strain toward this vision with eyes that the faith has not yet purified, since it has been promised as a reward to those alone who are clean of heart.[7] It is written: "By faith he cleanses men's hearts."[8] Therefore, since faith comes by hearing, and through faith the power of vision is clarified, it is but right to concentrate on adorning her ears, because reason here tells us that hearing is a preparation for seeing. They say: "You long, O bride, to gaze on the glory of your Beloved; but that belongs to another time. For now we suspend these pendants from your ears, to console you while you wait and even to prepare you for that vision to which you lay claim." Their words echo the Psalmist's: "Hear, O daughter, and see."[9] "You

3. Rom 12:3
4. Song 1:10
5. Rom 10:17
6. 2 Cor 5:7

7. Mt 5:8
8. Acts 15:9
9. Ps 44:11

long for the power to see, but you must first listen. To listen is
to move toward vision. Listen then, bow down you ear for the
pendants we are making for you, that by obedient listening
you may come to the splendor of the vision. We will make
your listening a thing of joy and gladness.[10] We cannot enable
you to see the vision that will be the fullness of your joy and
the fulfillment of your desire: to bestow that is the privilege
of the person you love.[11] To complete your happiness[12] he
will show you himself, he will fill you with gladness by let-
ting you see his face.[13] But for the moment, for your
consolation, take these pendants that we offer you; the delights that he holds in his right hand will remain for ever."[14]

III. 3. We should take note of the kind of pendants they offer
her: they are made of gold and studded with silver.[15] Gold
signifies the splendor of the divine nature, the wisdom that
comes from above.[16] The heavenly goldsmiths to whom this
work is committed, promise that they will fashion resplen-
dent tokens of the truth and insert them in the soul's inward
ears. I cannot see what this may mean if not the construction
of certain spiritual images in order to bring the purest intu-
itions of divine wisdom before the eyes of the soul that contemplates, to enable it to perceive, as though puzzling reflections in a mirror, what it cannot possibly gaze on as yet face
to face.[17] The things we speak of are divine, totally unknown
except to those who have experienced them. While still
in this mortal body,[18] while still living by faith, while the
content of the clear interior light is still not made clear, we
can, in part, still contemplate the pure truth. Any one of us
who has been given this gift from above[19] may make his own
the words of St Paul: "Now I know in part;"[20] and: "We
know in part and in part we prophesy."[21] But when the spirit

10. Ps 50:10
11. Song 1:6
12. Jn 16:24
13. Jn 14:21
14. Ps 15:11
15. Song 1:10

16. Jas 1:17
17. 1 Cor 13:12
18. Rom 6:12
19. Jn 19:11
20. 1 Cor 13:12
21. 1 Cor 13:19

is ravished out of itself[22] and granted a vision of God that suddenly shines into the mind with the swiftness of a lightning-flash, immediately, but whence I know not, images of earthly things fill the imagination, either as an aid to understanding or to temper the intensity of the divine light. So well-adapted are they to the divinely illumined senses, that in their shadow the utterly pure and brilliant radiance of the truth is rendered more bearable to the mind and more capable of being communicated to others. My opinion is that they are formed in our imaginations by the inspirations of the holy angels, just as on the other hand there is no doubt that evil suggestions of an opposite nature are forced upon us by the bad angels.[23]

4. Perhaps, too, we have here those puzzling reflections seen by the Apostle in the mirror[24] and fashioned, as I have said, by angelic hands from pure and beautiful images, which I feel bring us in contact somehow with the being of God, that in its pure state is perceived without any shadow of corporeal substances. The elegance of the imagery that so worthily clothes and reveals it I attribute to angelic skill. That this is so is more distinctly conveyed by another version: "We, the artificers, will make you images of gold, with silver decorations."[25] "With silver decorations" and "studded with silver" mean the same thing. To me they seem to signify not merely that the angels produce these images within us, but that they also inspire the elegance of diction which so fittingly and gracefully embellishes with greater clarity and keener enjoyment our communication of them to the audience. And if you ask me what connection there is between speech and silver, I give you the Prophet's answer: "The words of the Lord are pure words: silver refined in a crucible."[26] This is how these ministering spirits from heaven[27] fashion ornaments of gold studded with silver for the bride to wear during her earthly pilgrimage.

22. 2 Cor 5:13
23. Ps 77:49
24. 1 Cor 13:12

25. Song 1:10 (Septuagint)
26. Ps 11:7
27. Heb 1:14

IV. 5. Take note however that she yearns for one thing and receives another. In spite of her longing for the repose of contemplation she is burdened with the task of preaching; and despite her desire to bask in the Bridegroom's presence she is entrusted with the cares of begetting and rearing children. Nor is this the only time she has been so treated. Once before when she sighed for the Bridegroom's kisses and embraces she was told: "Your breasts are better than wine,"[28] to make her realize that she was a mother, that her duty was to suckle her babes, to provide food for her children. If indolence does not prevent you from trying, perhaps you too can discover further similar instances in other verses of this Song. Was it not prefigured long ago in the life of the holy Patriarch Jacob, when, instead of the long-awaited embraces of his desired Rachel, beautiful though barren, he was given, against his will and contrary to his plans, one who was fecund but blear-eyed?[29] So now too, the bride, as she is eagerly enquiring to learn where her Beloved pastures his flock and rests at noon,[30] is given instead ornaments of gold studded with silver, gifts of wisdom and eloquence, and committed to the work of preaching.

6. We learn from this that only too often we must interrupt the sweet kisses to feed the needy with the milk of doctrine. No one must live for himself but all must live for him who died for all.[31] Woe to those who are gifted with the power to think and speak worthily of God if they imagine that godliness is a means for gain,[32] if they make vain-glorious use of the talents given them for the winning of souls to God, if in their high-mindedness they refuse to associate with the lowly.[33] Let them fear what the Lord said by the mouth of his Prophet: "I gave them my gold and my silver; but they have used my gold and my silver in the service of Baal."[34] For your part, listen to the bride's reply when she receives on the one hand a reproof, on the other a promise. She is neither

28. Song 1:1
29. Gen 29:16-29
30. Song 1:6
31. 2 Cor 5:15
32. 1 Tim 6:5
33. Rom 12:16
34. Hos 2:8

puffed up by promises nor angered by the rebuke, but exemplifies the scriptural saying: "Reprove a wise man and he will love you."[35] With reference to gifts and promises we are also told: "The greater you are, the more you must humble yourself in all things."[36] That she was faithful to these principles will be clear from her reply. But a discussion on this must be postponed, if you do not mind, to await another sermon, and for what has been said so far let us give glory to the Church's Bridegroom, our Lord Jesus Christ, who is God blessed for ever. Amen.[37]

---

35. Prov 9:8
36. Sir 3:20

37. Rom 1:25

SERMON 42

FRATERNAL CORRECTION—TWO KINDS OF HUMILITY

"WHILE THE KING WAS ON HIS COUCH, my nard gave forth its fragrance."[1] These are the bride's words that we have left until today. This is the answer she gave when rebuked by the Bridegroom, not to the Bridegroom however but to his companions, as can easily be gathered from the words themselves. For since she does not address him directly and say: "When you were on your couch, O King," but: "when he was on his couch," it is clear that she does not speak to him but of him. Try to imagine therefore how the Bridegroom, seemingly after he had reproved or repulsed her, sees the blush of shame that covers her cheeks and departs from the room to give her the opportunity to express her feelings freely. If, as often happened, she yielded more than was becoming to dismay and depression, his companions would console and re-assure her. Not that he omits to do this himself, but he waits for the opportune moment. And to show clearly how pleasing to him she was even while correcting her, for she bore that correction becomingly and in the proper spirit, he could not depart till he had praised the beauty of her cheeks and neck in words that came from his heart. Hence those who remain with her, knowing what the Lord has in mind, try to charm her out of her sadness and present her with gifts. Her words then are addressed to them. This is how they fit within the context.

1. Song 1:11

210

2. But before attempting to extract the kernal of spiritual truth from this shell, I make one brief remark.

II. Happy the Superior who finds a reaction to his reprimand similar to the example given here. Far more desirable that there should never be a need to reprimand! That would be the better thing. But because "we all make many mistakes,"[2] and duty obliges me to correct those who err,[3] I may not remain silent; and indeed love impels me to act.[4] And if, in the fulfilling of my duty, I do correct someone only to see that my reprimand fails entirely to achieve its purpose, echoing its futility back to me like a javelin that strikes and recoils, what do you think, brothers, are my feelings then? Am I not frustrated! Am I not angered! Because of my own lack of wisdom let me quote the words of a Master:[5] "I am caught in a dilemma and know not what to choose." Should I be complacent about what I have said because I have done my duty, or perform a penance for what I have said because I have failed in my purpose? For I wished by overthrowing an enemy to rescue a friend, and did not do so; rather the contrary happened, I have offended him and set him deeper in the wrong.[6] He now despises me. "They will not listen to you," said the Prophet, "because they will not listen to me."[7] Note the greatness of him who is involved in this contempt. Do not imagine that you have despised only me. The Lord has spoken, and what he said to the Prophet[8] he also said to the Apostles: "He who despises you, despises me."[9] I am neither prophet nor apostle, but I dare to say that I fulfill the role both of prophet and apostle; and though far beneath them in merits I am caught up in similar cares. Even though it be to my great embarrassment, though it put me at serious risk, I am seated on the chair of Moses,[10] to whose quality of life I do not lay claim and whose grace I

2. Jas 3:2
3. 1 Tim 5:20
4. 2 Cor 5:14
5. St Paul: Phil 1:22-23
6. Prov 8:36

7. Ezek 3:7
8. Is 1:2
9. Lk 10:16
10. Mt 23:2

do not experience. What then? That one must withhold respect for the chair because the man sitting there is unworthy? But even though the Scribes and Pharisees be seated on it, Christ has said: "Do what they tell you."[11]

3. Quite often impatience is joined to the contempt, so that the man rebuked not only neglects to amend but is even angry with his corrector, like a madman who spurns his doctor's hand. What extraordinary perversity! While refusing to be angry with the archer who shot him, he is angry with his physician! That one who shoots in the dark at the spright of heart[12] has now shot the death-blow into your own self; and you fail to react against him? Yet you are annoyed with me when all I want is to put you right! "Be angry but do not sin,"[13] Scripture says. If your anger is directed against your sin, not only do you not sin but you destroy the sin you had committed. Now however you add sin to sin[14] by spurning the remedy in this senseless fit of anger; this is a sin of special malice.[15]

4. Sometimes the anger is spiced with impudence, as when the correction is not only met with impatience but the error impudently defended. This is obvious recklessness. God can say to such a man: "You have a harlot's brow, you refuse to be ashamed;"[16] and again: "My jealousy will depart from you, I shall be angry with you no more."[17] Merely to hear these words makes me shudder. Do you not feel how perilous it is, how horrible and frightening, to defend one's sin? For God also says: "All whom I love I reprove and discipline."[18] If God's jealous anger has turned away from you, so also has his love; if you think yourself unfit for his chastisement, you will not be fit for his love.[19] It is when God does not show his anger that he is most angry: "We have shown favor to the wicked," he says, "and he does not learn righteousness."[20] This kind of favor is not for me. To be spared on these terms is worse than any anger, it leaves me shut off from the paths

---

11. Mt 23:3
12. Ps 10:3
13. Ps 4:5; Eph 4:26
14. Ps 77:17
15. Rom 7:13

16. Jer 3:3
17. Ezek 16:42
18. Rev 3:19
19. Eccles 9:1
20. Is 26:10

of righteousness. Better for me to follow the Prophet's advice and learn discipline, lest the Lord be angry and I fall away from the true path.[21] I prefer that you be angry with me, O Father of Mercies,[22] but with that anger by which you put the sinner right rather than drive him off the path. A correction benignly administered begets the former, an ominous concealment of your anger leads to the latter. It is not when I am ignorant of your anger but when I feel it, that I trust most in your goodwill for me, because when you are angry you will remember to be merciful.[23] "You were a forgiving God to your people," according to the Psalmist, "but an avenger of their wrong-doings."[24] He is speaking of Moses and Aaron and Samuel whom he had previously mentioned, and considers it a mercy that God did not spare their waywardness. But you? Go on defending your error and condemning the correction, and cut yourself off from this mercy forever! But that is surely to call evil good and good evil. And out of this odious impudence shall we not soon see emerging the buds of impenitence, the mother of despair? For who will repent of what he thinks good? Woe to them, the Prophet says.[25] And that woe is for eternity. It is one thing for a person to be tempted when he is lured and enticed by his own desire,[26] but quite another to freely pursue evil as good, to speed toward death with a false security as if on the way to life.

III.   For this reason I should sometimes prefer to remain silent and pretend I had not seen some wrong being done, rather than to bring about so great a calamity by a reprimand.

5. Perhaps you will tell me that my good deed will redound to my welfare;[27] that I have freed my own soul and am innocent of the blood of that man[28] in speaking and warning him to turn away from his evil path that he might live.[29] But though you give me countless reasons they will not comfort

21. Ps 2:12
22. 2 Cor 1:3
23. Hab 3:2
24. Ps 98:8
25. Is 5:20

26. Jas 1:14
27. Is 55:11
28. 2 Sam 3:28
29. Ezek 3:18

me because my eyes rest on a son who is dying. It is as if by that reprimand I sought to achieve my own salvation rather than his. Where is the mother who will be able to restrain her tears when she sees her ailing son at the point of death, even if she knows she has devoted all possible care and attention to him, but in vain, since all her efforts now come to nothing? She weeps because death takes him from her for a time. How much more should I weep and lament for the eternal death of a son of mine even if I am conscious of no failure on my part, even though I have warned him? You see then how great the evils from which a man delivers both himself and me when he responds with meekness on being corrected, submits respectfully, obeys modestly, and humbly admits his fault. To a man like this I shall in all things be a debtor, I shall minister to and serve him as a genuine lover of my Lord, for he is one who can truly say: "while the king was on his couch, my nard gave forth its fragrance."[30]

6. How good the fragrance of humility that ascends from the valley of tears, that permeates all places within reach, and perfumes even the royal couch with its sweet delight.

IV. The nard is an insignificant herb, said by those who specialize in the study of plants to be of a warm nature. Hence it seems to be fittingly taken in this place for the virtue of humility, but aglow with the warmth of holy love. I say this because there is a humility inspired and inflamed by charity, and a humility begotten in us by truth but devoid of warmth. This latter depends on our knowledge, the former on our affections. For if you sincerely examine your inward dispositions in the light of truth, and judge them unflatteringly for what they are, you will certainly be humiliated by the baseness that this true knowledge reveals to you, though you perhaps as yet cannot endure that others, too, should see this image. So far it is truth that compels your humility, it is as yet untouched by the inpouring of love. But if you were so moved by a love of that truth which, like a radiant light, so

30. Song 1:11

wholesomely discovered to you the reality of your condition, you would certainly desire, as far as in you lies, that the opinions of others about you should correspond with what you know of yourself. I say, as far as in you lies, because it is often inexpedient to make known to others all that we know about ourselves, and we are forbidden by the very love of truth and the truth of love to attempt to reveal what would injure another. But if under the impulse of selflove you inwardly conceal the true judgment you have formed of yourself, who can doubt that you lack a love for truth, since you show preference for your own interest and reputation?

7. Convicted by the light of truth then, a man may judge himself of little worth, but you know this is far from the equivalent of a spontaneous association with the lowly[31] that springs from the gift of love. Necessity compels the former, the latter is of free choice. "He emptied himself, taking the form of a servant,"[32] and so gave us the pattern of humility. He emptied himself, he humbled himself, not under constraint of an assessment of himself but inspired by love for us. Though he could appear abject and despicable in men's eyes, he could not judge himself to be so in reality, because he knew who he was. It was his will, not his judgment, that moved him to adopt a humble guise that he knew did not represent him; though not unaware that he was the highest he chose to be looked on as the least. And so we find him saying: "Learn from me for I am gentle and humble in heart."[33] He said "in heart;" in the affection of the heart, which signifies the will, and a decision arising from the will excludes compulsion. You and I truly know that we deserve disgrace and contempt, that we deserve the worst treatment and the lowest rank, that we deserve punishment, even the whip; but not he. Yet he experienced all these things because he willed it;[34] he was humble in heart, humble with that humility that springs from the heart's love, not that which is exacted by truthful reasoning.

31. Rom 12:16
32. Phil 2:7
33. Mt 11:29
34. Is 53:7

V. 8. So then, I have said that we attain to this voluntary humility not by truthful reasoning but by an inward infusion of love, since it springs from the heart, from the affections, from the will; you must judge whether I am right. But I also submit to the scrutiny of your judgment the rectitude by which I attribute this to the Lord, who under love's inspiration emptied himself,[35] under love's inspiration was made lower than the angels,[36] under love's inspiration was obedient to his parents,[37] under love's inspiration bowed down under the Baptist's hands,[38] endured the weakness of the flesh, and became liable to death, even the ignominious death of the cross. And one more thing I ask you to consider: whether I have been correct in assuming that this humility, aglow with love, is symbolized by that lowly plant, the nard. And if you do assent to all these opinions—and you must give assent to evidence that is so manifest—then if you feel humiliated by that inescapable sense of unworthiness implanted by the Truth that examines both heart and mind[39] in the very being of one who is attentive, try to use your will and make a virtue of necessity, because there is no virtue without the will's co-operation. You will achieve this if you do not wish to appear externally in any way different from what you discover in your heart. Otherwise you must fear that you will read your fate in words like the following: "He flatters himself in his own eyes that his iniquity cannot be found out and hated."[40] For "diverse weights and diverse measures are both alike an abomination to the Lord."[41] What am I getting at? Will you despise yourself in your own heart when you weigh yourself in the balance of God's truth, and yet deceive the public with a different estimate by selling yourself to us at a greater weight than Truth has indicated? Let the fear of God prevent you from attempting anything so despicable[42] as to commend the man whose unworthiness is revealed by God's truth: for this is to resist the truth, to fight against God.[43]

35. Phil 2:7
36. Heb 2:9
37. Lk 2:51
38. Mt 3:15
39. Ps 7:10

40. Ps 35:3
41. Prov 20:10
42. Prov 3:7
43. 2 Mac 7:19

You must rather submit to God and let your will be docile to the Truth;[44] and more than docile, even dedicated. "Was not my soul subject to God," said the Psalmist."[45]

9. It counts for little, however, that you are submissive to God, unless you be submissive to every human creature for God's sake,[46] whether it be the abbot as first superior or to the other officers appointed by him. I go still further and say: be subject to your equals and inferiors. "It is fitting," said Christ, "that we should in this way do all that righteousness demands."[47] If you seek an unblemished righteousness, take an interest in the man of little account, defer to those of lesser rank, be of service to the young. Doing this you may dare to say with the bride: "My nard gave forth its fragrance."[48]

VI.   That fragrance is the fervor of your life, the good repute in which all men hold you, so that you might be the good odor of Christ in every place, seen by all, loved by all.[49] Such influence is beyond the man whose humility is compelled by the truth; he is so caught up in self-interest that it cannot flow out so that it will spread abroad. His life bears no fragrance because he lacks fervor, his humility is neither free nor spontaneous. But the bride's humility, like the nard, spreads abroad its fragrance, the warmth of its love, the vigor of its fervor, the inspiring power of its good name. The bride's humility is freely embraced, it is fruitful and it is forever. Its fragrance is destroyed neither by reprimand nor praise. She has heard: "Your cheeks are beautiful as the turtle dove's, your neck like strings of jewels."[50] When promised pendants of gold she acquiesced with humility; the more she is honored the more she humbles herself in all things. She does not boast of her merits nor forget her humility when she hears her praises multiplied. Under this name of nard she humbly vows her lowliness in the spirit of the Virgin Mary's

44. 2 Tim 2:25
45. Ps 61:2
46. 1 Pet 2:13
47. Mt 3:15

48. Song 1:11
49. 2 Cor 2:15
50. Song 1:9

words: "I am unaware of any merit that would warrant all this honor, except that God has been pleased with the lowliness of his handmaid."[51] What else can she mean by saying: "My nard gave forth its fragrance," than that my lowliness was pleasing to him? It was not any wisdom of mine, not any nobility, not any beauty, for these meant nothing to me; it was my humility alone that gave forth fragrance, in its accustomed way. God is habitually pleased with humility; the way of the Lord is to look down lovingly on the humble from the heights of heaven;[52] and therefore while the king was on his couch, in his dwelling-place in the heavens,[53] the fragrance of my humility mounted even to the presence of him of whom the Psalmist says: "He dwells on high and takes account of the lowly things in heaven and on earth."[54]

10. Therefore: "while the king was on his couch, my nard gave forth its fragrance."[55]

VII. The king's couch is the heart of the Father,[56] because the Son is always in the Father.[57] Never doubt of the mercy of this king, whose eternal resting place is the abode of the Father's love. What wonder that the cry of the humble should reach to him whose dwelling-place[58] is at that source of all kindliness, where his happiness is most intimate and his goodness consubstantial with that of the Father; for he receives all that he is from the Father, and the timorous glance of the lowly will see in his royal power nothing that is not fatherly. Therefore the Lord says: "Because the poor are despoiled, because the needy groan, I will now arise."[59] The bride knows this because she is a well-loved member of his household; she knows that her Bridegroom's favors will not be limited by the poverty of her merits, for she puts her trust solely in her lowliness. Yet she gives him the title of king, for while smarting from the reprimand she does not dare to call

51. Lk 1:48
52. Ps 137:6
53. Deut 26:15
54. Ps 112:5-6
55. Song 1:11

56. Jn 1:18
57. Jn 10:38; 14:10-11
58. Ex 2:23
59. Ps 11:6

him Bridegroom. He is said to dwell on high,[60] but this does not weaken the trust that permeates her humility.

11. You may very suitably apply the text of this sermon to the early church, if you recall those days when, after the Lord had ascended to where he was before and seated himself at the Father's right hand,[61] on that ancient, magnificent and glorious couch, the disciples came together in one place, persevering with one mind in prayer along with the women and Mary the mother of Jesus and his brothers.[62] Do you not feel that was a time when the nard of the tiny and timorous bride gave forth its fragrance? And when suddenly a sound came from heaven like the rush of a mighty wind and filled all the house where they were sitting,[63] could she not say in her littleness and indigence: "While the king was on his couch my nard gave forth its fragrance"?[64] All who lived in that place clearly perceived the ascent of that fragrance of humility, so agreeable and so welcome, and the immediate response of a rich and glorious reward. Nor was the bride ungrateful for that favor. For hear: no sooner is she possessed by the ardor then she professes herself ready to endure any evil for the sake of his name, for the following text runs: "My beloved is to me a bunch of myrrh that lies between my breasts."[65] But I feel too weak to speak any further. I shall say that under the name of myrrh she includes all the bitter trials she is willing to undergo through love of her beloved. Some other time we shall continue with the remainder of the text, provided that the Holy Spirit will be attentive to your prayers and enable me to understand the words of the bride, since he himself has inspired and composed them in a way befitting the praises of him whose Spirit he is, the Church's Bridegroom, our Lord Jesus Christ, who is God blessed for ever. Amen.[66]

---

60. Ps 112:5
61. Mk 16:19
62. Acts 1:14
63. Acts 2:2

64. Song 1:11
65. Song 1:12
66. Rom 1:25

SERMON 43

THE SUFFERINGS OF CHRIST

"MY BELOVED IS TO ME a little bundle of myrrh that lies between my breasts."[1] Recently he was king, now he is the beloved; recently he was on his royal couch, now he lies between the breasts of the bride. This illustrates the great power of humility, to which the God of majesty will so gladly yield. In a moment reverence has given way to friendship, and he who seemed so distant has been quickly brought close.[2] "My Beloved is to me a little bundle of myrrh." Because myrrh is a bitter herb it symbolizes the burdensome harshness of afflictions. Foreseeing that the service of her beloved makes them inevitable, she speaks with a sense of gladness, trusting that she will undergo them all with courage. "The disciples left the presence of the council, rejoicing that they were counted worthy to suffer dishonor for the name of Jesus."[3] Hence she refers to the beloved by the diminutive endearment, "bunch," not bundle, to indicate that the love she bore him would make light of imminent hardship and pain. How apt the word bunch, for he is born to us an infant.[4] Apt, too, in another sense, because "the sufferings of this present time are not worth comparing with the glory that is to be revealed to us.[5] For this slight momentary affliction is preparing for us an eternal weight of glory beyond all comparison."[6] What today

1. Song 1:12
2. Eph 2:13
3. Acts 5:41

4. Is 9:6
5. Rom 8:18
6. 2 Cor 4:17

220

is a bunch of myrrh will become one future day an immense profusion of glory. A bunch surely, if its yoke is easy and its burden light.[7] Not that it is of its nature light —there was nothing light about the cruel passion or the bitter death —only the lover finds it light. Hence she does not say: "My Beloved is a bunch of myrrh;" but rather he is a bunch of myrrh "to me," because I love. That is why she calls him "beloved," to show that the power of love can prove superior to all the miseries of suffering for "love is strong as death."[8] As proof, too, that she does not glory in herself but in the Lord,[9] that she does not presume on her own strength but on his, she says that he will lie between her breasts. To him she sings with safety: "Even though I should walk in the midst of the shadow of death I will not fear evil because you are with me"[10]

II.   2. I remember saying in one of my previous sermons[11] that the breasts of the bride signified a sharing in joy and a sympathy in suffering, like the Pauline prescription to rejoice with those who rejoice and to weep with those who weep.[12] And because her life swings between extremes of good fortune and bad, with peril lurking on both sides, she wants to find her beloved midway between these breasts, so that fortified against both by his unceasing protection, she may not be proud in prosperity nor depressed in sorrow. You too, if you are wise, will imitate the prudence of the bride, and never permit even for an hour that this precious bunch of myrrh should be removed from your bosom. Preserve without fail the memory of all those bitter things he endured for you, persevere in meditating on him and you in turn will be able to say: "My beloved is to me a little bunch of myrrh that lies between my breasts."[13]

3. As for me, dear brothers, from the early days of my conversion, conscious of my grave lack of merits, I made sure

---

7. Mt 11:30
8. Song 8:6
9. 1 Cor 1:31; 2 Cor 10:17
10. Ps 22:4

11. Serm. 10: par. 2; CF 4:62
12. Rom 12:15
13. Song 1:12

to gather for myself this little bunch of myrrh and place it between my breasts. It was culled from all the anxious hours and bitter experiences of my Lord; first from the privations of his infancy, then from the hardships he endured in preaching, the fatigues of his journeys, the long watches in prayer, the temptations when he fasted, his tears of compassion, the heckling when he addressed the people, and finally the dangers from traitors in the brotherhood,[14] the insults, the spitting, the blows, the mockery, the scorn, the nails and similar torments that are multiplied in the Gospels, like trees in the forest, and all for the salvation of our race. Among the teeming little branches of this perfumed myrrh I feel we must not forget the myrrh which he drank upon the cross[15] and used for his anointing at his burial.[16] In the first of these he took upon himself the bitterness of my sins, in the second he affirmed the future incorruption of my body. As long as I live I shall proclaim the memory of the abounding goodness contained in these events;[17] throughout eternity I shall not forget these mercies, for in them I have found life.[18]

4. These are the mercies that King David once begged for with tears as he said: "Let your mercies come to me that I may live."[19] And another of the saints sighed as he recalled these, and said: "The mercies of the Lord are many."[20] What a multitude of kings and prophets desired to see, and did not![21] They worked hard, and I have entered into the reward of their labors.[22] I have reaped the myrrh that they had planted. This life-giving bunch has been reserved for me; no one will take it away from me,[23] it shall lie between my breasts.

III. I have said that wisdom is to be found in meditating on these truths. For me they are the source of perfect righteousness, of the fullness of knowledge,[24] of the most

---

14. 2 Cor 11:26
15. Mt 27:48
16. Jn 19:39
17. Ps 144:7
18. Ps 118:93
19. Ps 118:77

20. Ps 118:156
21. Lk 10:24
22. Jn 4:38
23. Jn 16:22
24. Is 33:6

efficacious graces, of abundant merits. Sometimes I draw from them a drink that is wholesomely bitter, sometimes an unction that is sweet and consoling. When I am in difficulties they bear me up, when I am happy they regulate my conduct. For anyone traveling on God's royal road, they provide safe guidance amid the joys and sorrows of this life, warding off impending evils on every side. These win me the favor of him who is the world's judge, revealing him, despite his awesome powers, as one who is gentle and humble. Though beyond the reaches of princes and filling kings with fear,[25] he is yet not one who only forgives but even offers himself as an example to follow. Hence as you well know, these sentiments are often on my lips, and God knows they are always in my heart. They are a familiar theme in my writings, as is evident. This is my philosophy, one more refined and interior, to know Jesus and him crucified.[26] I do not ask, as the bride did, where he takes his rest at noon,[27] because my joy is to hold him fast where he lies between my breasts. I do not ask where he rests at noon for I see him on the cross as my Savior. What she desired is the more sublime, what I experience is the more sweet. Her portion was bread that satisfies the hunger of children, mine is the milk that fills the breasts of mothers;[28] therefore I shall keep it between my breasts.

5. Dear brothers, you too must gather this delectable bunch for yourselves, you must place it in the very center of your bosom where it will protect all the avenues to your heart. Let it abide between your breasts. Always make sure it is not behind you on your shoulders, but ahead of you where your eyes can see it, for if you bear it without smelling it the burden will weigh you down and the fragrance will not lift you up. Be mindful that this is the Christ that Simeon took in his arms;[29] whom Mary bore in her womb, fostered in her lap, and like a bride placed between her breasts. And not to leave anything out, he was present too in the prophetic words

25. Ps 75:13
26. 1 Cor 2:2
27. Song 1:6
28. 1 Cor 3:2
29. Lk 2:27

of Zechariah[30] and of many others.[31] And I can imagine how Mary's husband Joseph[32] would often take him on his knees and smile as he played with him. For all these people he was to the fore, not behind. They are an example for you, do as they did.[33] If you carry him where your eyes can rest on him you will find that the sight of his afflictions will make your burdens lighter, helped as you will be by him who is the Church's Bridegroom, God blessed for ever. Amen.[34]

30. Lk 1:67
31. Is 38:4; Jer 1:2; etc
32. Mt 1:16

33. Jn 13:15
34. Rom 1:25

SERMON 44

THE SOUL'S BEAUTY—ITS DIALOGUE WITH THE WORD

"MY BELOVED IS TO ME a cluster of grapes of Cyprus among the vines of En-gedi."[1] If he is beloved, while on the myrrh-tree, how much more in the sweet cluster of grapes. My Lord Jesus dead is a myrrh-tree for me; risen, a cluster of grapes. He has given himself to me as the most wholesome of drinks, bringing tears in full measure.[2] He died for our sins and rose for our justification,[3] that we might die to sin and live in holiness.[4] Hence if you have been truly sorry for your sin you have swallowed the bitter drink; but if a holier life has already refreshed you with the hope of eternal life,[5] the bitterness of myrrh has been changed for you into the wine that gladdens man's heart.[6] Perhaps this is the meaning to be derived from the wine mixed with myrrh offered to the Savior:[7] he refused to drink it because he thirsted for the true wine. You too, once you have tasted the sweet wine after the bitter myrrh, may say without any presumption: "My beloved is to me a cluster of grapes of Cyprus among the vines of En-gedi." The name En-gedi has two interpretations but both meanings can be harmonized. One meaning is "the fountain of the kid," and this manifestly designates the baptism of the nations and the tears of the sinners. It is also called "an eye

1. Song 1:13. En-gedi, "the fountain or well of the kid," was situated on the west shore of the Dead Sea.
2. Ps 79:6
3. Rom 4:25
4. 1 Pet 2:24
5. Tit 1:2
6. Ps 103:15
7. Mt 27:34

for temptation," for along with producing tears it foresees the temptations that are never absent from man's life on this earth.[8] The pagan peoples who lived in darkness[9] could never of their own power perceive the traps of temptation, and therefore could not escape them until they received the light of faith as a gift from him who gives light to the blind;[10] until they entered the Church which has the power to discern what temptation is; until they listened to the instructions of spiritual men who, enlightened by the spirit of wisdom and taught by their own experience, can truly say: we are not ignorant of the designs of the devil.[11]

II. 2. Balsam shrubs grow in En-gedi and the natives cultivate them after the manner of vines; this is perhaps why she referred to them as vines. Otherwise what would a cluster of grapes of Cyprus be doing among the vines of En-gedi? Who ever transported bunches of grapes from one vineyard to another? When something is lacking one supplies it from another source, but not where it is present. By the vines of En-gedi therefore we may understand the peoples of the Church, which possess a liquid balsam, the spirit of gentleness, to soothe and cherish the tenderness of those who are still "babes in Christ,"[12] and to ease the sorrows of repentent sinners. So if a brother sins,[13] let a man of the Church, who has already received this spirit, come to his assistance with all gentleness, not forgetting that he himself may be tempted. It is to typify this that the Church anoints with oil the bodies of all whom she baptizes.

3. But let us consider the man who fell into the hands of brigands and was carried by the good Samaritan to that inn which is the Church.[14] His wounds were healed not by oil alone but by wine and oil, to show that the spiritual physician must possess the wine of fervent zeal as well as the oil of gentleness, since he is called not only to console the timid[15]

8. Job 7:1
9. Is 9:2
10. Ps 145:8
11. 2 Cor 2:11

12. 1 Cor 3:1
13. Gal 6:1
14. Lk 10:30-37
15. 1 Thess 5:14

but to correct the undisciplined. For if he sees that the wounded man, the sinner, rather than improving through the exhortations so gently addressed to him, rather disregards the kindness and becomes gradually more negligent, resting more securely in his sins, then, since the soothing oils have been tried in vain, the physician must use medicines with a more pungent efficacy. He must pour in the wine of repentance,[16] that is, accost him with severe threats and warnings, and if his persistent obduracy demands it in the circumstances, he must beat the contemptuous with the rod of ecclesiastical censure. But where is this wine to come from? In the vineyards of En-gedi one finds oil, not wine. Let him look for it therefore in Cyprus, an island that abounds with wine, the best wine; let him take from there a huge cluster of grapes such as the spies of Israel once carried on a pole between two bearers:[17] that long procession of prophets to the forefront, the band of apostles to the rear, and in between them Jesus, beautifully prefigured by the grapes. Let him take possession of this cluster and say: "My beloved is to me a cluster of grapes of Cyprus."

III. 4. We have seen the cluster, let us see how the wine of zeal is pressed from it. If any man, conscious of his own sins, refuses to be angry when he sees a fellowman committing an offence, but instead approaches him with a love and sympathy that comfort him like the sweetest balsam, here is something whose source we know, about which you have already heard,[18] but perhaps without grasping its significance. What I said is, when a man reflects on his own conduct he ought to feel impelled to be gentle with all.[19] Following the wise counsel of St Paul, he must learn to love those who are caught in habits of sin,[20] not forgetting that he himself is open to temptation. Is it not in this very thing that love of neighbor is rooted, as the commandment reveals: "You must love your neighbor as yourself"?[21] For it is in intimate

16. Ps 59:5
17. Num 13:24
18. Num 13:24

19. 2 Tim 2:24
20. Gal 6:1
21. Lk 10:27; Lev 19:18

human relationships like this that fraternal love finds its
origins; the natural inbred pleasure with which a man esteems
himself is the nourishing soil that gives it growth and
strength. Then, influenced by grace from above, it yields the
fruits of loving concern, so that a man will not think of
denying to a fellowman who shares the same nature, the good
that he naturally desires for himself. When the opportunity
offers, let him freely and spontaneously do as the occasion
demands, urged by his humane instinct. Where human nature
has not been perverted by sin it possesses this choice and
pleasant balsam that induces compassionate tenderness toward sinners and not an angry severity.

5. We are told in Ecclesiastes that "dying flies spoil this oil
of sweetening,"[22] and since nature lacks the power within
itself to restore what it has lost, it knows it has undergone a
regrettable change. It finds itself in that condition of which
Scripture very truly states: a man's senses and thoughts are
prone to evil from his youth.[23] One cannot commend that
adolescence in which the younger son asks for a portion of
the paternal estate for himself,[24] desiring to have in his private possession goods that are more happily possessed in
common, to have for himself alone the goods that common
use would not have diminished but by personal use will be
squandered. Thus says Scripture: "He squandered all his
goods with prostitutes in a life of debauchery."[25] Who are
these prostitutes? Surely they are those desires of the flesh
that destroy the oil of sweetness of which Scripture so wisely
warns you when it says: "Do not follow your lusts."[26]
Wisdom properly describes them as dying, for the world and
its lusts are passing away.[27] And so when we try to find our
own personal satisfaction in them, we deprive ourselves by this
selfish indulgence of the good that is enjoyed in communal
sharing. These foul and malodorous flies mar the beauty that
nature gives us, they tear the mind with cares and anxieties,
and destroy the pleasure of social intercourse. This man is

22. Eccles 10:1
23. Gen 8:21
24. Lk 15:12

25. Lk 15:13
26. Sir 18:30
27. 1 Jn 2:17

called the younger son because his nature, corrupted by the lusts of thoughtless youth, has forfeited the virile energy and wisdom of mature manhood. Grown churlish in manner and barren of intellect he displays a contempt for everybody but himself and has become a man devoid of love.[28]

IV. 6. From his earliest youth, base and miserable, a man's thoughts and imagination are prone to evil.[29] By nature he is more prompt to dissension than to compassion. Like one who has divested himself entirely of that humanity by which he would wish others to assist him in time of need, he himself will not assist them in their need. He who bears the name of man judges, spurns, ridicules other men; the guilty one condemns the sinners, failing to consider himself lest he himself be tempted.[30] As I have pointed out, nature can never shake off this evil by its own strength, nor regain the oil of innate kindness once it has been destroyed. But what nature cannot do, grace can. And therefore the man on whom the merciful unction of the Holy Spirit deigns to pour out again the grace of its gentleness, will be immediately restored to a truly human condition, and will obtain from grace gifts far greater than nature could bestow. In his faith and gentleness it will make him holy[31] and will endow him with something more than oil, with balsam in the vineyards of En-gedi.

7. There is no reason to doubt that the better gifts[32] flow from the fountain of the kid, whose sprinkling changes kids into lambs and transfers sinners from the left side to the right,[33] so abundantly are they bedewed with the graces of mercy, so that where sin was multiplied, grace now abounds.[34] Is he not restored to true manhood, the man who has abandoned his undisciplined worldliness and been clothed with a human gentleness that is embellished by grace: a disposition that the flies of his carnal lusts had totally destroyed? Out of this humanity that now clothes him —that

---

28. Rom 1:31; Tit 3:3
29. Gen 8:21
30. Gal 6:1
31. Sir 45:4

32. 1 Cor 12:31
33. Mt 25:33
34. Rom 5:20

is, his real self— he draws the inspiration and the insight to
compassionate other men, so that he abhors as he would a
barbarous rite not only the infliction on other men of things
he himself would not endure, but even the omission to do
for all of them all the good he would wish done for himself. [35]

8. That then is the source of the oil. But whence the wine?
From the cluster of grapes of Cyprus. For if you love the
Lord Jesus with all your heart, all your mind, all your
strength,[36] can you see him endure injuries and contempt and
keep a quiet mind? Surely not. Carried away by a burning
ardor for justice,[37] "like a hero fighting-mad with wine,"[38]
with the resolute zeal of Phinehas,[39] you would say with
David: "My zeal consumes me because my foes forget your
words;"[40] or with the Lord: "Zeal for your house devours
me."[41] The wine then is that burning zeal pressed from the
grape-cluster of Cyprus: the love of Christ — a cup that in-
toxicates.[42] Again, "our God is a consuming fire,"[43] and
when the Prophet feels inflamed with divine love he describes
it as a fire sent from heaven into his bones.[44] So when fraternal love gives you gentleness like oil, and divine love
inspires you with zeal like wine, you may feel secure in your
purpose to heal the wounds of the man who fell among brigands, you are equipped for the work of the good
Samaritan.[45] You may repeat, too, with the assurance of the
bride: "My beloved is to me a cluster of grapes of Cyprus
among the vines of En-gedi;"[46] meaning that the fraternal
love that I exercise, my zeal for righteousness, is the fruit of
my beloved's love in me. And let me finish there. As often
happens my weakness reminds me that I must cease, so that,
as you know, I am frequently compelled to leave my sermons
unfinished and to postpone the rest of the chapter to another

35. Mt 7:12
36. Mk 12:30
37. Is 4:4
38. Ps 77:65
39. Num 25:6 -8
40. Ps 118:139
41. Ps 68:10
42. Ps 22:5
43. Deut 4:24
44. Lam 1:13
45. Lk 10:30-37
46. Song 1:13

day. But does it matter? I am ready for the lash,[47] knowing
that what I have suffered till now is far less than I deserve.
Let him strike then, strike me as a useless workman;[48] if the
lashes can be reckoned as merits perhaps he will have mercy
on the victim even when he finds in me no good worth rewarding — he who is the Church's Bridegroom, our Lord
Jesus Christ, who is God blessed for ever. Amen.[49]

47. Ps 37:18   49. Rom 1:25
48. 2 Tim 2:9

SERMON 45

THE WINE OF ZEAL AND THE OIL OF MERCY

"BEHOLD, HOW BEAUTIFUL YOU ARE, my dearest, O how beautiful, your eyes are like doves!"[1] How beautifully said, how excellent. The bride's presumption springs from her love, the Bridegroom's anger from his love. The circumstances prove this. For correction followed the presumption, amendment the correction, and reward the amendment. The master is gone, the king has disappeared, dignity is put off, reverence is laid aside, only the Beloved is present. As love grows strong, pride melts away. And just as Moses once spoke to God as a friend to a friend and God answered him,[2] so now the Word and the soul converse with mutual enjoyment, like two friends. And no wonder. The two streams of their love have but a single source from which they are equally sustained. Winged words honey-sweet fly to and fro between them, and their eyes like heralds of holy love, betray to each other their fullness of delight. He calls her his dearest one, proclaims her beauty, repeats that proclamation, only to win a like response from her. It is no idle repetition that gives firm assurance of love, and hints at something that demands investigation.

2. Let us see what is meant by the soul's twofold beauty, for that is what seems to be intimated here. Humility is the soul's loveliness. This is not my opinion merely, the Prophet

---

1. Song 1:14   2. Ex 33:11

has already said: "Sprinkle me with hyssop and I shall be cleansed,"[3] symbolizing in this lowly herb the humility that purifies the heart. He who was once both king and prophet trusts that this will wash him clean from his grave offence, and give him back the snowy brightness of his innocence. But though we are attracted by the humility of one who has gravely sinned, we may not admire it. If, however, a man retains an innocence now graced with humility, do you not think that his soul is endowed with loveliness? Mary never lost her holiness, yet she did not lack humility; and so the king desired her loveliness,[4] because she joined humility to innocence. As she said: "He looked graciously upon the lowliness of his handmaid."[5] Happy then are those who keep their garments clean, who guard their simplicity and innocence, but on condition that they strive for the loveliness of humility. One so endowed will hear words like these: "Behold, how beautiful you are my dearest, O how beautiful."[6] Lord Jesus, if only you would once say to my soul: "How beautiful you are." Safeguard my humility! For I have poorly kept my robe of innocence. I am your servant.[7] I cannot presume to profess myself your friend, for I fail to hear your voice repeat its witness to my beauty. It would be enough for me to hear it even once. But what if this too should be questionable: I know what I will do:[8] servant though I am I shall have recourse to her who is the friend. In my dwarfish ugliness I shall be filled with wonder by her multiform loveliness; I shall rejoice at the voice of the Bridegroom[9] as he too marvels at a beauty so great. Who knows but I may so find favor in the eyes of the bride, and with her support be numbered among the friends. Then as the Bridegroom's friend I shall stand and experience the greatest joy at hearing the Bridegroom's voice,[10] the voice that is meant for the ear of his beloved.[11] Let us listen and be glad. They are present

3. Ps 50:9
4. Ps 44:12
5, Lk 1:48
6. Song 1:14
7. Ps 118:125

8. Lk 16:4
9. Jn 3:29
10. Jn 3:29
11. Song 2:14

to each other, they speak together. Let us also attend; no worldly cares, no carnal pleasures must distract us from this conversation.

II. 3. "Behold, how beautiful you are, my dearest," he said, how beautiful."[12] "Behold," is an expression of his admiration; the rest, his praise. And how worthy of admiration she is, in whom not the loss but the preservation of holiness fostered humility. Rightly too is this beauty praised twice over, since she lacked neither of the two sources of beauty. This is a rare bird on earth,[13] where neither innocence is lost nor humility excluded by innocence. Consequently she who retained both is truly blessed. The proof is that though conscious of no fault[14] she did not reject the connection. We, when we sin gravely, can scarcely tolerate reproof; she on the contrary listens with equanimity to bitter reprimands,[15] and does not sin. If she did long to see her Bridegroom's glory, what harm in that? It is a praiseworthy desire. And yet when reproved she repented and said: "My beloved is to me a little bundle of myrrh that lies between my breasts."[16] As much as to say: It is enough for me; I desire to know nothing any longer except Jesus and him crucified.[17] What great humility! Though actually innocent she adopts the attitude of the penitent, and though conscious of nothing for which to repent, she still had the will to repent. But why then, you ask, was she reprimanded if she did nothing wrong? But listen now to the plan and the prudence of the Bridegroom. In the same way that Abraham's obedience was put to the test long ago, so now the humility of the bride. And just as Abraham, when he carried out the command was told: "Now I know that you fear God;"[18] so she is equivalently told: Now I now that you are humble. What he actually says is: "Behold, how beautiful you are." And he repeats this encomium to show that the grace of humility is joined to the

12. Song 1:14
13. Juvenal, *Satires* 6:165
14. 1 Cor 4:4
15. Job 13:26
16. Song 1:12
17. 1 Cor 2:2
18. Gen 22:12

glory of holiness: "Behold, how beautiful you are, my dearest, how beautiful."[19] Now I know that you are beautiful, not merely because of my love for you but also because of your humility. I am not now praising your beauty among women[20] nor the beauty of your cheeks and neck as I have previously done.[21] I make no comparison of your beauty, nor qualification nor any other distinction. I speak of your beauty as such.

4. He continues: "Your eyes are like doves."[22] He is still obviously paying tribute to her humility. He takes account of the fact that when he disapproved of her ambitious enquiry she did not hesitate for a moment but turned her mind to matters less exalted. She exclaimed: "My beloved is to me a little bundle of myrrh."[23] There is a vast difference between the vision of his glory and the little bundle of myrrh; and therefore an unmistakable sign of humility in her acceptance of the summons from the one to the other. So, "your eyes are like doves."[24] You no longer occupy yourself with great affairs or marvels beyond your scope,[25] but like that guileless bird who builds her nest in the crevices of the rock,[26] you are content to be unpretentious, to linger near my wounds, happy to contemplate with dove-like eyes the mysteries of my Incarnation and Passion.

III. 5. However, since the Holy Spirit appeared in the form of this bird,[27] the vision commended to us under the sign of a dove is not mere simple gazing but spiritual contemplation. I think too that we should refer this present text back to the one where the companions promise to make ornaments for her ears,[28] not, as I pointed out, with the purpose of adorning her bodily ears but to prepare the ear of her heart. As a consequence, with a heart made purer by the faith that comes from hearing,[29] she is more fully equipped to see

19. Song 1:14
20. Song 1:7
21. Song 1:9
22. Song 1:14
23. Song 1:12
24. Song 1:14
25. Ps 130:1
26. Song 2:14
27. Mt 3:16
28. Song 1:10
29. Rom 10:17

where previously she failed. And since by accepting the
ornaments she notably acquired a keener power of spiritual
understanding, she became pleasing to the Bridegroom who
always prefers to be seen in a spiritual manner. Adding this to
the list of her praises he says: "Your eyes are like doves."
"From now on," he says, "contemplate me in the spirit,
because Christ the Lord is a spirit before your face.[30] And
you have the power to do this, for 'your eyes are like doves.'
Formerly you did not have it, and so you incurred a rebuke;
now you may gaze as you please, because 'your eyes are like
doves,' they are spiritually enlightened. Admittedly this is
not the favor that you sought, for even now you are not
equipped for that, but it suffices for you in the meantime.
You will be led on from brightness to brightness,[31] so exert
to the full the power you now possess, and when you can,
you will see more."

6. My brothers, I do not think that this kind of vision is to
be lightly esteemed, nor that it is common to all, though it
cannot match the one destined for us in the next life. Note
carefully then what is to follow.

IV. The bride speaks in her turn: "Behold, how beautiful
you are, my love, how beautiful."[32] See how she takes her
stand on the heights,[33] see how her loftiest aspirations reach
into the heavens, how with a personal right she claims as her
beloved him who is Lord of the universe. Take note that she
does not simply say "love," but "my love," as if insisting on
a special prerogative. A tremendous vision indeed that endows
her with such confidence and prestige that she greets this
Lord of all things not as her lord but as her beloved. For I
believe that in this vision images of his flesh, or of the cross,
or in any way suggestive of physical frailty, were not im-
printed on her imagination, since the Prophet tells us that
under these forms he possessed neither beauty nor majesty.[34]
But as she now contemplates him, she declares him both

30. Lam 4:20
31. 2 Cor 3:18
32. Song 1:15

33. Bar 5:5
34. Is 53:2

beautiful and majestic, making it clear that her present vision transcended all others. He speaks to her face to face as once he spoke to Moses,[35] and she for her part sees God plainly, not through riddles and symbols. Her words declare what her mind perceives in that sublime vision so full of delight. Her eyes beheld the king in his beauty,[36] though to her he was not king but her beloved. One man has seen him sitting on a lofty and exalted throne,[37] another testifies that he appeared to him face to face;[38] but for me this vision of the bride surpasses them, for there we read that he was seen as Lord, here as the beloved. One text runs: "I saw the Lord seated on a high and lofty throne;"[39] another: I have seen God face to face and yet my life is preserved."[40] But he says: "If I am a master, where is my fear?"[41] If the revelation accorded to them was accompanied by fear, since where the Lord is there too is fear of him, I for my part, given the choice should embrace with greater willingness and love the vision seen by the bride, because it comes about through a more wonderful passion, that of love. For to fear is to expect punishment, but perfect love casts out fear.[42] There is a vast difference between him who appears so terrible in his deeds among men,[43] and him who surpasses men in beauty of form.[44] "Behold, you are beautiful, my beloved, truly lovely." These words are vibrating with love, not fear.

V. 7. But perhaps you are thinking and asking yourselves with increasing doubt: "How can the words of the Word be spoken to the soul and those of the soul to the Word, so that she hears his voice telling her that she is beautiful, and she in return offers a similar compliment to him? How can this happen?[45] It is not the word that speaks, it is we who speak the word. So too, the soul has no means of uttering speech

35. Num 12:18
36. Is 33:17
37. Is 6:1
38. Gen 32:30
39. Is 6:1
40. Gen 32:30
41. Mal 1:6
42. 1 Jn 4:18
43. Ps 65:5
44. Ps 44:3
45. Jn 3:9

unless the body's mouth forms and speaks the words." It is a good question; but take note that it is the Spirit who speaks, and whatever is said must be spiritually understood. So whenever you hear or read that the Word and the soul converse together, and contemplate each other, do not imagine them speaking with human voices nor appearing in bodily form. Listen, this is rather what you must think about it: The Word is a spirit,[46] the soul is a spirit; and they possess their own mode of speech and mode of presence in accord with their nature. The speech of the Word is loving kindness, that of the soul, the fervor of devotion. The soul without devotion is a speechless infant that can never enjoy such intercourse with the Word. But when the Word addresses such a soul, desiring to speak to it, that soul cannot but hear, for "the word of God is living and active, sharper than any two-edged sword, piercing to the division of soul and spirit."[47] And again when the soul decides to speak, much less can the Word hide from it, not merely because he is present everywhere, but rather because without his inspiration the soul will lack the devotion that urges speech.

8. When the Word therefore tells the soul, "You are beautiful," and calls it friend,[48] he infuses into it the power to love, and to know it is loved in return. And when the soul addresses him as beloved and praises his beauty, she is filled with admiration for his goodness and attributes to him without subterfuge or deceit the grace by which she loves and is loved. The Bridegroom's beauty is his love of the bride, all the greater in that it existed before hers. Realizing then that he was her lover before he was her beloved, she cries out with strength and ardor that she must love him with her whole heart and with words expressing deepest affection. The speech of the Word is an infusion of grace, the soul's response is wonder and thanksgiving. The more she feels surpassed in her loving the more she gives in love; and her wonder grows when he still exceeds her. Hence, not satisfied to tell him

46. Jn 4:24   48. Song 1:14
47. Heb 4:12

once that he is beautiful, she repeats the word, to signify by that repetition the pre-eminence of his beauty.

VI. 9. Again, this repetition may have expressed her admiration at the beauty in each of Christ's natures, the beauty of nature and the beauty of grace. How beautiful you appear to the angels, Lord Jesus, in the form of God,[49] eternal, begotten before the daystar amid the splendors of heaven,[50] "the radiant light of God's glory and the perfect copy of his nature,"[51] the unchanging and untarnished brightness of eternal life?[52] How beautiful you are to me, my Lord, even in the very discarding of your beauty! When you divested yourself[53] of the native radiance of the unfailing light, then your kindness was thrown into relief, your love shone out more brightly, your grace was wider in its sweep. Star out of Jacob,[54] how brilliant your rising above me! How fair the flower, as you spring from the root of Jesse![55] How pleasant your light as you come to me in darkness, rising from on high![56] How stupendous, how admirable in the sight of the angelic hosts, is your conception from the Holy Spirit, your birth from the Virgin, your sinless life, your wealth of doctrine, your glorious miracles, your revelation of mysteries. And how you rose from the heart of the earth,[57] gleaming after your setting, Sun of Righteousness![58] And finally, with robes of splendor,[59] how you ascended to the heights of heaven, the King of Glory! Because of all these marvels shall not all my bones cry out: Lord who is like you?[60]

10. These are the qualities, and others like them, that the bride contemplated in her beloved when she said: "Behold, how beautiful you are, my Love, how beautiful." And not these alone, but beyond them she must have glimpsed something of the beauty of his higher nature, something that

49. Phil 2:6
50. Ps 109:2
51. Heb 1:3
52. Wis 7:26
53. Phil 2:7
54. Num 24:17
55. Is 11:1
56. Lk 1:78
57. Mt 12:40
58. Mal 4:2
59. Is 63:1
60. Ps 34:10

wholly transcends our vision, that eludes our experience. And therefore repetition is her tribute to the loveliness of the two natures. Hear then how she dances at the sight and words of her Beloved, as her love spills over in song to him to celebrate their betrothal: "Our bed is covered with flowers; the beams of our houses are of cedar, the panelling of cypress."[61] But this song of the bride we will save for a new discourse, so that when quiet rest has made us more eager we shall more willingly rejoice and be glad with her,[62] to praise and glorify her Bridegroom, our Lord Jesus Christ, who is God blessed for ever. Amen.[63]

61. Song 1:15-16
62. Ps 117:24

63. Rom 1:25

SERMON 46

THE CHURCH AND ITS MINISTERS
THE VIRTUES THAT LEAD TO CONTEMPLATION

"OUR BED IS COVERED with flowers; the beams of our houses are of cedar, the panelling of cypress."[1] She is singing her marriage-song, describing in beautiful language the marriage bed and bridal suite. She invites the bridegroom to repose: for the better thing is to remain at ease and be with Christ;[2] but necessity drives one forth to help those who are to be saved. So now when she feels that the opportunity presents itself, she announces that the bridal suite has been furnished, and pointing to the bed with her finger she invites, as I have said, the Beloved to rest there. Like the disciples on the way to Emmaus she cannot contain the ardor in her heart,[3] but entices him to be the guest of her soul, compels him to spend the night with her. With Peter she says: "Lord it is good for us to be here."[4]

2. Let us now seek the spiritual content of these words. And indeed in the Church the "bed" where one reposes is, in my opinion, the cloisters and monasteries, where one lives undisturbed by the cares of the world and the anxieties of life.[5] This bed is seen to be adorned with flowers when the conduct and life of the brothers brightly reflect the examples and rules of the Fathers, as if strewn with sweet smelling flowers. By "houses" understand the ordinary communities of Christians. Those who enjoy high office,[6] the

1. Song 1:15-16
2. Phil 1:23
3. Lk 24:13-29

4. Mt 17:4
5. Lk 8:14; 21:34
6. 1 Tim 2:2

241

Christian leaders of both orders, strongly bind them together with laws justly imposed, as beams bind the walls, lest living by their own law and will, they should fall apart from each other like tilting walls and tottering fences,[7] and thus the whole building fall to the ground and be destroyed. The panelling however, which is firmly attached to the beams, and impressively adds to the beauty of the house, seems to me to designate the courteous and disciplined behavior of a well-trained clergy, who carry out their duties correctly. For how shall the clerical orders stand and fulfill their duties unless they are sustained, as by beams, by the beneficence and munificence of those who govern and protect by their power?

3. Since the beams are described as cedar and the panelling as cypress, these timbers must possess natural properties that liken them to the aforesaid orders. The cedar, an incorruptible and fragrant wood of great height, sufficiently indicates the qualities of the men who ought to be selected for the role of beams. Hence it is necessary that those who are appointed over others should be strong and reliable, tenacious in hope, their minds directed to supernatural truths, radiating everywhere the good odor of their faith and conduct. With the Apostle they can say: We are the incense offered by Christ to God in every place.[8] The cypress, too, a wood that is equally incorruptible and fragrant, shows that every cleric ought to be of unblemished life and faith, that he may be seen as an ornamental panelling for the beauty of the house. For it is written: "Holiness befits your house, O Lord, for evermore,"[9] which expresses both the beauty of virtue and the constancy of unfailing grace. It is necessary therefore that the man who is chosen for the adornment and beauty of the house should have an excellent moral character, and though living always within, nevertheless be well thought of by those outside.[10] There are yet other qualities in the nature of these timbers that suit the spiritual themes under discussion, but for the sake of brevity I pass them over.

7. Ps 61:4   9. Ps 92:5
8. 2 Cor 2:15   10. 1 Tim 3:7

4. It is worth noting how beautifully every state of the Church is comprehended in one brief expression: the authority of prelates, the good repute of the clergy, the dutifulness of the people, the peacefulness of the monks. As she reflects on these, holy Mother Church rejoices when everything is right; and then she presents them to the beloved to contemplate, since she refers everything to his goodness as the author of all things, attributing nothing of them all to herself. The fact that she says "our" and "ours" is not a sign of usurpation but of love: for with the confidence of superabundant charity she considers nothing belonging to the one she loves so much to be alien to her. She who was accustomed to pursue always not her own concerns but his,[11] will not imagine that she is to be excluded from the Bridegroom's dwelling or from the companionship of his repose; and this is the reason why she dares to proclaim that the bed and the houses are common to herself and the Bridegroom. For she said "our bed," and "the beams of our houses," and "our panelling," thus boldly uniting herself in ownership to one with whom she knows she is united in love. It is not so with one who has not yet renounced her own will. She lies down by herself, she dwells by herself. Or rather not by herself, for she lives licentiously in the company of prostitutes,[12] I mean the lusts of the flesh, on which she squanders her goods, and that share of the estate which she demanded to be set aside for her.

II. 5. For the rest, when you hear or read these words of the Holy Spirit, do you think you can apply to yourself some of what is said? Can you recognize in yourself any share in the happiness of the bride that is celebrated by the Holy Spirit himself in this song of love? Otherwise you also may be told that you hear his voice, but know not whence he comes or whither he goes.[13] Perhaps you too long for the repose of contemplation, and you do well; only do not forget the flow-

11. 1 Cor 13:15
12. Lk 15:11-32

13. Jn 3:8

ers with which you read the bed of the bride is strewn.[14]
Therefore you must take care to surround yours with the
flowers of good works, with the practice of virtues, that precede holy contemplation as the flower precedes the fruit.
Otherwise, instead of seeking rest after labor you will want to
slumber on in luxurious ease. Indifferent to the fertility of
Lia you desire the pleasure of Rachel's embraces only.[15] But
it is a perversion of order to demand the reward before it is
earned, to take food and not to work, for the Apostle says:
"If anyone will not work, let him not eat."[16] "From your
precepts I learn wisdom"[17] said the Psalmist, that you may
know that the grace of contemplation is never owed except
to the commandments. Do not imagine that love of your own
repose is to become an obstacle to the way of obedience and
the traditions of the seniors.[18] If so, the Bridegroom will not
sleep in the same bed with you, especially if, instead of the
flowers of obedience, you have bestrewn it with the hemlock
and nettles of disobedience. Because of this he will not listen
to your prayers. When you call he will not come. Nor will
this great lover of obedience who preferred to die rather than
disobey,[19] put himself into the power of one who will not
obey. He will not approve the empty repose of your contemplation, for he said through the Prophet: "I have labored
with patience,"[20] referring to the time when, an exile from
heaven and the homeland of supreme peace, he performed
saving acts throughout the earth.[21] I fear indeed that the
terrible judgment that he thundered forth against the perfidy
of the Jews may also involve you: "Your new moons and
sabbaths and other assemblies I will not endure;" and again:
"Your new moons and appointed feasts my soul hates; they
have become a burden to me."[22] And the Prophet will mourn
over you and say: "The enemies saw her, and mocked at her

---

14. Prov 7:17
15. Gen 29:31
16. 2 Thess 3:10
17. Ps 118:104
18. Mt 15:2

19. 2 Mac 7:2
20. Is 1:14; Jer 6:11
21. Ps 73:12
22. Is 1:13-14

sabbaths."[23] For why should not the enemy deride that which the beloved repudiates?

6. I am exceedingly astonished at the shamelessness of some who are not among us, who, after they have troubled us all with their impatience, and infected us with their disobedience, dare nevertheless to invite the Lord of all purity, with most urgent prayers, to the bed of a conscience that is so polluted. "When you spread forth your hands," he said, "I will turn my eyes from you; and when you multiply prayers, I will not listen."[24] And why? The bed is not covered with flowers, it is even filthy; and you would woo there the King of Glory? Are you doing this in order to rest or in order to wrangle? The centurion whose faith breathes forth a perfume throughout Israel, forbids him to enter this house because of his own unworthiness;[25] and do you, defiled with the filth of vices so great, compel him to come in to you? The Prince of the Apostles cries out: "Depart from me, O Lord, for I am a sinful man;"[26] and do you say: "Come in to me, O Lord, because I am holy? "[27] "Be you all of one mind in prayer," he says, "love the brotherhood."[28] And the Chosen Vessel[29] speaks of "lifting holy hands without anger or quarreling."[30] Do you not see how the Prince of the Apostles and the Teacher of the Nations agree with each other, and speak with the same mind about the peace and tranquillity of soul which the man who prays should possess? Continue then all day to raise your hands to God, you who all day disturb your brothers, undermine concord and stand apart from unity.

7. "And what do you wish me to do? "[31] you ask? Certainly in the first place, cleanse your conscience of every defilement of anger and quarreling,[32] and murmuring and envy. Hasten to eliminate from the heart's dwelling-place

---

23. Lam 1:7
24. Is 1:15
25. Mt 8:5-8
26. Lk 5:8
27. Ps 85:2

28. 1 Pet 3:8; 1 Pet 2:17
29. St Paul, Acts 9:15
30. 1 Tim 2:8
31. Acts 9:6
32. Heb 9:14

whatever is known to be entirely hostile either to the peace of the brothers or to obedience to the seniors. Then surround yourself with the flowers of good works of all kinds and praiseworthy desires, with the perfumes of the virtues, that is, of whatever is true, whatever is just, whatever is holy, whatever is lovely, whatever is of good repute, whatever is strong and to the praise of discipline. Think about these things, strive to put them into practice.[33] Then you may confidently invite the Bridegroom because when you lead him in you also can truly say: "Our bed is covered with flowers,"[34] since the conscience undeniably breathes forth affection, peace, meekness, righteousness, obedience, joyfulness, humility. This suffices for the bed.

III.   8. A spiritual house is what each one should recognize himself to be,[35] provided he walks in the Spirit and not in the flesh.[36] "The temple of God is sacred," says the Apostle, "and you are that temple."[37] Therefore, Brothers, take care of this spiritual building that you are,[38] lest perhaps when it begins to rise upward it should totter and fall because it was not supported and fastened together with strong beams. Take care to supply it with girders that are incorruptible and immovable, with the fear of the Lord which remains for ever;[39] with patience of which it is written that "the patience of the poor shall not perish forever;"[40] with forbearance also, that endures inflexibly no matter what the weight of the building, and reaches out to the endless ages of the life of the blessed. The Savior said in the Gospel: "He who endures to the end will be saved."[41] But before all else take care of charity which will never come to an end,[42] for love is strong as death, jealousy as relentless as the grave.[43] Study then how to cover these girders and bind them with woods that are also precious and beautiful, provided they are available, to form a paneling for the embellishment of the house. Such are words of

33. Phil 4:8
34. Song 1:15
35. 1 Pet 2:5
36. Gal 5:16
37. 1 Cor 3:17
38. 2 Cor 6:16
39. Ps 18:10
40. Ps 9:19
41. Mt 10:22
42. 1 Cor 13:8
43. Song 8:6

wisdom or knowledge,[44] prophecy, the gift of healing, the interpretation of words. These are more fittingly regarded as ornaments than as necessary for salvation. Concerning them I have no command,[45] but I give my opinion: because it is evident that timbers of this kind must be arduously sought for, are discovered with difficulty, and wrought into shape with risk —for in these times especially they are found to be rare products on our earth— I advise and admonish that they be not too eagerly sought for. The paneling should rather be prepared from other timbers which, though less splendid in appearance are proved nevertheless to be no less strong and moreover are found more easily and safely.

9. Would that I possessed an abundance of these trees that grow so thickly in the Bridegroom's garden, the Church: peace, goodness, kindness, joy in the Holy Spirit,[46] cheerful compassion, open-hearted alms-giving,[47] rejoicing with those who rejoice, weeping with those who weep.[48] Does it not seem to you that the house whose ceiling you perceive to be adequately and skilfully covered with these timbers is adorned richly enough? "Lord, I love the beauty of your house."[49] I desire that you will always give me wood like this, so that I may exhibit my conscience to you as a room that is always adorned: both my own conscience and my neighbor's. With this I shall be content. And there will be those who will wish to follow my guidance in this matter, because I think that it contents you, too; the rest I leave to the holy apostles and to apostolic men. As for you, dearly beloved, although you may not have those rarer timbers, nevertheless if you have these less splendid ones, be confident. Approach with full trust to that chief stone, the corner-stone, chosen, precious.[50] Build yourselves up as living stones[51] on the foundation of the apostles and prophets.[52] Be, in fact, houses in which to offer spiritual sacrifices pleasing to God, through Jesus Christ, the Church's Bridegroom, our Lord, who is blessed forever. Amen.[53]

44. 1 Cor 12:8
45. 1 Cor 7:25
46. Gal 5:22
47. Rom 12:8
48. Rom 12:15

49. Ps 25:8
50. 1 Pet 2:6
51. Eph 2:20
52. 1 Pet 2:5
53. Rom 1:25

ABBREVIATIONS

Apo   *Apologia ad Guillelmum Abbatem,* OB 3:81-108; tr. *Cistercians and Cluniacs: St Bernard's Apologia to Abbot William,* CF 1:13-69.

ASOC   *Analecta Sacri Ordinis Cisterciensis* (Rome, 1935).

BSJ   *The Letters of St Bernard of Clairvaux,* tr. Bruno Scott James (London: Burns Oates, 1953).

C Cist   *Collectanea Cisterciansea* (Rome, 1935).

CF   Cistercian Fathers Series (Spencer, Mass., Washington, D.C., 1970).

CS   Cistercian Studies Series (Spencer, Mass., Washington D.C., 1969).

CSEL   Corpus Scriptorum Ecclesiasticorum Latinorum (Vienna: Hoelder-Pichler- Tempsky).

Ep   Letter(s)

Études   Jean Leclercq, *Études sur s. Bernard et le texts de ses écrits* (Rome, ASOC 9, 1953).

OB   *Sancti Bernardi Opera,* edd. J. Leclercq, C. H. Talbot, H. M. Rochais (Rome: Editiones Cistercienses, 1957).

PG   Patrologiae cursus completus, series Graeca (Paris, 1844-1855).

PL   Patrologiae cursus completus, series Latina (Paris, 1878-1890).

SC   *Sermones super Cantica canticorum,* OB 1 and 2; tr. *On the Song of Songs,* CF 4 and 7.

SCh   Sources Chrétiennes (Paris: Cerf, 1948)